Voices of Change

Voices of Change: Race, Racism, and Colonization in Accounting

EDITED BY

ANTON LEWIS

Governors State University, USA

ADAM J. SAATKAMP

Illinois Central College, USA

AND

JOANNE SOPT

San Francisco State University, USA

emerald PUBLISHING

United Kingdom – North America – Japan – India – Malaysia – China

Emerald Publishing Limited
Emerald Publishing, Floor 5, Northspring, 21-23 Wellington Street, Leeds LS1 4DL

First edition 2025

British Library Cataloguing in Publication Data
A catalogue record for this book is available from the British Library

ISBN: 978-1-83753-031-1 (Print)
ISBN: 978-1-83753-030-4 (Online)
ISBN: 978-1-83753-032-8 (Epub)

Printed and bound by CPI Group (UK) Ltd, Croydon, CR0 4YY

INVESTOR IN PEOPLE

Contents

Foreword

During my doctoral studies, when I was tearing through texts on the history of accounting and the experience of African Americans, trying to deconstruct the newly discovered bits of whiteness that framed my understanding of the world and the profession, I wish the interlibrary gods had sent me this book. As the prototypical pale and male accountant, I was wrestling with questions about the profession's identity and the experience of folks who weren't like me. The data, limited though it were and are, revealed that only 2% of CPAs at US firms were Black or African American. I wanted to know why.

As in any research endeavor, I searched for someone who had the answer. Unsurprising to those who have sought the same, I happened upon the revelatory work of Theresa Hammond. Rather than providing *the* answer to my question, *A White-Collar Profession: African American Certified Public Accountants Since 1921* pointed to a multitude of answers for the profession's persistent racial imperviousness. To comprehend our present reality, one must understand the historic exclusion and racial opportunity costs faced by accountants of color, the diversity of values contained in various cosmologies or ways of being, and the disconnect between inclusion and accounting education. If you're like me and possess an imperfect understanding of each, this book is a gift – a source of edification and enlightenment. If you're not like me – if you have an intimate understanding of racial issues – this book is for you, too, a source of encouragement and an exhortation to keep fighting for change.

The individuals whose words fill the chapters of this text, while writing from Australia and Africa, the United States and the United Kingdom, Canada and the Caribbean, use their experience and position to collectively call for change – a global initiative.

When I was asked to serve as co-editor, alongside the influential Anton Lewis and the assiduous Joanne Sopt, I was, admittedly, unsure I'd measure up. And yet, what I've learned from my fellow editors and from each of our contributing authors, and what you, too, will likely take away, can be summed up in the words of James Baldwin: 'Not everything that is faced can be changed, but nothing can be changed until it is faced'. This book represents a part of the change being sought. It stands as a witness of those who are facing what must be changed and calling others to join them. It offers a glimpse at how resistance can be overcome, how unchangeable things can be changed, no matter how much one knows or how they feel they measure up to the task.

It is by no means premature to celebrate the ripples of change this book will produce. Some of the ripples will be small – a curricular change here or a pedagogical change there – and some of the ripples may be larger, changes in perspective or changes in policy or practice. Whether big or small, and regardless of impediments or obstructions, the ripples of change will be positive, leaving in their wake a new or renewed willingness to face what must be changed.

Adam J. Saatkamp

Introduction

Anton Lewis

Governors State University, USA

"What is this book?" – was a question posed by an esteemed scholar who writes within this volume. Initially, it surprised the lead editor, as most straightforward questions often do. Why is it, indeed? Is it a call for the repudiation of race and racism in accounting? Or a safe space for critical accounting scholars of race to publish their work without fear of reprisal? Is it to prove the salience of race and racism in the field of accounting, highlighting its importance as a field of study to detractors? It is all these things and more. Ultimately, text is a voice, one long ignored by the field, just as those racialized as Other have been ignored for the longest time. Our hope as the editors of this volume is that this collective voice, comprising varied research from across the globe, inspires those who read it to challenge what is possible and to be brave in thought and deed when challenging race and racism in the accounting academy. More importantly, the tenor of this work is that of the personal. As researchers, we are warned to be wary of the bias of the personal; as accountants, we are guided to be impassionate as a proxy for impartiality. This divorce from self is no small thing; it comes at no small cost. It is the sacrifice of passion needed to drive change forward. This book opposes this, instead unapologetically reintroducing passion and self, eschewing positivism as antithetical to explaining and exploring race and racism within the borders of accounting.

The genesis of this approach began several years ago with the establishment of the Accounting and Race Forum, a safe space where accounting scholars researching race, racism, and diversity, equity, and inclusion (DEI) can find support, informed academic debate, and companionship in what is often the loneliest of journeys.[1] Over the years, the Forum has found its voice, but as Lewis often quips, "a voice is not a voice unless it is heard." Meetings take the form of debates and presentations fostering a myriad of ideas and creative thinking, which leaves those who partake all the better because of their involvement. Nevertheless, such creative output requires a home. This book showcases the variety of Outsider accounting and race scholarships that now exist – exploring the edges of

[1]Also known simply as the Forum.

Voices of Change, 1–7

Published under exclusive licence by Emerald Publishing Limited
doi:10.1108/978-1-83753-030-420251003

accounting imagination because dreams of what can be are the life force of any profession that seeks to stay relevant in changing times.

Alas, the voice of race and accounting research is muted by many ranked journals eager to dismiss such research as "not of accounting" and inherently sociological. Outsider scholarship needs to be more in accounting. Worse, reports consistently surfaced in the group of rejections out of hand from established journals, which affected tenure and promotion opportunities to the detriment of junior academics. The Forum became a repository of tales of harm within accounting academe, a narrative outlining punishments to be expected for challenging the status quo in the pursuit of knowledge earmarked as taboo. Doctoral candidates, particularly those of Color, most often experience this as an insidious inference that they will not attain their PhD should they follow such a path, let alone gain employment or tenure in research or teaching schools. Scaremongering, to be sure. So, it was decided to refrain from running the gauntlet of accounting journals and instead publish a volume of research based on the work of the Accounting and Race Forum and others interested in the area.

Happily, matters seem to be changing. Some journals now publish race and diversity work since the global movement of Black Lives Matter took hold in 2020, seeking racial redress across societies globally after the premature death of George Floyd in the streets of Minnesota at the hands of racist police. However, retrenchment is on the horizon, if not already here. As Lewis has stated, a DEI Winter blows across the United States and elsewhere, dismantling DEI offices across universities and dismissing corporate DEI directors (Lewis, 2023). Several states, such as Florida and Texas, have implemented restrictive legislation spearheaded by Republican Governors, such as Governor De Santis of Florida and Abbot of Texas, legally mandating the removal of DEI initiatives. The legislation has influenced businesses, schools, and universities to remove Affirmative Action policies and DEI education activities. The fear is that DEI classes and research agenda are damaged by anti-Critical Race Theory legislation meant to curb its teaching in schools (Hernandez, 2024). An example is the cancellation of fully enrolled courses on race and ethnicity, pending legislation review by Oklahoma Community College (Faison, 2023) – a taste of things to come.

Nevertheless, the fight still needs to be fought. Voices of Change: Race, Racism, and Colonization in Accounting is also a resistance text, moving beyond the theoretical, and technical. Each chapter, in some way or form, has social justice as a core theme, illustrating its importance across numerous places where accounting as a topic is present. Nonetheless, risk exists in any act of resistance, and central to the core of this book is the need to shake up accounting's cautious and staid nature in the areas of race, racism, and DEI. Action is required more than ever because the profession has sleepwalked itself into an existential crisis. Minimal entry of students into accounting classes is central to the dwindling number of junior accountants, which is not just a matter of low representation of accountants of color but now a worrying trend of dwindling numbers of white accountants as well, particularly in the United States. This will reach catastrophic proportions if matters do not change. In terms of identity and the supply of diverse accountants, the profession's inability to see new perspectives and ways forward is laid bare. The actual value of this text lies in its innovative nature and eagerness to challenge what is considered standard accounting practice. In this way, accounting academe can, as it always should have, choose to lead the industry in resolving its most intractable problems with original modes of thought. Solutions are called for now, not more of the same that has proved ineffective at increasing the numbers of Black and Brown accountants over decades, now leaking to all would-be accountants who are currently looking elsewhere. Even though this text is an ode to risk, it is necessary if the profession is to gain meaningful racial representation and a new mode of being. However, in the realm of race and diversity, risk is necessary if old patterns are to change for a brighter future and a diversity return earned.

On the Present

What follows is an ode to the new and the varied as chapter authors within the first section of the book explore accountings of the racial present, beginning with the experience of what accounting has been and is now. In their chapter, which starts proceedings, "Overcoming Obstacles to certified public accountant (CPA) Status in the United States of America," Theresa Hammond and Denise Streeter, pioneers of the field, give an overview of the historical difficulties that have beset Black accountants from the beginning. While outlining the profession's wretched history of African American disenfranchisement, Streeter counters this reality with her own successful lived experience as a jobbing CPA. Noting that, with the help of trailblazers before her, excellent mentorship from Black innovators, and the proper support from firms, she saw a prosperous life come to fruition as a Black accountant. Both authors charge that if the profession can do it once, it can do it again. If it can do it for one, it can do it for all. Leaving the lingering question in the air, "So why doesn't it?"

Phoebe Culler explores a possible answer in "Ascending the Invisible Caste of The US Accounting Industry," viewing racial practice in accounting firms as a de facto occupational caste system. It is one that forever dooms those cast as Other to subordinate status. Culler explores this at a deeper level through her own subjugated racial experience within the industry as an accountant, decrying the present state of DEI as the delusion of inclusion, leaving accounting today for the racial Other as unwelcoming as it ever was. Denial is not a solution. Moving across the pond to the United Kingdom, Jonathan Ashong-Lamptey, in his chapter – "The Intersection of Race, Ethnicity, and Class in the UK Accounting Profession" – takes us on a journey through a differing accounting locale. His insightful study reveals the contested intersectional terrain of race, ethnicity, and class of Black British accountants, which takes salience when striving for professional success while Black. Lamenting Carl Sagan's famous quote "You have to know the past to understand the present," Adam Saatkamp's chapter critiques the parlous state of accounting DEI in "The Railroad Connection: The Liners, the Muckers and Me." It is a profoundly personal narrative, which locates him steadfast in Peralta's fascinating research finding, showing accounting to be one of the least diverse professions (Peralta, 2022). Of particular alarm is the penchant for accountants to be least concerned with DEI as an imperative, with the least enthusiastic response to diversity policy. Saatkamp posits that to answer this thorny issue, we as professionals must hold ourselves accountable for who we are, why we are, and why this came to be in accounting's past. Intriguingly, accounting's past possesses deep colonial roots and suspect moral standing, as seen in many studies of its role in the Plantocracy and valuation of slave assets in the antebellum south and British West Indies, as highlighted by Rosenthal and Fleischman, among others (Fleischman, 2004; Rosenthal, 2018). Here, Gittens reminds us in her study "Accounting Practices in the Public Sector in the Eastern Caribbean: Do They Reflect Caribbean Realities?" that the colonial shadow stays up to the present day. She sketches Caribbean accounting still in the thrall of postcolonial influence to their detriment. International bodies decide what is beneficial, demanding deadlines be satisfied on their terms and representing a continuation of the white Westen hijacking of autonomy from independent nations without consent. Here, accounting practice is set by outside global interests and needs, leaving them as suspect tools, which Bakre has alluded to, that are not fit for internal native needs. It brings to mind the uselessness of the master's tools from the far-sighted Audry Lorde, where taking down the master's house is concerned (Bakre, 2008; Lorde, 2007) – showing all the while that the pervasive reach of racial hegemony is far from ahistoric, existing as our troubling companion right here and right now.

Perhaps it is best seen in the DEI winter we experience, the chilling wind of rolled-back diversity initiatives and policy, as mentioned earlier. It is a sign of the times. In Akolisa Ufodike's chapter, why this is the case is reflected upon in "The Evolution of Accounting Science: COVID-19 Pandemic Lessons on Anti-Black Racism," propelling us back in time to the global lockdown period of COVID-19, where difficult lessons and personals victories accrued in equal measure. Ufodike's story of this time is personal, exploring the difficulties of research during this period; the elation of his production of a groundbreaking paper, placed in the context of isolation and racism(s), varied in scope, which threatened to tear one's soul asunder. To this end, he unpacks attacks against DEI as PESTS – public interest, equity, supply-side, temporal, and spatial rationales. In doing so, he illustrates that the anti-diversity landscape we find ourselves in was well-formed years ago.

Moreover, what we do now matters. If we take our eyes off the ball for a moment, that we hold dear can often be taken from us. Education is one such valuable asset, one in which accountability is paramount but often lacking, as Chevonne Alston's study "Does Fraud Risk in the Charter School Industry Disproportionately Affect Minority Students?" reveals. All too typically to the cost of Under-Resourced Minorities (URMs) in Charter school settings. Internal controls in this educational environment currently fail at this juncture, encouraging fraud to rear its inevitable head to the detriment of Black and Brown communities. Still, neutrality imbricates what is and can be conceived in the accounting realm; reproduction of the accountant is the process, among other things, of creating the dispassionate professional, a byword for the authentic professional. It is an archetype for Saatkamp that alludes to what is most pale, male, and stale, a state of existence he once inhabited, detailed in his second chapter "From 'Civilized' to 'Professional': A Critique of Accounting Education and the Business Case for Diversity." Nonetheless, Saatkamp admonishes the profession for producing a curriculum which generates more of what is not needed, a less diverse, more homogenous white profession. To summarize, if the word public in the acronym CPA is to ring true, then it must reflect all of the public, not a Gentlemanly select few.

Toward the Future

The second section of the book examines what must be improved to remake the profession in the image of the populace it serves, mirroring their values and serving their needs. However, not all agree that this is the path forward. As a DEI expert in the field, Jina Etienne problematizes critical issues she sees day-to-day in accounting organizations in her chapter "Un-Triggered." Usefully, she poses alternate solutions to typically intractable problems using conceptual models of her devising. Meanwhile, Ufodike continues our journey, providing a rebuttal of PESTS outlined in his first chapter and meeting DEI naysayers where they stand.

Still, if continued attacks against critical race theory have proved anything, a theoretical base is paramount to weather the storms of disinformation, uninformed detractors, and racial cynicism. To this end, Twfyford, Tanima, and George's chapter –"Critical Perspectives on Accounting and Race: Shifting the Focus from Periphery to Centre using a Critical Race Theory and Critical Dialogic Accounting and Accountability approach" – provides an excellent application and explanation of the theoretical tenets of both Critical Race Theory and Critical Dialogic Accounting and Accountability as it pertains to deep analysis of race and racism and the emancipatory potential of accounting as a discipline, respectively. When seeking conceptual tools to use in racial analysis, the fluidity of any given model is critical. Race is a slippery construct, and the theoretical lance used to skewer it must be multifaceted and sharp enough to match it. To this end, Orthodoxia Kyriacou's piece "Exploring the spaces in between professional accounting practice and academia: What could a Transdisciplinary Approach offer diversity in accounting?" provides a multidisciplinary praxis of how to combine opposing canons into a unified whole and apply it to engender real-world results. Bringing accountants together with other professionals, such as lawyers and diversity experts, is one practical example explained by Kyriacou.

Another is the call for the use of Oral History by Sedzani Musundwa and Theresa Hammond in their chapter, "Operationalising Oral History for Social Justice in Accounting." Its use as methodology, combined with a social justice lens, is a powerful transdisciplinary tool with which to discover the lived experience of the marginalized other. The authors demonstrate its effectiveness as a tool to solicit new racialized knowledge from Black accountants against the backdrop of a predominantly white South African accounting profession. In essence, this is an act of privileging differing ways of knowing within the accounting academy, ensuring that epistemically, for once, the way of white

Western knowledge is not the only way, nor always the right way. Within this frame, Joanne Sopt, Nadra Pencle, and Jean Wells drive home the importance of decentering whiteness and Western ways of knowing in their chapter, "Decolonizing the Accounting Curriculum." There is a call for a deeper probing of what colonization and decolonization mean on a curricular level, situating them within the accounting paradigm and troubling white domination in their wake.

Finally, toward the end of the second section of the text, our experiences as race-critical accounting scholars invite the reader to be comrades in arms in the struggle for social justice. Lauren Rukasuwan takes the lead with an impassioned plea to move beyond neoliberal capitalism in her chapter, "Going Beyond Business-as-usual," where accountings customary function has been the championing of pecuniary interest over and above the needs of everything and everyone else. It is to admit, like so many chapter authors in this volume, that our innocence about the accounting conspiracy of somatic Native exploitation (past and present) and land theft is a sham. Only after some time, do we see a more distressing picture of a profession we once called home; similarly to Sopt, Pencle, and Wells, Rukasuwan calls for decolonizing the accounting curriculum to stop accounting hegemony. Hers is an upbeat call for those in accounting to assume an anti-oppressive praxis for the good of all. Lewis and Hurt contribute "The Racially Conscious Accountant," a call for anti-racist accountants, individuals who seek to do no racial harm and who have been prepared for the profession in a new and different way. Submerged within Voices of Change: Race, Racism, and Colonization in Accounting lies a call for caring and connection. One which says let us look out for one another, for at its heart, racism divides and steals our inherent gift for connection for one another. Our last author, Iwi Ugiagbe-Green, illustrates this perfectly with a truly poignant tale of connection, hurt, and sorrow while existing as a Black woman within accountings borderlands. Her concluding chapter, "The cost that comes with not caring: An autoethnographic critical reflection of race equity in education" implores we who work and teach within accounting's Hinterland to be cognizant of what is taught, by whom, and for what reason. Ours is a sacred task of teaching, sharing, and caring in an environment that traditionally recognizes neither to its detriment.

We, the editors, hope that those consuming this text enjoy the content within and look forward to the inevitable challenges it will pose. In the same measure, we look for this book to be an intellectual safe space that supports query and inquisitiveness.

References

Bakre, O. M. (2008). Financial reporting as technology that supports and sustains imperial expansion, maintenance and control in the colonial and post-colonial globalisation: The case of the Jamaican economy. *Critical Perspectives on Accounting*, *19*, 487–522.

Faison, W. (2023). The impact of CRT bans on southern public universities: An analysis of the response of PWIs and HBCUs to anti-CRT legislation and a way forward. *Peitho*, *26*(1). https://wac.colostate.edu/docs/peitho/files/2023/12/Faison_26.1.pdf

Fleischman, R. K. (2004). Confronting moral issues from accounting's dark side. *Accounting History*, *9*(1), 9–23.

Hernandez, T. (2024). Can CRT save DEI?: Workplace diversity, equity & inclusion in the shadow of anti-affirmative action. *UCLA Law Review*, *71*(2). https://papers.ssrn.com/sol3/papers.cfm?abstract_id=4666156

Lewis, A. (2023, November/December). Keeping our promise. *The CPA Journal*, 1–80. https://www.cpajournal.com/2024/02/07/keeping-our-promise/

Lorde, A. (2007). *Sister outsider*. Crossing Press.

Peralta, P. (2022). *The ROI on DEI*. Arizent Research.

Rosenthal, C. (2018). *Accounting for slavery. Masters and management*. Harvard University Press.

Section 1

On the Present

Chapter 1

Overcoming Obstacles to CPA Status in the United States of America

Denise W. Streeter[a] *and Theresa Hammond*[b]

[a]Howard University, USA
[b]San Francisco State University, USA

Introduction

To commemorate the 20th anniversary of the National Association of Black Accountants (NABA), Denise Streeter and her team researched and identified the first 100 Black CPAs in the United States for a book published by NABA in 1990 (Streeter, 1990). Subsequently, she and Theresa Hammond interviewed one-third of those pioneers to document their stories, identify the barriers they faced, and discover the characteristics that led them to overcome obstacles and achieve CPA certification. In this chapter, we examine the progress (and lack thereof) that has been made over the past 30 years to make the composition of the CPA profession a better reflection of the diversity of US society.

Currently, only approximately 2% of certified public accountants are Black – a proportion that has not changed much in recent decades. The persistent under-representation is dismaying, and our intent with this chapter is to both draw attention to this important issue and to encourage our readers to work to effect change. Public accountancy is intended to serve the public; this is futile when the profession does not reflect the composition of the society in which it is situated. The absence of Black CPAs has distressing real-world results, including exacerbating the shortage of accountants as well as limiting the number of perspectives – less Black voices – in policy setting (Brown, 2021; Elzayn et al., 2023; Minogue, 2022; Washington, 2021).

Historical Context

As Streeter (1990) documented, in 1965 – at a time when there were almost 100,000 CPAs in the United States – only 100 were Black. In some southern states, Black people were not permitted to attend the flagship public universities, were not permitted to take the CPA exam in the venues chosen by their states, and were not

Voices of Change, 11–21

Published under exclusive licence by Emerald Publishing Limited
doi:10.1108/978-1-83753-030-420251005

permitted to join the state societies of CPAs if they did manage to earn the CPA credential.

In a follow-up study (Hammond & Streeter, 1994), we interviewed one-third of the first 100 Black CPAs in the United States to hear their story of moving forward in their career. No matter what their state of residence, all those we interviewed faced stiff challenges in obtaining the required experience for certification.

Before the 1960s, almost no firms – and certainly not the major white-owned firms (with a handful of exceptions, who were almost exclusively Jewish) – would hire Black recruits, a supremely effective use of the experience requirement as a barrier to exclude Black accountants from earning CPA status. Therefore, several Black accountants moved hundreds of miles to work for one of the pioneering Black CPAs who had started firms. Most prominently, many traveled to Chicago to work under Mary T. Washington, who had become the first Black female CPA in the United States in 1943.

Most of those we interviewed were exceptionally well educated: several had master's degrees – exceptional credentials in decades when most states did not even require a college education to become a CPA. Despite their intelligence, ingenuity, and perseverance, many of those we interviewed found that their careers were restricted to teaching. A disproportionate number became professors at Black colleges (now historically Black colleges and universities, HBCUs), where they inspired new generations of students, hoping that the opportunities they had been denied would be open to their students. It is striking how many of them devoted their careers to shaping a more equitable future for other Black CPA candidates.

One such Black CPA candidate is coauthor Denise Streeter. In reflecting on her journey to CPA status, Denise credits our pioneers with the relative "ease" of earning her credential 65 years after the first Black CPA, John Cromwell, earned his in 1921. It is clear that the first 100 Black CPAs paved the way for her career in public accounting and beyond, as she tells her story.

> As I began to compare my journey to those of our pioneers, I realized that there were support systems and mentors in place for me that they did not have. Though our CPA pioneers had to petition and/or move to another state to get into a university to study accounting, I applied, was admitted, and enrolled in Howard University in a seamless manner in 1980. I studied accounting in the School of Business with both schoolwide and AACSB accreditation under then Dean, Milton Wilson; Associate Dean, Joe Cramer; and with Frank Ross, one of the founders of NABA and former partner at KPMG, as my auditing professor! The array of esteemed faculty is a long list and encouragement abounded. The support that I received at Howard provided me with insightful internships each summer and led me to graduate in 1984 with magna cum laude honors and a job awaiting me at then Coopers & Lybrand (now PricewaterhouseCoopers [PwC]).

> My career at Coopers & Lybrand also was uneventful from the corporate perspective. I did not have to find a Black CPA firm to hire me or take a position with the Internal Revenue Service to meet the two-year experience requirement. I was hired by one of the "Big 8" accounting firms after many recruitment calls, interviews, and advice from a white female recruiter. She was more than a recruiter and became a mentor as she guided me through decisions on everything from makeup to not moving to Minnesota with my then boyfriend (now husband) (long story).
>
> The first day of work at Coopers & Lybrand (C & L) was even more amazing as our diverse group of about 12 "Staff Bs" included two of us from Howard, along with an African American woman from James Madison University. I recall that we all went out front to take a photo together to celebrate with our new Hispanic colleague, whose family was there with him. C & L changed the trajectory of his and many families.
>
> Later, we were greeted by (perhaps the firms' first) Black female partner, Carolyn Smith, who encouraged us to success. We did not have to figure it out on our own as our CPA pioneers had to do, but we had a mentor to help us navigate the profession. When the time came for us to take the CPA exam, her incentive for us to pass the CPA exam was tickets to a Prince concert in the C & L sky suite at the arena! Who could pass up that kind of deal? I will tell you that studying never seemed easier with that incentive. The firm provided time for us to study between engagements, we took prep courses at a location near the office, and many of us passed the CPA exam, including me, on the first attempt! Such support from the firm really made the long nights of exam study worth it (and the Prince concert was incredible)!

That experience is an example of how universities and accounting firms can make a difference in the success of accounting students to attain the CPA credential and diversify the profession. Are we ready to remove the barriers to an accounting education through scholarships and support systems? Are we ready to open our firms to people from families who will be so proud that they will take photos in front of the building? Are we ready to give incentives for passing the CPA exam and assignments that align with the interests of the new staff accountants? It is our hope that after 102 years since the first Black CPA, John Cromwell, attained his credential in 1921, that we are ready to diversify the accounting profession to serve all companies with all people. Her experience fostered great hope that the positive trajectory between the 1960s and 1980s would continue in the following decades.

Recent Research Findings

After the 100th Black accountant was certified in 1965, the Civil Rights Movement led to changes in all professions, including accounting. In 1968, the American Institute of Certified Public Accountants (AICPA) created the Minority Recruitment and Equal Opportunity Committee to address the absence of Black people in the profession. In 1969, Frank Ross and eight of his colleagues founded the NABA (Ross, 2006). A few years later, in 1973, Howard University created the Center for Accounting Education (CAE).

Advancements plateaued in the 1980s, however, with Supreme Court decisions that pushed back against Affirmative Action and the nation's election of Ronald Reagan as the 40th President of the United States. Nevertheless, two important institutions designed to increase the diversity of the profession persisted. The CAE conducted several insightful surveys of Black accountants and maintained some attention from the profession, with many publications in practitioner journals to ensure ease of access for implementation of the findings (*e.g.,* Ross, 2011; Ross & Traub, 2008; Ross et al., 2014). In 1994, we both participated in the founding of the PhD Project, which was formed by the KPMG Foundation with the goal of diversifying the front of the business-college classroom, starting with African-American doctoral students in accounting. The PhD Project is one of the few sustained DEI programs in diversity; by the time it celebrated its 25th anniversary, it had quintupled the number of Black, Latinx, and Indigenous professors of business.

With few exceptions, the progress plateaued until recent years (see Table 1.1); it has only been since the murder of George Floyd in 2020 that attention has refocused on Black participants in the profession. Despite the consistent support of the Diversity Section of the American Accounting Association (AAA), publishing research on race in academic accounting journals in the United States has been a formidable goal. (See Hammond et al., 2023.) Without support for such research, the ability to understand, address, and rectify the disparities we discuss is severely constrained. Fortunately, recent studies and efforts have helped to illuminate current conditions in our field.

Several AAA journals, including *Issues in Accounting Education* and *Accounting Horizons*, have announced special issues on Race and Accounting. This book itself is an example of the recent increased attention to the importance of this issue.

Table 1.1. Key Dates in History of Black CPAs.

1968	Minority Initiatives Committee created by AICPA
1969	National Association of Black Accountants founded
1973	Center for Accounting Education created at Howard University
1994	PhD Project formed by KPMG Foundation
2020	National Society of Black CPAs founded
2020–2021	Eight of the 10 largest firms released DEI transparency reports
2020–2021	Major accounting journals introduced special issues on DEI

One study that helped usher in this new momentum is Pelzer and Nkansa (2022), which addressed the challenges facing Black accounting students. They examined students' perceptions of their abilities and how those perceptions affect their career decisions. As have other studies (*e.g.*, Madsen, 2013, 2020), they document the disparity between the percentage of Black and Latinx accounting graduates (22%) and the percentage hired by CPA firms (14%). All student respondents had a positive view of the auditing profession and believed that they had the ability to succeed in it. The Black and Latinx students interviewed perceived that their identities would provide challenges, but none thought it would be worse in audit than in other fields they were considering.[1] The white students perceived no challenges regarding their race and reported being more likely to have mentors in the field.

The findings of Pelzer and Nkansa (2022) reflect the history of Black CPAs as uncovered by Hammond and Streeter (Hammond & Streeter, 1994; Streeter, 1990). The denial of admission to the profession for the first two-thirds of the 20th century inevitably led to the persistence of fewer role models and mentors, especially family-based insights and mentoring.

Madsen (2020) notes that the largest disparity in Black versus non-Black entrance into the accounting profession happens not at the point at which students are choosing their majors, but at the point at which they are hired out of college. We call for both archival and qualitative research in the field: Madsen's archival approach (2013, 2020), helps reveal the severity of the disparities; qualitative research helps unearth their causes and opens avenues to addressing those disparities.

Black college students are directly impacted by the backgrounds of their professors. As a result, Smith et al. (2023) undertook a study of faculty at HBCUs. HBCUs play a crucial role especially because they are unique among accounting university programs in providing a constant source of role models, mentors, peers, and Black success stories. Crucially, Smith et al. (2023) examine job satisfaction. The importance of role models and mentoring found in earlier studies is underscored in this study as the authors found that the most satisfying aspect of these HBCU faculty positions is the daily ability to promote the success of the Black community by promoting the success of their Black students. The faculty surveyed reported that their ability to teach, interact with, and serve as role models for underserved students were the most satisfying aspects of their jobs.

The study recommends more support for faculty at HBCUs, which suffer from chronic underfunding. According to the United Negro College Fund (UNCF, 2023), HBCUs produce 20% of all Black college graduates. The UNCF (2023) also reports that 33% of white Americans over 25 have college degrees, but only 19% of Black Americans do – this disparity underscores the important role of HBCUs.

Turning from education to experiences in the profession, Davis et al. (2021) produced groundbreaking research that sheds light on the experiences of internal

---

[1]While our focus is on Black CPAs, some studies combine their examination of Black accountants with other under-represented groups.

auditors. They note that most people are unaware of their biases, and that – because auditing is dominated by white people – this means that many Black auditors do not feel a sense of belonging in the field. This can be particularly sensitive in internal auditing, where more junior people (the internal auditors) might be providing negative feedback to higher ranking members of the same organization – people who could potentially be their future bosses.

Several of the Black internal auditors interviewed believed – or sometimes worried – that they had been under more scrutiny than their white counterparts, both at the time of being interviewed as well as when it was time to be given responsibilities or be considered for promotion. Many felt that their self-reported accomplishments were questioned more skeptically than the accomplishments of white colleagues. Davis et al. (2021) recommend that nonminority accountants and auditors make intentional efforts to learn about Black history and contemporary inequities, in order to make them more fully appreciate their Black colleagues.

Initiatives to Address the Dearth

The research we surveyed reveals themes that have been applicable throughout the history of the profession: More research needs to be done on why Black accounting graduates are not hired in proportionate numbers, Black students need to be exposed to the profession at an earlier age, sincere and effective mentoring is needed by Black candidates, majority professionals should take on the responsibility of learning about marginalized communities, and more support should be directed to HBCUs. Both of us are involved in programs to increase the awareness of high school students regarding opportunities in accounting and business, through the NABA's Accounting Career Awareness Program (ACAP). Most often, this entails a weeklong summer residency at a local university, where students learn about applying to college, the opportunities that open up with various majors, and the various fields in accounting. Howard University, where Denise is chair of the Accounting Department, hosts its own ACAP program every summer. Theresa serves on the board of ACAP San Francisco, and the summer residential program is usually held at the University of California at Berkeley or California State University East Bay.

ACAP in the Bay Area has expanded to reach out to the diverse public high schools in Oakland, California. Theresa and her colleagues lead volunteers who work in small groups with the students where they do tax returns, audit exercises with LEGOs, make decisions related to financing a car versus taking public transportation, and play a stock-market game. The volunteers are a mix of NABA members, the Association of Latino Professionals (ALPFA) members, members of Black and Latinx affinity groups at the larger public accounting firms in the area, and college students. Many young people we encounter think that if they don't like geometry or calculus, they aren't going to like (or be good at) accounting. We encourage them to recognize the ways in which they and their families are constantly making financial decisions, and that this is an excellent preparation for working in the field.

There are dozens of ACAP programs in the United States; each is unique. Denise and Theresa have been active members of NABA for over three decades, and we both know that throughout that period, there has been an emphasis on raising young people's awareness of the field, especially at the high school age. These dozens of programs are not sufficient, though, and we encourage readers of this chapter to reach out to us if they are willing to start similar programs.

The National Society of Black Certified Public Accountants (NSBCPA) was founded in 2020 specifically to address the dearth that is the topic of this paper. More specialized than NABA, which is concerned with all accounting careers, NSBCPA provides not only CPA exam review and preparation by members of the Black academic accounting community but also the assignment of Black CPA mentors. This is a direct way to address the challenges uncovered by Pelzer and Nkansa (2022), who repeatedly underscore the importance of mentoring.

Why so Little Progress?

Both of us are frequently asked how it is possible that we have made so little progress since the initiatives to end discrimination started over half a century ago. Lewis (2020, p. 40, and 2021, p. 9) straightforwardly states that the industry has both "run out of effective ideas" (2020, p. 40) and "[lacks] impetus, even now" (2021, p. 9). It is true that many of the same ideas have been circulating for decades: sincere and effective mentoring, high-school outreach to raise awareness, transparency reports. These efforts, however, have been short lived and narrow in scope. The PhD Project has been the one enduring and effective program, increasing Black, Latinx, and Indigenous representation in front of the business classroom for nearly three decades. Seeing a professor who looks like them has been demonstrated to increase the interest of students of color.

The PhD Project, however, is not sufficient, as is evident from recent surveys as well as from the transparency reports many major firms have adopted. The recent rise in public concern about discrimination against Black Americans has had ripple effects in our industry. The Institute of Management Accountants (IMA) (the Association of Accountants and Financial Professionals in Business) partnered with the California Society of CPAs to conduct the most extensive research project to date on the state of the profession with regard to DEI (IMA, 2021). They surveyed more than 3,000 individuals and interviewed 50 HR and other accounting leaders. The persistent under-representation they reveal is striking: although Black people make up 13.4% of the US population, in 2018, Black people were only 1.0% of partners in CPA firms (p. 7). These data were enriched in this extensive study by detailed surveys as well as interviews. They found that 73% and 70% of "Nonwhite, Hispanic, Latino" (the group in which Black professionals were included), respectively, reported that they did "not consistently receive fair treatment in the recruitment process" and that they did "not have equitable access to sponsors or mentors within their organization" (p. 9; Table 2).

This group was the *least* likely (compared with Female, LGBTQIA, and white male, non-LGBTQIA respondents) to agree with the statements "I believe the profession is equitable" (26%) and "I believe the profession is inclusive" (30%). In contrast, 67% and 69% of white male, non-LGBTQIA respondents agreed with the two statements (p. 18, Table 4).

Clearly, if white male professionals believe that the profession is equitable, they have no incentive for change. Further surveys underscore this finding. The parent company of *Accounting Today* recently surveyed the banking, accounting, wealth management, insurance, and other industries and found that nonwhite employees were less likely to feel valued, to feel they belonged, and experience requests for their input in decision-making at work than were their white counterparts (Peralta, 2022, p. 2). While leading accounting and race researcher Anton Lewis has called for "the Black voice to take the lead in policy and action" (2020, p. 40), unfortunately, power and "voice" in the profession remain out of reach. Peralta (2022, p. 5) found that Black, Indigenous, and people of color (BIPOC) and Latinx men were twice as likely as their Anglo, white counterparts to disagree that their input is requested on important topics, and 1.5 times as likely to state that they "don't feel comfortable disagreeing" (Peralta, 2022, p. 5). Women of color are even more likely to report negative experiences. These women of color also report experiencing more stress at work and are less likely to report that they work in a supportive atmosphere (Peralta, 2022, pp. 7–8).

Of the industries surveyed, Peralta found that accounting is the least diverse (Peralta, 2022, p. 12) and that on many dimensions, accountants were least concerned with diversity, equity, and inclusion. Accounting employees were the group most likely to think DEI received too much attention and to express very negative attitudes toward recent efforts to be more inclusive (Peralta, 2022, p. 14). Written answers and interviews found that approximately 10% of respondents' answers included comments such as that DEI is no longer an issue, there is no pipeline to recruit from, or that DEI efforts undermine white, non-LGBTQ males (p. 22). The survey also found that white men were the group that was the least likely to agree that diversity leads to better decisions and the most likely to say that the company for which they work is truly interested in promoting DEI. In this influential report, the authors called for increased transparency in reporting demographic and promotion data by the firms (pp. 40–41) and that it would lead to improved accountability.

The mounting calls for transparent reporting of accounting demographics (*e.g.*, Hammond, 2004; Lewis, 2020; Schultz, 2020) finally generated a response after the 2020 murder of George Floyd. Within two years, eight of the 10 largest CPA firms began publishing DEI "transparency" reports (see Appendix). The reports are welcome – and, we hope, a catalyst for change. Nevertheless, the results demonstrate a continued under-representation, especially at the upper levels of the firms.

Frequently, the "Big Four" claim that they are more diverse than are the smaller big firms, and that is reflected in Table 1.2 at least at the senior manager and partner level. Theresa met with a recruiting partner at a large (not Big Four) firm who stated that the Big Four could "afford" to hire more Black and Latinx

Table 1.2. Black American Participation in Major CPA Firms 2021.

	Deloitte	**PwC**	**EY**	**KPMG**	**McGladrey (RSM)**	**Grant Thornton**	**BDO**	**Crowe Horwath**
Associates	9.2%	7%	6%	7%	3.20%	8.9%	6%	5.35%
Senior associates	8.3%	6%	7%	8%	3.28%	8.1%	7%	4.41%
Managers	5.4%	5%	5%	6%	3.29%	6%	5%	2.82%
Senior managers	3.8%	4%	4%	3%	1.90%	1.1%	3%	2.22%
Partners	2.1%	2%	2%	2%	0.69%	1.3%	1%	0.94%

Source: Transparency Reports 2021 by the various firms.

Note: Two of the 10 largest firms, CBIZ and CLA, did not share detailed reports.

associates because they could "hide" them in large audits, but that her firm could not because the audit teams were too small, and a Black or Latinx associate would stand out. This dispiriting conversation reflects very little change from the "our clients won't tolerate a Black auditor" attitude that was prevalent in the early years of Black CPAs (Hammond, 2002; Hammond & Streeter, 1994).

While transparency reports do not solve the problem, without some accountability, we fear that the trajectory established in the 1980s and 1990s – stasis – would persist. So, we welcome this response – after decades of calls for it – and hope that it is one more step in the right direction.

Nonetheless, we both continue the *fight* for a more inclusive profession, taking inspiration from Stacey Abrams, who said, "I'm not optimistic or pessimistic. I'm determined."

References

Brown, D. A. (2021). *The Whiteness of wealth: How the tax system impoverishes Black Americans—And how we can fix it*. Crown.

Davis, P. L., Dickins, D., & Reid, J. D. (2021, April). Illuminating the Black experience in auditing. *Internal Auditor*, *22*, 57–61.

Elzayn, H., Smith, E., Hertz, T., Ramesh, A., Fisher, R., Ho, D., & Goldin, J. (2023). *Measuring and mitigating racial disparities in tax audits*. Stanford Institute for Economic Policy Research. https://siepr.stanford.edu/publications/measuring-and-mitigating-racial-disparities-tax-audits. Accessed February 12, 2023.

Hammond, T. (2002). *A white-collar profession: African American certified public accountants since 1921*. University of North Carolina Press.

Hammond, T. (2004, July 15). *Diversity in the financial services industry and access to capital for minority-owned businesses: Challenges and opportunities*. Committee on Financial Services, United States House of Representatives.

Hammond, T., & Streeter, D. (1994). Overcoming barriers: Early African-American certified public accountants. *Accounting, Organizations and Society*, *19*(3), 271–288.

Hammond, T., Streeter, D., & Musundwa, S. (2023). Using qualitative research to effect change: African/American accountants in Black and White. *Critical Perspectives on Accounting*, *89*(6–7). https://doi.org/10.1016/j.cpa.2021.102358

IMA. (2021). *Diversifying US accounting talent a critical imperative to achieve transformational outcomes.* IMA and CalCPA.

Lewis, A. (2020, September). When will we be able to breathe in accounting: Provoking an honest conversation about Race and racism in the profession. *The CPA Journal*, 36–41.

Lewis, A. (2021, December). Smoke and mirrors: Race and the Black CPA. *The CPA Journal*, 6–9.

Madsen, P. E. (2013). The integration of women and minorities into the auditing profession since the Civil Rights period. *The Accounting Review*, *88*(6), 2145–2177.

Madsen, P. E. (2020). Research initiatives in accounting education: Transforming today's students into accounting professionals. *Issues in Accounting Education*, *35*(4), 35–46. https://doi.org/10.2308/ISSUES-2020-016

Minogue, A. (2022, December 23). Diversity is critical to the future of the CPA profession. *AICPA Insights Blog*. https://www.aicpa-cima.com/news/article/diversity-is-critical-to-the-future-of-the-cpa-profession

Pelzer, J. E., & Nkansa, P. (2022). Why aren't more minority accounting students choosing auditing? An examination of career choice and perceptions. *Accounting Education*, *31*(4), 347–369. https://doi.org/10.1080/09639284.2021.1991404

Peralta, P. (2022). *The ROI on DEI.* Arizent Research.

Ross, F. K. (2006). *Quiet guys can do great things too: A Black accountant's success story*. Writing Our World Press.

Ross, F. (2011). The uncomfortable truths about improving diversity. *The CPA Journal*, *81*(4), 12.

Ross, F. K., & Traub, L. (2008). Expanding the ranks of African-American CPAs. *Journal of Accountancy*, *205*(2), 48–51.

Ross, F., Wells, J., & Clarke, A. (2014). A pipeline for diversity: Initiative spearheads profession wide effort to attract underrepresented minorities to accounting. *Journal of Accountancy*, *218*(2).

Schultz, D. (2020, July 31). Black CPAs are a rarity, and that's no coincidence (Podcast). *Bloomberg Tax*. https://news.bloombergtax.com/daily-tax-report/black-cpas-are-a-rarity-and-thats-no-coincidence-podcast

Smith, K., Davis, M., Malone, C. F., & Owens-Jackson, L. A. (2023). Faculty that look like me: An examination of HBCU accounting faculty motivation and job satisfaction. *Issues in Accounting Education*, *38*(1), 35–58. https://doi.org/10.2308/ISSUES-2020-090

Streeter, D. (1990). *The history of Black accountancy: The first 100 Black CPAs*. The National Association of Black Accountants.

United Negro College Fund (UNCF). (2023). *Numbers don't lie: HBCUs are changing the college landscape*. https://uncf.org/the-latest/the-numbers-dont-lie-hbcus-are-changing-the-college-landscape. Accessed February 12, 2023.

Washington, K. (2021, June 3). Covid-19 has had a disproportionate financial impact on Black small businesses. *Forbes Advisor*. https://www.forbes.com/advisor/personal-finance/covid19-financial-impact-on-black-businesses/. Accessed February 12, 2023.

Appendix: Transparency Reports Websites

BDO: https://www.bdo.com/insights/bdo-usa-diversity,-equity-and-inclusion-transparency-report
CBIZ: https://www.cbiz.com/about-us/diversity-inclusion
CLA: https://www.claconnect.com/en/who-we-are/dei
Crowe Horwath: https://www.crowe.com/about-us/diversity-equity-inclusion
Deloitte: https://www2.deloitte.com/content/dam/Deloitte/us/Documents/about-deloitte/dei-transparency-report.pdf
EY: https://www.ey.com/en_us/diversity-inclusiveness/ey-us-2022-dei-report
GT: https://www.grantthornton.com/content/dam/grantthornton/website/assets/content-page-files/careers/pdfs/2021-diversity-equity-and-inclusion-report-article.pdf
KPMG: https://www.kpmg.us/content/dam/global/pdfs/2021/kpmg-us-2021-dei-report.pdf
PwC: https://www.pwc.com/gx/en/services/people-organisation/global-diversity-and-inclusion-survey.html
RSM: https://rsmus.com/about/dei.html

Chapter 2

Ascending the Invisible Caste of the US Accounting Industry

Phebian Davis

Clemson University, USA

Introduction

When one hears the word caste, the default visualization is that of a social hierarchy that governed Indian society for hundreds of years. Rarely would anyone equate the idea of caste to the United States. This writing links the concept not only to a US set in the past but also to the present-day accounting occupation. I specifically compare the accounting industry to an occupational caste system and pose the question of whether caste can be ascended. My accomplishments and career trajectory in accounting suggest that I ascended caste, but my personal experiences may paint a different reality.

Racially motivated law enforcement incidents, before and during 2020, called to the surface a swelling of social justice and equity demands challenging corporations, universities, and other institutions to re-examine their commitment to diversity and inclusion. Many organizations made promises to change and become more inclusive to Black Americans. In a brief reflection of guilt, some companies even acknowledged their role and complicity in silently reducing the perceived value of Black Americans. Other organizations ignored the call entirely.

The AICPA, accounting firms, business schools, State CPA societies, and other accounting stakeholders lacked diversity in accounting, specifically in relation to African Americans, well before the COVID pandemic period of reflection and have continued to struggle with how to address the issue. With efforts such as targeted recruiting, designated minority scholarships, The PhD Project, The National Association of Black Accountants' (NABAs') Accounting Career Awareness Program (ACAP) program, and other recent programs created by the larger accounting firms, progress for Black Americans in the accounting space has amounted to barely

Voices of Change, 23–34

Published under exclusive licence by Emerald Publishing Limited
doi:10.1108/978-1-83753-030-420251008

a few drops of water in a bucket of clear water.[1–3] The true impact of these programs on increasing the numbers and ranks of African Americans in accounting in the United States remains to be seen. So far, the resulting image is one that continues to mirror what has always been, which is an industry created by, for and dominated by white men. Without addressing the structural issues of the profession, the accounting industry will continue with just an illusion of inclusion.

Caste and Occupation

A caste by any other name is still a caste. Caste traditionally refers to a system of social hierarchy in India. Hereditary status and occupation are fundamental characteristics of the Indian caste system that specifically ascribe the status of a person. As such, an individual's status and expected occupation are determined at birth by the caste into which that person was born rather than being earned from hard work and merit. In the United States, slavery and Jim Crow laws created a two-tier caste system that relegated slaves and their offspring to the lowest caste, specifically as human capital to serve those in the higher caste. Despite having distinct different social structures with different historical contexts, the American slavery system and the Indian caste system are similar in several ways (Wilkerson, 2020). Both systems are hierarchical in nature, classifying different groups of people based on birth or descent. They both involve the inheritance of status from parents to children. Additionally, both systems justified and perpetuated social discrimination and control over certain groups. Each system was legitimized through religious or legal frameworks. And both systems faced strong resistance and efforts at reform.

An integral feature of a caste system includes a degree of superiority from a sense of being placed at the top of the caste hierarchy while having all the controlling power, or on the other hand, being placed at the bottom of the caste and having no power at all. To create a hierarchy of power and control in a caste system, there needs to be a basis upon which to separate humans. In the United States, physical features (i.e., race) separated people into higher and lower castes.

[1]The PhD Project is an initiative, launched in 1994 to raise the numbers of African Americans, as well as other under-represented minorities attaining doctoral degrees and become accounting educators. Notably, it has significantly diversified the business academic environment by helping over 1,200 minority business faculty members earn doctoral degrees.

[2]The NABA aims to advance the careers of Black professionals through the implementation of various programs, scholarships, and events.

[3]The Accounting Career Awareness Program (ACAP) is an initiative of NABA which aims to grow the amount of under-represented minorities in the accounting profession through increasing student knowledge of the skills and resources needed to succeed in careers in accounting, finance, and other business fields. It includes a week-long placement at a college or university, where students join in accounting themed workshops, seminars, and networking events.

Blacks were relegated to the lowest caste having to serve the whites, who made up the higher caste.

The anthropologist and race critic, Montagu (1945), suggests that the idea of race resulted from exploitation by a class of people (i.e., upper caste) to retain and support their privilege and profitability against what they deemed and labeled an inferior social caste. Wilkerson (2020, p. 19) writes "race, in the United States, is the visible agent of the unseen force of caste." Race became the basis for a caste system in the United States that divided humans based on perceived value. While caste predates race, the two are innately interwoven in the United States.

Wilkerson (2020, p. 19) notes that what we look like or the race we have been assigned is the visible link to our caste in the United States. This in turn leads to a determination by the superior caste of how the inferior caste should be treated, where they should live, what kind of jobs they are expected to have, whether they should or can be considered experts of subject matter, etc. (Wilkerson, 2020). As recent as the first 2024 US presidential debate, one of the candidates made a blatantly racist comment that immigrants are taking Black jobs. This public comment by one of the most powerful men in the United States further supports the notion that a perceived hereditary link between race and occupation persists in the United States by promoting the perception that Blacks are only capable of doing certain jobs (Wile & Adams, 2024).

The concept of a US caste system, a result of slavery and Jim Crow laws, through murder, physical abuse, fear tactics, and discriminatory laws, relegated Black people to the lowest caste for hundreds of years (Wilkerson, 2020). "The state of South Carolina, right after the Civil War, explicitly prohibited black people from performing any labor other than farm or domestic work, setting their place in the caste system" (Wilkerson, 2020, p. 133). As a result, we cannot expect today that individuals from the lowest US-made caste believe they can truly be part of and accepted by those in the highest caste. Nor can we expect that those with inherited privilege from the highest caste would openly embrace the offspring of the lowest caste. This lack of acceptance and inclusion extends beyond social status and occupation.

The US Accounting Industry

Essential to *self-awareness is the ability for honest and transparent introspection* (Avolio & Gardner, 2005). By acknowledging both the bad and good of our lives, we may see ourselves more clearly for who we really are. Current leaders in the US accounting industry inherited an occupational caste system from the forefathers of the country. Slavery created a hierarchy based on the social construct of race. Naturally, race became akin to occupation, initially based on who could own property and who was the property. In the United States, those in what would be considered the upper caste owned land and owned the slaves who performed work on the land and were in the lowest caste. This naturally created occupational caste system ensured that Blacks would be kept out of professional job roles for a long time.

The US accounting industry by all accounts is considered an industry of prestige and one that would naturally be afforded to those of the higher caste. If the current leaders of the US accounting industry are truly honest about what they inherited and continue to perpetuate, the industry will reveal an inherent occupational caste system. This can only be done by looking deeper into the hierarchical structures and silent systems of privilege within the institutions.

Some of the similarities that the accounting industry and top castes share include prestige, an assumption of competence, access to resources, respect accorded, and the benefit of the doubt. After slavery ended in the United States, Jim Crow laws still prevented Blacks from making gains in life that would possibly give them a path from the bottom caste to the top caste. Post Jim Crow, African Americans struggle to reach the level of a professional, and when they do, the treatment they endure is insufferable. Accounting is no exception. The accounting profession did not have a Black CPA until 1921 and the second in 1946.

In her book, *A White-Collar Profession*, Hammond (2003) describes accounting as the whitest profession. She notes that in the 1930s, 1960s, and 1997, among the three professions of lawyers, doctors, and CPAs, African American representation was the lowest for CPAs with less than one percent. Barriers including education and work experience kept Blacks out of the accounting profession. While some of the barriers to entry have been removed, the number of African American CPAs sadly remains meager today at an estimate of barely one percent (National Society of Black CPAs, 2023).

Hammond (1997) reports that in the late 1960s and early 1970s, the accounting industry went from a total exclusion of African Americans to experiencing a high in recruitment. The inclusion resulted from the Civil Rights Act and affirmative action initiatives during the period. Accounting firms attempted to appease the social climate of the time only to see the trend reverse in the 1980s, reflecting once again minimum inclusion. Once support for social justice and equity waned, the gains made earlier were reversed and the same firms barely reflected the inclusion of African Americans. We are currently experiencing a similar pattern of retracting diversity initiatives that were previously embraced. The enthusiastic efforts after the 2020 George Floyd incident and related social justice initiatives have been thwarted by efforts to eliminate DEI initiatives and thus the related gains from prior efforts.

Dey et al. (2019) find that even though the profession has made efforts to increase opportunities for minority employees, the treatment of African Americans in the workplace presents ongoing challenges in retention. They note that some of the greatest challenges of Blacks in the accounting work environment include navigating corporate politics (soft skills), establishing credibility of technical skills and being included in informal networks. African Americans felt less welcome and accepted by colleagues in 2017 than in 2006 (Dey et al., 2019). Similarly, Davis, Dickins, Reid, and Higgs (2021) find that Black internal auditors often face in-group and out-group biases in the workplace. Another study by McKinsey and Co. (2020) also finds that minorities were more likely to report being excluded from social activities with coworkers as well as having to correct false assumptions that colleagues made about them and their personal lives.

Blacks feel isolated from informal networks in the workplace, yet they acknowledge the necessity of being part of the in-group to advance within the organization. Not being invited to or included in social gatherings outside of the office puts Blacks at a disadvantage when it comes to receiving key information, creating bonds with colleagues and gaining access to those in power.

Davis et al. (2024) highlight the inequality in accounting academia, which reflects a similar dynamic as other areas in accounting. The authors find that racial microaggressions contribute to the under-representation of Blacks in the academy. Unfortunately, this leads to less Black students majoring in accounting and creates a continuous cycle of under-representation of Blacks in accounting. In his article "When Will We Be Able to Breathe in Accounting," Lewis (2020) calls for the accounting industry to do more and stop turning a blind eye to their racist acts and start calling out racist practices in the workplace and within their organizations.

While there are many plausible explanations for the lack of Blacks in accounting, Davis, Dickins, Higgs, and Reid (2021) find that the persistence of macro- and microaggressions in the workplace might be the larger problem. They report stories by Black auditors that include verbal and nonverbal behaviors that degrade Blacks in the workplace. Additionally, policies and practices at the firm level tend to exclude Black auditors and negatively impact their success.

I applaud efforts of various accounting organizations to increase minority representation. However, if true impact is to be made, the accounting industry must not only look externally to fill the void (i.e., scholarships, nontraditional recruiting paths, etc.) but must look deeply within at its own policies, written and implied, which are clearly impacting their ability to not only recruit but retain Blacks in the accounting industry.

> The problem is not inclusion. Everybody's included in the plantation.
>
> The problem is that there is a hierarchy and there's an exploitative mode.
>
> There's a way women are positioned... and Black folks.
> (C. Kumanyika, former Clemson professor, as cited in Nicholson & Hamilton, 2022)

Ascending Caste

Post slavery and Jim Crow, after hundreds of years of oppression in the United States, Blacks were still expected to perform domestic and agricultural occupations. There was never any expectation or allowance for Blacks to become more or aspire to perform any type of professional role. Even to this day, Blacks who have attained wealth well beyond that which would be expected of the lowest caste have done so mostly as entertainers or athletes but rarely as owners or CEOs. *Black Entrepreneurs & Executives* (2023) magazine reports that only 26 Blacks have reached the level of Chairman or CEO within the Fortune 500 companies. Currently, there are only eight Black CEOs inclusive of two Black women of Fortune 500 companies. Even more telling is that while Black athletes comprise the bulk of the rosters of the National Football League (NFL), National Basketball Association (NBA), and the Women's National Basketball Association (WNBA), Michael Jordan is the only Black majority owner of a major sports franchise (The Charlotte Hornets), at the time of this writing. In the Black community, ascending caste can be synonymous to "making it." Attaining a Fortune 500 CEO position or owning a professional sports franchise is clearly indicative of that, but whether it truly breaks through the levels of caste is questionable. There are many examples of Blacks ascending to various levels of the corporate ladder and other advanced positions within various institutions. Sometimes, merely obtaining an occupation better than your parents' (or a nonservice role) can be seen as "making it." I was born in a small, poor farming town located in one of the richest counties in Florida. My hometown is surrounded by agriculture and sits on the eastern side of Lake Okeechobee, the largest freshwater lake in Florida. My parents worked mostly as seasonal farm workers for the large agricultural companies in the area.

My hometown did not have many employment opportunities, and as such, most parents and often their offspring were relegated to fieldwork and other service-type occupations. It was a normal way of life to work in the fields, and for a very long time, no one was expected to do much more. As a child, I was a good student, read a lot, and was smart by most accounts. Most importantly, I dreamed of a world so much bigger than my everyday surroundings. One day while I was in high school, a female banker visited our classroom as part of her role with Junior Achievement. I was so intrigued with this professional, from her appearance to everything she shared about her job. It was then that I decided I wanted to be a businesswoman. I continued to work hard as a student, and even after several missteps, I was eventually accepted into several colleges. I chose to go to a Historically Black College/University (HBCU) outside of Florida. At this point, it was clear that I had "ascended caste" from an educational perspective. I would no longer be expected to work the farmland as my parents did.

> Caste may be elusive for some who have distanced from their social and cultural roots, but for others... caste is enduring, and it is there in practice in one way or other. At times, caste-based outbursts surface... (Sharma, 2012, p. 1)

There are some unexpected truths about those "outbursts" and "making it" that no one tells you. When you leave what is comfortable and pursue something greater, at times, it might not feel like success. When you enter an environment that was not created for people like you, you do not know the rules of engagement and often find yourself in situations in which you are not equipped to properly handle.

The true meaning of caste suggests that I will always be part of the lowest caste, no matter the level of education I attain or success I achieve in my career. In the remainder of this narrative, I reflect on my accounting career and highlight a few of the moments in which I feel were, or caste-based outbursts or reminders in some way that I was not part of, nor would ever truly be accepted by the dominant caste. Though in many ways I moved up in the social hierarchy due to education and job experience, someone always found a way to remind me otherwise. I can look back at my experiences and clearly recall the invisible cuts, macro and microaggressions, and slights I have experienced while remaining steadfast in my pursuit of being successful in accounting.

Education

The first sign that accounting might not be the welcoming career I envisioned came as I completed my education at the HBCU I chose to attend for my undergraduate education. Once I learned that the most coveted accounting positions were with the larger accounting firms, I realized that none of them recruited at my college. As a result, I had no choice but to pursue additional education at a predominantly white institution (PWI) to gain access to the major accounting firm recruiters. The exclusion of students from many HBCUs in the recruiting process of the major accounting firms sends a message that we are in a nonfavored group. The larger accounting firms have since established recruiting efforts with more HBCUs.

Public Accounting

> Caste is the granting or withholding of respect, status, honor, attention, privileges, resources, benefit of the doubt and human kindness to someone on the basis of their perceived rank or standing in the hierarchy. (Wilkerson, 2020, p. 70)

My introduction to and early entry into public accounting was not a warm experience. I was granted an interview with a Big-Six firm for an internship prior to completing my graduate degree.[4] I did not know or understand at the time what to expect from the interview process. After arriving at the firm's office for the scheduled interview, I was basically dismissed by the person I was told to ask for. He immediately said that he was not expecting me, though a national recruiter for the firm arranged the interview, nor did he have time to meet with me. He then gave me cash to reimburse me for the drive and my time and sent me on my way. The naïve person I was at the time did not realize how abnormal this was. In this instance, I was not afforded the attention, respect, and kindness that is normally granted during the interview process. Similarly, after graduating from a college in the south in 1973, Gwendolyn McFadden was told by a Big-Eight recruiter in the south that his office was not ready for someone like her (Hammond, 2003).

---

[4]Arthur Andersen, Coopers and Lybrand, Deloitte and Touche, Ernst and Young, KPMG, and Price Waterhouse were the six largest accounting firms before a series of mergers cut down them to the Big 4.

As noted by Wilkerson (2020), caste systems endure *because the dominant caste ascribes to it, upholds the restrictions that come with it, and reminds those from the lower caste that they are not and will never be accepted by the dominant caste.* Another reminder that public accounting might not be welcoming to people like me was when I learned during an internship that the firm I was working for was having an offsite event at a country club that did not allow Black people (in 1995). As such, I was informed by a senior that I could not attend and should just take that day off. I was shocked and appalled. I knew right then that I would not work for that firm after the internship, even after receiving a fulltime offer for employment. So, when firms struggle to retain Black talent, they might need to turn the magnifying glass on their own institutional practices.

One might ask after these two distinct early negative accounting firm experiences why I would continue with a career in accounting. I had to. I could not let my parents, my family, nor my community down. I had to finish what I started. After all, working in public accounting was the coveted dream job for accounting students/majors.

> What people look like (their race) determines the caste to which they have been relegated and what kind of positions they are expected to hold. (Wilkerson, 2020, p. 18)

As a staff auditor, I had a client make it clear that he did not respect me or my role on the audit team. While working on the client, the controller told my manager that "he did not want that black girl asking his people questions." I was the black girl. As an auditor, asking questions was part of my job but he did not care. He did not see an educated auditor and young woman working hard to complete her tasks. He just saw a Black girl that he felt should not have the authority to question his employees, white or otherwise.

Corporate Accounting

> Caste pushes back against an African American woman who, without humor or apology, takes a seat at the head of the table... Yet it sees as logical a sixteen-year-old white teenager serving as store manager over employees from the subordinate caste three times his age. (Wilkerson, 2020, p. 70)

An invisible caste rears its ugly head in the workplace and in our everyday lives without notice. After a few years of public accounting, I decided to pursue a corporate accounting path. It was not long before I was again reminded that I was perceived to be out of my league and should not expect equitable treatment. I was working as a senior financial analyst, and a few months after starting the job, I realized I knew a lot more than my colleagues in the same role and quickly felt stifled. I had more experience and education than most on the team. Soon a position opened to manage the team that I was part of. I thought the role was perfect for me. When I expressed interest to my supervisor, the VP of Finance, about the position, he stated that while I had the public accounting experience they desired, they preferred to hire someone with a CPA. I thought that was fair and accepted his explanation without further concern as I had not yet earned the CPA certification. Soon they hired someone, a white female, who did not have a CPA and did not have public accounting experience. To make matters worse, the VP asked me to train her which was a clear indication that he knew I could do the job. I refused to train her and soon left the company. At that same company, I recall a previous conversation with an older white woman in the breakroom one day. I do not remember how the topic came up, but I remember her telling me that I would never get promoted at that company because I looked too young. Please note that I was in my mid-30s at the time. I remember saying that was a ridiculous reason not to promote someone. After the hiring situation, I reflected on her comments and felt that she really meant that I would not get promoted because I was Black. This experience took me back to the day the controller said that he did not want me, the Black girl, asking his people questions. I realized after this last incident that I would probably not be successful in accounting in corporate America, and to be honest, I was getting tired of the fight. I guess I was starting to have post-traumatic stress disorder because of my negative experiences in the industry. As a result, I started to re-evaluate my personal and professional goals.

Academia

After deep self-reflection and reassessment of my career goals, I remembered that as a little girl, I always wanted to be a teacher. However, my high school teachers urged me not to become a teacher because I would not make much money. I fell in love with accounting in college, but it was not until my senior year at the HBCU I attended, while taking an auditing class with a Black female professor, that I realized that I could achieve my childhood dream of being a teacher and still remain in accounting. I could do two things I loved at the same time. But I was initially set on a path to a public accounting career, so I tabled that idea. After my frustrating experiences with public and corporate accounting, I decided to pursue an academic career. I eventually earned a PhD in accounting and started teaching at the college level.

While I have been mostly happy with my academic career, it has not come without challenges. My first position was with the HBCU that I attended for my undergraduate degree. Though I started this position with excitement and wanting to make a difference, I eventually found myself overworked and underpaid due to the limited resources of the school. I eventually left for a nontenure track position at a PWI in the south. While my choice of a nontraditional career path was frowned on by many, I have been very happy with my decision. However, my start at the PWI was not without another reminder that there was a perception that I should not be teaching at the school. Students had no problem expressing their dissatisfaction with having a Black female professor. Most of the white students in my classes had never had a Black teacher during their entire education process. However, I persisted and eventually the racially tinged comments flipped to students expressing gratitude for having me during their education process. As the only Black female faculty member in our College of Business, I find it necessary to seek out in-group support networks outside of my work environment, such as The PhD Project. While my department and supervisor are supportive of my work and goals, it often still feels very lonely being the only one like me.

Everyone knows that research is the currency of academia. Having chosen a nontraditional path, I am lucky to be able to do the kind of research that I find meaningful and not what the academy necessarily deems valuable. In recent years, I have taken on projects that explore the Black experience in different areas of accounting, specifically DEI research. I have found that the academy is not openly receptive to such critical research. Though my coauthors and I have had publishing success with our research, the comments included in some of the rejections made it clear that not everyone in the academy thought there was an equity problem. However, the stories needed to be told, and I am happy to be a medium for Black accountants to share their experiences in hope for changes in the industry. I think I have found my happy medium with a career in academia. I can influence the next generation of accountants, impact change in the industry, and elevate my community by showing those that come behind me that they too can break through their assigned caste and be happy doing it. It is hard to be what you can't see.

Closing

One might ask why I continue to pursue a career in accounting after all the slights, microaggressions, and injustices I have experienced. In total, I have a storied career. I have earned my place in the accounting industry. I am not doomed to the caste in which I was born. I believe I have ascended caste by attaining the highest level of education in accounting and attaining coveted jobs in the industry. I believe that by remaining in accounting, an industry that I have grown to love, I am making a difference for the next generation of Black accountants. Nonetheless, issues remain. I have shared a few examples of when I was reminded of my caste or perceived place in this society, and it is in such instances I feel that I will never be accepted by my peers or truly break from the caste that I was relegated to at birth, no matter the contributions I make to this industry.

The US accounting industry has strong traits of an occupational caste system. While I understand and even support some of the recent efforts of the larger accounting firms, I worry that some continue to unknowingly caste minority employees. With minority recruitment efforts that create special internship programs for minorities before accepting them into regular internships, along with different starting titles, such efforts might successfully recruit Blacks in the short term, but these employees will eventually recognize the differential treatment and more often than not, they will leave. Such a stigma will be difficult to shed while at the firm. So, until industry leaders are honest with themselves and take accountability for what is, accounting will continue to present the illusion of inclusion but never truly reflect an inclusive environment for Black accountants. Yet, I remain hopeful that it can be done.

For those individuals of privilege who are quick to say that they are not responsible for the past wrongs of their ancestors, I will use an analogy from Isabel Wilkerson (2020) in which she eloquently explains why it is still *your* problem today. Imagine purchasing a used house and receiving an inspector's report that clearly outlines severe issues with the foundation of the house, roof issues, and other structural problems that need correcting to make the house stable and livable. While you, the new homeowner, are not responsible for the damage caused by the previous homeowners, if you choose to do nothing and do not correct the problems noted in the inspection report, you then become responsible for any further deterioration of the house.

One can choose to not get an inspection of the preowned home and disregard any visible cracks in the walls, ceiling, and foundation. However, your willful blindness will not make the house any better, and you, the new owner, will eventually pay the price for your ignorance. So, for the residuals of slavery and continued institutional segregation that you believe are not your fault or problem, they will eventually become your problem. So, when our non-Black colleagues ignore obvious wrongs perpetrated against Black Americans in accounting, they too become part of the problem. It is never one small cut that kills the soul of a person; it is death by a 1,000 cuts.

References

Avolio, B. J., & Gardner, W. L. (2005). Authentic leadership development: Getting to the root of positive forms of leadership. *The Leadership Quarterly*, *16*(3), 315–338.

Black Entrepreneurs & Executives. (2023, April 10). https://www.blackentrepreneurprofile.com/collections/black-fortune-500-ceos

Davis, P. L., Dickins, D., Higgs, J. L., & Reid, J. (2021). Auditing while Black: Revealing microaggressions faced by Black professionals in public accounting. *Current Issues in Auditing*, *15*(2), A24–A33.

Davis, P. L., Dickins, D., Higgs, J., & Reid, J. (2024). Microaggressions in the accounting academy: The Black experience. *Journal of Business Ethics*, *192*(3), 627–654.

Davis, P. L., Dickins, D., Reid, J., & Higgs, J. (2021, April 22). Illuminating the Black experience in internal auditing. *Internal Auditor*. https://internalauditor.theiia.org/en/articles/2021/april/illuminating-the-black-experience-in-internal-auditing/

Dey, M., Lim, L., Little, C., & Ross, F. (2019, January). Challenges continue for African-American accountants. *Journal of Accountancy*. https://www.journalofaccountancy.com/issues/2019/jan/challenges-continue-for-african-american-accountants.html

Hammond, T. A. (1997). From complete exclusion to minimal inclusion: African Americans and the public accounting industry, 1965–1988. *Accounting, Organizations and Society*, *22*(1), 29–53.

Hammond, T. A. (2003). *A white-collar profession: African American certified public accountants since 1921*. University of North Carolina Press.

Lewis, A. (2020, September). When will we be able to breathe in accounting? *The CPA Journal*, 36–41. https://www.cpajournal.com/2020/09/30/when-will-we-be-able-to-breathe-in-accounting/

McKinsey & Co. (2020, June 23). *Understanding organizational barriers to a more inclusive workplace*. https://www.mckinsey.com/capabilities/people-and-organizational-performance/our-insights/understanding-organizational-barriers-to-a-more-inclusive-workplace?cid=other-eml-alt-mip-mck&hlkid=0a0b998626ef4713b02c14ce226d6ee3&hctky=2799396&hdpid=4eaa142d-de5f-46b3-aa50-423380d53597

Montagu, A. (1945). *Man's most dangerous myth: The fallacy of race*. Columbia University Press.

National Society of Black CPAs. (2023). https://www.nsbcpa.org/

Nicholson, Z., & Hamilton, A. (2022, September 20). Low pay, toxic work culture fueled exodus of employees of color from Clemson. *Greenville News*. Black employees face steeper climb, toxic culture at Clemson University. https://www.greenvilleonline.com/story/news/local/south-carolina/2022/09/21/minorities-black-employees-face-toxic-work-culture-clemson-university-sc/5291747001/

Sharma, K. L. (2012). Is there today caste system or there is only caste in India? *Polish Sociological Review*, *178*, 245–263.

Wile, R., & Adams, C. (2024). 'Black jobs'? Trump draws pushback after anti-immigration rant. https://www.nbcnews.com/news/nbcblk/trumps-anti-immigration-black-jobs-reactions-presidential-debate-rcna159375

Wilkerson, I. (2020). *Caste: The origins of our discontents*. Random House.

Chapter 3

The Intersection of Race, Ethnicity and Class in the UK Accounting Profession

Jonathan Ashong-Lamptey

Independent Researcher, UK

Research on professional identities has primarily explored how organisations and occupations influence and control people's work-related identities (Alvesson & Willmott, 2002) but has focused less on whether or how this control is mitigated by the influence of non-work identities (Ramarajan & Reid, 2013). This chapter is concerned with how minority racial and ethnic individuals experience their ethnic identity in the workplace.[1] More specifically, this chapter will investigate how ethnic identity is enacted through heritage culture and what this means in terms of workplace behaviours. The result is a typology illustrating how an individual's heritage culture intersects with race, class and professional identity to influence their work-based behaviours.

The motivations for this chapter stem from first re-examining the predominant conception of minority individuals' heritage culture as a burden that must be, or actively, reduced or eliminated in order to flourish in a professional work environment (Lewis, 2011; Pearce, 2005; Sommerlad, 2008). This chapter can help guide future research concerning how minority racial and ethnic professionals experience their heritage culture within the workplace.

I have chosen to study Black accountants in the United Kingdom for several reasons. Blacks have been shown to experience a high ethnic penalty (Berthoud, 2000) and are more likely to be employed in lower paying occupations than other

[1]I use the term minority racial and ethnic individuals to refer to individuals who are members of a minority racial group or members of a minority ethnic group and those individuals who may identify as belonging to both. This term is used to describe people that are referred to as BAME in the United Kingdom (Bhopal, 2004) and 'people of color' in the United States (Quintana, 2007). In a manner similar to (Kenny & Briner, 2013), I will refer to race when I cite work by those who use that term, and I will use ethnicity when citing scholars who use that term. My use of the term minority refers to a specific work-based context that recognises not only the size of the populations of the particular racial and ethnic groups of interest but a lack of influence and power too (Wellman, 2001).

Voices of Change, 35–46

Published under exclusive licence by Emerald Publishing Limited
doi:10.1108/978-1-83753-030-420251010

ethnic groups (Elliott & Lindley, 2008). Moreover, Blackaby et al. (2002) found that Blacks had the lowest employment rate of all ethnic groups. In the context of professional work, Black identity may be considered to be a lower status ethnic identity than some other ethnic groups because negative stereotypes exist about the intellectual ability and competence of Black people (Kenny & Briner, 2013). Accounting is a suitable location for this study because it is a form of social control that has aided the construction of dominant class hegemony (Moore, 1991). Evidently, accounting has come to occupy an ever more significant position in modern industrial societies (Burchell et al., 1980).

A History of Accounting in the United Kingdom

Accounting in the United Kingdom has developed from being an ill-defined group of commercial occupations in the late 19th century (Kirkham & Loft, 1993) to an occupational group with a membership over 405,000 members (Financial Reporting Council, 2024). In attempting to evolve into a recognised profession, the dominant institutions used a variety of practices to reflect existing gender and class relations (Lehman, 1992). These acts combined with the marginalisation of competing professional bodies helped to exclude whole classes of people from membership such as women and those from lower socio-economic groups (Kirkham & Loft, 1993). Through a combination of stigma and impression management (Goffman, 1959; Jeacle, 2008), the accounting profession deliberately cultivated the image of the chinless, nervous, bespectacled pen pusher in order to construct an identity perceived to be congruent with conservatism, accuracy, and competence (Bougen, 1994; Friedman & Lyne, 2001). This secured the trust of the public legitimising the profession and over time establishing a normative identity that is white, male and middle class (Lewis, 2011, 2015).

Much of the literature is centred upon the US accounting profession (Hammond, 1997, 2002; Hammond & Streeter, 1994). These take the form of historical accounts of the experiences of African-American Certified Public Accountants (CPAs) pursuing a career in accounting in the midst of the legacy of slavery and the Civil Rights movement (Hammond, 2002). The accounting profession actively excluded Blacks from participation for most of the 20th century through its restrictive practices (Hammond & Streeter, 1994).

There is a need for more research outside of the United States (McNicholas & Barrett, 2005). The literature regarding the experiences of minority ethnic accountants in the United Kingdom is limited, indicating that it is a neglected area of research (Hammond & Sikka, 1996). Johnston and Kyriacou (2007) suggest that the UK Accounting profession operates processes that are institutionally racist and sexist. Lewis (2011) challenges notions of colour blindness in accounting suggesting that racism is resilient in UK accounting, arguing that the myth of meritocracy obscures the racialised reality of inequality experienced by Black accountants.

Methodology

In order to achieve my research aims, I wanted to describe and understand the actual human interactions, meanings and processes that constitute real-life organisational settings (Gephart, 2004). The use of qualitative research methods when exploring minority ethnic accountant experiences is prevalent (Hammond & Sikka, 1996; Johnston & Kyriacou, 2007). Much of the accounting literature concerning race and ethnicity provides insightful narratives through this research methodology and reveals experiences that may not have been revealed (Kyriacou & Johnston, 2006; Lewis, 2011; Ram & Carter, 2003).

Grounded theory was used to better understand the unexplored dynamics of how accountants with a similar cultural background benefit from their heritage culture within their professional careers. Grounded theory seems appropriate given the need to build theory on complex, multifaceted processes that is firmly based in the data collected (Martin & Turner, 1986). The cases being studied here are qualified Black accountants located within the United Kingdom. The case study approach is particularly suitable where there is little or no prior theory (Riege, 2003). Given the difficulties other researchers have experienced in collecting data in this field (Johnston & Kyriacou, 2007; Lewis, 2011) and the limited number of potential cases available to be studied, it seemed fitting to choose extreme cases to study where I could ensure that the phenomenon of interest was 'transparently observable' (Pettigrew, 1990).

I recruited participants using a snowball approach which was appropriate given that my participant population of interest is small and hard to reach. This approach has been successfully used in similar studies when access to the sample has been difficult (Hammond, 2002; Johnston & Kyriacou, 2007). All the participants had parents born in Africa or the Caribbean or were born in Africa or the Caribbean themselves. I also included participants of mixed heritage who had one parent born in Africa or the Caribbean. I chose to study individuals who were qualified with any of the accounting bodies recognised by the Financial Reporting Council. I interviewed 14 accountants in total with 20 hours of recorded interviews (See Table 3.1). The analysis procedure followed the grounded theory approach formulated by Glaser and Strauss (1967). This approach requires that the data and theory be constantly compared throughout the data collection and analysis process (Miles & Huberman, 1994).

My personal experience as a Black chartered accountant of West African heritage makes my role as a researcher in this study uniquely valuable and well informed. During the project, it helped to build rapport with respondents quickly and develop social bonds that may have resulted in responses that researchers unfamiliar with accounting may not have achieved. I do not have to consider issues of white privilege (Wellman, 2001) in explaining the experiences of groups disadvantaged in this field, but I do need to consider my privilege as a researcher to shape research experiences (Anderson, 1993). I perceive my role in this research process as an opportunity rather than an intrusion (Lincoln & Guba, 1985).

Table 3.1. List of Participants.

Number	Pseudonym	Job Title	Sector	Qualification	Gender	Heritage
1	Beatrice	Art Curator	Arts	ACA	Female	Ghanaian
2	Chantel	Project Manager	Public Sector	ACA	Female	Guyanese
3	Daniel	Property Developer	Property	ACCA	Male	Nigerian
4	Edward	Gym Owner	Leisure	CIMA	Male	Nigerian
5	Anne	Senior Manager	Accounting	ACA	Female	South African
6	Andy	Senior Manager	Accounting	ACCA	Male	Nigerian
7	Bill	Senior Associate	Accounting	ACA	Male	Sierra Leonean
8	Charles	Business Partner	Banking	ACA	Male	Ghanaian/Jamaican
9	Frank	Accountant	Recruitment	ACCA	Male	Ugandan
10	Gavin	Senior Audit Manager	Accounting	ACA	Male	Ghanaian
11	Henry	Partner	Accounting	ACA	Male	Jamaican
12	Ian	Associate	Accounting	ACA	Male	Nigerian
13	James	Senior Associate	Accounting	ACA	Male	English/Zimbabwean
14	Gemma	Manager	Accountancy	ACA	Female	Nigerian

Notes: ACA: Associate Chartered Accountant; ACCA: Association of Chartered Certified Accountants; CIMA: Chartered Institute of Management Accountants.

Research Findings

The findings show that participants believed that their workplace behaviour was influenced to a large extent by their heritage culture. I identified three distinct pathways: professional attributes, cultural performance management, and cultural inspiration. See Table 3.2 which also includes additional explanations of the identified themes and notable quotes from the participants.

Professional Attributes

The participants provided evidence that indicated how their heritage culture prepared them for entry into a competitive professional environment and promoted behaviours that were considered necessary for their success. In particular, this pathway was fundamental in explaining the core influences in preparing individuals for the workplace. Participants were able to identify the influence of their heritage culture from their childhood regarding attitudes towards education, the choice of subjects to study in school and expectations after leaving formal education. The influence of the heritage culture was also reflected in individual career choices and workplace behaviour. Four themes emerged from the data analysis: the importance of education, postgraduate achievement, professional membership and strong work ethic.

Cultural Performance Management

Participants also described the influence of their heritage culture on their attitudes towards themselves as individuals and the meanings associated with this in the workplace. Two themes emerged from the data: self-knowledge and cultural performance. The participants indicated that their heritage culture motivated them to manage their cultural identity within a professional context.

Cultural Inspiration

Participants described how their culturally motivated interests encouraged them to pursue activities or modes of thought that supported their professional aspirations; this had the potential to accelerate professional development to the benefit of the organisation and the individual. Here, heritage culture of individuals provided an alternative lens to observe phenomena within the workplace. The data revealed two types of attributes that participants describe as being of long-term benefit to the individuals: culturally inspired interests and cultural wisdom.

Discussion on Intersectionality

The typology that emerged may not be the exclusive result of the influence of the heritage culture as initially conceptualised but the intersection of race, ethnicity

Table 3.2. Typology for Heritage Cultural Influence on Professional Careers.

Theme	Sub-theme	Explanation	Example
Professional Attributes	Importance of Education	Education is considered important as a path to future success.	'They were strict parents, very keen on education, which a lot of African families are.' Daniel
	Postgraduate Achievement	There is a clear expectation of academic and career success.	'I feel like there's maybe an inherent or maybe an emerging pressure to succeed.' James
	Professional Membership	Individuals are encouraged to enter a prestigious profession.	'You know the next step from that is to be qualified to be a professional, highly rated, Doctor, Lawyer… Accountant.' Andy
	Strong Work Ethic	Hard work is necessary and may mitigate potential discrimination.	'My mum said "you're going to have to work twice as hard as anyone else."' Beatrice
Cultural Performance Management	Self-knowledge	Culture provides a way for individuals to learn about themselves.	'I was certainly very aware of my culture and of maybe how it determines or it tells or informs someone else of who or what I am. It's difficult not to be.' Anne
	Cultural Performance	Culture must be performed subject to the social context.	'Obviously I'm very clear about my heritage but I'm British, so can relate on that level and you kind of leave other things at the door. It's not really relevant at work.' Chantel
Cultural Inspiration	Culturally Inspired Interests	Interests pursued as a consequence of culturally specific knowledge.	'My destination has always been push for the best and see what happens, but now its push for the best in Africa.' Bill
	Cultural Values and Wisdom	Culture as a source of values and wisdom.	'Just knowing where you're from, where they say – in English it will sound bad – but where your umbilical cord is buried. That is important and that kind of helps or influences.' Anne

and class within a professional context. The notion of intersectionality is used to address multiple forms of identity and inequality in different contexts and at different times (Rollock et al., 2015). The term is attributed to Crenshaw (1991) and avoids the issues of attributing social experiences to a single identity category. I propose that the research findings can be attributed to members of a Black middle class pursuing their class driven professional aspirations within a racialised labour market. Research on minority racial and ethnic middle classes have received little attention to date, and this reflects the wide disparity in the way the term 'Black middle class' has been conceptualised (Maylor & Williams, 2011; Rollock et al., 2012).[2]

Research has shown that accounting is normatively a middle-class occupation (Kirkham & Loft, 1993). In a study of class status among the Black middle class, Rollock et al. (2012) used Office of National Statistics socio-economic classifications NS-SEC1 and NS-SEC2 to define members of the Black middle class. It included those employed in clerical and skilled manual roles. Given this definition, the qualified accountants in this study satisfy the occupational criterion for belonging to the Black middle class. Another benchmark is used by Pattillo (2005) who described earnings of at least two times the poverty line in the United States. This was deemed inappropriate for the United Kingdom by Rollock et al. (2015) who suggest that this would equate to a salary of £23,000 per annum. In contrast, the lower end of earnings of the Black middle-class participants in the Rollock et al. (2015) study was £36,000. Given that newly qualified accountants can expect to make £48,100 and £59,000 per annum, respectively (Institute of Chartered Accountants in England and Wales, 2016), the participants in this study satisfy the earnings criteria for belonging to the Black middle class in the literature.

With respect to the educational achievement and attitudes of the Black middle class, participants in this study held postgraduate vocational qualifications. Archer (2010) suggests that Black middle class parents are involved and engaged in their children's education. This behaviour could be observed in the typology for professional attributes. If defined in terms of professional aspirations and attitudes towards education, then the participants appear to have parents that were involved and engaged in their education. Archer (2010) posited that race plays a significant and complicated role in education for minority middle-class families suggesting that due to racism, their class resources may protect against failure but their racial position curtails key aspects of any class advantage. This means that 'minority ethnic families must work disproportionately harder to achieve success' (Archer, 2010, p. 466). This phenomenon can be observed in the data under the strong work ethic sub-theme and the quote provided by Beatrice.

Viewed through an intersectional lens, the participants are members of a Black middle class seeking to benefit from their class resources by reproducing existing class structures from one generation to the next. In this regard, the goals of

---

[2]I am going to characterise the study participants as Black middle class using three criteria from the existing literature. The first criterion is based upon their occupation, the second is based upon their earnings and the third is based upon educational achievement and attitudes.

accounting are congruent with the participant's personal goals. As discussed, accounting has been shown to reproduce existing class structures and social stratification (Kirkham & Loft, 1993). As members of the Black middle class, participants can be described as seeking to benefit from the social closure of professional membership in obtaining social and economic benefits (Richardson, 1997). It is unclear if participants were able to distinguish between the influence of their class membership and that of their heritage culture. Individuals were clear that the attributes they were describing were attributed to their heritage culture as identified in the typology. There was however a clear understanding that their racial identity was a potential disadvantage, and this reflects the intersection between class and race in a profession.

Viewed through an intersectional lens, access to the professions was granted to participants through their middle-class aspirations and attributes discussed; however, within the workplace, they are required to remove elements of their identity that correspond with their racial identity. The need for individuals to perform their identity was a consequence of the intersection of race, ethnicity and the classed professional environment. The experience of race was something that participants raised only when considering the perceptions of others. This is indicative of a double consciousness (Du Bois, 1903) that emerges as a result of their negotiation through a racialised professional environment. The participants are describing their attempts to view themselves through the eyes of a member of the majority group to avoid reinforcing negative stereotypes. In contrast, their personal experience of their heritage culture reflected knowledge, pride and self-esteem regarding their ethnic identity. Participants were so familiar with the necessity to perform their identity that participants identified it as both a feature and consequence of their heritage culture.

Race and ethnicity were dismissed as irrelevant to the workplace by the participants; however, the attributes of being middle class meant that the participants were exhibiting traits consistent with the professional identity through their attempts to bleach out their own racial identities (Levinson, 1993). This requirement also explains why so few participants were able to enjoy the cultural inspiration pathway in the workplace. Participants were only able to benefit from these experiences if their racial and or ethnic identity was salient and acceptable within the workplace. Only one participant achieved this within an organisation, and he was a member of a team specifically concerned with African organisations. His knowledge and experiences were a rare competitive advantage.

Conclusion

The purpose of this chapter was to examine the role ethnicity plays in shaping the work-based behaviour of minority racial and ethnic professionals. Specifically, my focus was on how ethnic identity is enacted through heritage culture, and what this means in terms of workplace behaviours.

In this study, I used a Grounded Theory approach to focus on extreme case studies of Black accountants and identified a typology of three distinct pathways through which participants believed their heritage culture influenced their behaviour: professional attributes, cultural performance management and cultural inspiration. The approach led to using an intersectional lens to analyse the findings which resulted in uncovering a complex process of race, class, ethnicity and professionalism.

The data revealed that the participants were members of a Black middle class which was exhibited in their attitudes towards education, professional membership and general career aspirations. This had contradictory implications which meant that their collective experience was characterised by their class-driven aspirations for professional membership with its associated socio-economic benefits and at the same time a recognition of their ethnic identity in terms of self-knowledge and esteem for their heritage culture. This was mitigated by their experiences in a profession in which they believed it was necessary to exclude their racial identity. The participants perceived their ethnic identities as being congruent with their professional identities; however, they recognised that what they considered to be their ethnic identities was likely to be perceived as their racial identities by others. In other words, their racial identities were not considered to be congruent which explains why the participants shape their work-based behaviours in a manner that bleaches out their ethnic identities. To an observer, their racial and ethnic identities may appear to be identical. Instead, the result is a complex and challenging form of identity management on behalf of Black professionals.

It seems that the extent to which the heritage culture of Black professionals shapes their behaviour is great; however, it is mitigated by the role of class and race which may influence behaviour to a greater extent. This is achieved through the pathways identified in the typology and suggests that Black professionals have a complex and often contradictory experience within the workplace. This may be alleviated over time by the extent to which the normative professional identity remains white, male and middle class. However, given the history of accounting reproducing existing class structures (Kirkham & Loft, 1993), I suggest that the extent to which the normative professional identity remains intransient is itself influenced by the general identity of members of the middle class in the United Kingdom. This may be possible as a consequence of social mobility, and accounting itself may have a role to play. Research has found that the UK professions have become increasingly socially exclusive over the past 30 years. In particular, accounting was identified as the most socially exclusive profession in the United Kingdom, second only to journalism (Cabinet Office, 2009). This suggests that in the foreseeable future, existing normative identities and the challenges of being a Black professional may persist.

While challenges exist, there are several exciting lines for future research to pursue. Class emerged as being an important source of identity and inequality that was not originally considered in this study. Moreover, participants rarely discussed it. Not enough is known about the experiences of Black middle-class professionals in the workplace. Research on minority racial and ethnic professionals is primarily concerned with their ethnic, racial and professional experiences. The literature may benefit from future research that considers the challenges and complexity surrounding being part of a Black middle class particularly for individuals who are seeking social mobility. Future research should also consider gender and other potentially salient identities such as sexual orientation.

The theoretical developments in this chapter are intended to encourage further studies of this nature. It may be possible for the normative identity within high-status professions like accounting to change over time given the ongoing legitimation processes of the professions, the increasing number of minority groups entering the labour market and the emergence of a global economy. This may have a profound impact on the experiences of minority racial and ethnic professionals in the workplace.

References

Alvesson, M., & Willmott, H. (2002). Identity regulation as organizational control: Producing the appropriate individual. *Journal of Management Studies*, *39*(5), 619–644.

Anderson, M. (1993). Studying across difference: Race, class, and gender in qualitative research. In M. Fine & L. Weis (Eds.), *The craft of research* (pp. 39–52). Sage Publications.

Archer, L. (2010). 'We raised it with the head': The educational practices of minority ethnic, middle-class families. *British Journal of Sociology of Education*, *31*(4), 449–469.

Berthoud, R. (2000). Ethnic employment penalties in Britain. *Journal of Ethnic and Migration Studies*, *26*(3), 389–416.

Bhopal, R. (2004). Glossary of terms relating to ethnicity and race: For reflection and debate. *Journal of Epidemiology & Community Health*, *58*(6), 441–445.

Blackaby, D. H., Leslie, D. G., Murphy, P. D., & O'Leary, N. C. (2002). White/ethnic minority earnings and employment differentials in Britain: Evidence from the LFS. *Oxford Economic Papers*, *54*(2), 270–297.

Bougen, P. D. (1994). Joking apart: The serious side to the accountant stereotype. *Accounting, Organizations and Society*, *19*(3), 319–335.

Burchell, S., Clubb, C., Hopwood, A., & Hughes, J. (1980). The roles of accounting in organizations and society. *Accounting, Organizations and Society*, *5*(1), 5–21.

Cabinet Office. (2009). *Unleashing Aspiration: The Final Report of the Panel on Fair Access to the Professions [Milburn Report]*. HMSO.

Crenshaw, K. (1991). Mapping the margins: Intersectionality, identity politics, and violence against women of color. *Stanford Law Review*, *43*(6), 1241.

Du Bois, W. E. B. (1903). *The souls of Black folks*. A. C. McClurg & Co.

Elliott, R., & Lindley, J. (2008). Immigrant wage differentials, ethnicity and occupational segregation. *Journal of the Royal Statistical Society*, *171*, 645–671.

Financial Reporting Council. (2024). *Key facts and trends in the accountancy profession 2023*. https://media.frc.org.uk/documents/Key_Facts_and_Trends_in_the_Accountancy_Profession_2024.pdf. Accessed March 11, 2025.

Friedman, A., & Lyne, S. (2001). The beancounter stereotype: Towards a general model of stereotype generation. *Critical Perspectives on Accounting*, *12*, 423–451.

Gephart, R. P. (2004). Qualitative research and the *Academy of Management Journal*. *Academy of Management Journal*, *47*(4), 454–462.

Glaser, B. G., & Strauss, A. L. (1967). *The discovery of grounded theory: Strategies for qualitative research*. Aldine.

Goffman, E. (1959). The presentation of self in everyday life. *Teacher*, *21*(5), 259.

Hammond, T. (1997). From complete exclusion to minimal inclusion: African Americans and the public accounting industry, 1965–1988. *Accounting, Organizations and Society*, *22*(1), 29–53.

Hammond, T. A. (2002). *A white collar profession: African American certified public accountants since 1921*. University of North Carolina Press.

Hammond, T., & Sikka, P. (1996). Radicalizing accounting history: The potential of oral history. *Accounting, Auditing & Accountability Journal*, *9*(3), 79–97.

Hammond, T., & Streeter, D. W. (1994). Overcoming barriers: Early African-American certified public accountants. *Accounting, Organizations and Society*, *19*(3), 271–288.

Institute of Chartered Accountants in England and Wales. (2016). *Salary Survey 2015*. http://www.icaew.com/~/media/corporate/files/about%20icaew/ICAEWSALARYSURVEY2015-amended.ashx?utm_source=ICAEWjobs&utm_medium=ArticleLink&utm_campaign=SalarySurveyReport. Accessed September 26, 2016.

Jeacle, I. (2008). Beyond the boring grey: The construction of the colourful accountant. *Critical Perspectives on Accounting*, *19*(8), 1296–1320.

Johnston, R., & Kyriacou, O. (2007). Figuring masculinities: Exploring ethnic masculinities in the institutions of UK accounting. *Accountancy Business and the Public Interest*, *6*(2), 75–113.

Kenny, E. J., & Briner, R. B. (2013). Increases in salience of ethnic identity at work: The roles of ethnic assignation and ethnic identification. *Human Relations*, *66*(5), 725–748.

Kirkham, L., & Loft, A. (1993). Gender and the construction of the professional accountant. *Accounting, Organizations and Society*, *18*(6), 507–558.

Kyriacou, O., & Johnston, R. (2006). Accounting for (in)visibilities: Resistance, gender and control. *Accountancy Business and the Public Interest*, *5*(2), 54–88.

Lehman, C. (1992). "Herstory" in accounting: The first eighty years. *Accounting, Organizations and Society*, *17*(3), 261–285.

Levinson, S. (1993). Identifying the Jewish lawyer: Reflections on the construction of professional identity. *Cardozo Law Review*, *14*, 1577–1579.

Lewis, A. (2011). *A study of the Black accounting experience in the UK* (Doctoral dissertation). Leeds Metropolitan University.

Lewis, A. M. (2015). A pilot study of the Black British professional accounting experience. *European Scientific Journal*, *11*(13), 1–16.

Lincoln, Y. S., & Guba, E. G. (1985). *Naturalistic enquiry*. Sage Publications.

Martin, P. Y., & Turner, B. A. (1986). Grounded theory and organizational research. *The Journal of Applied Behavioral Science*, *22*(2), 141–157.

Maylor, U., & Williams, K. (2011). Challenges in theorising 'Black middle-class' women: Education, experience and authenticity. *Gender and Education*, *23*(3), 345–356.

McNicholas, P., & Barrett, M. (2005). Answering the emancipatory call: An emerging research approach 'on the margins' of accounting. *Critical Perspectives on Accounting*, *16*(4), 391–414.

Miles, M. B., & Huberman, A. M. (1994). *Qualitative data analysis: An expanded sourcebook*. Sage Publications.

Moore, D. C. (1991). Accounting on trial: The critical legal studies movement and its lessons for radical accounting. *Accounting, Organizations and Society*, *16*(8).

Pattillo, M. (2005). Black middle-class neighborhoods. *Annual Review of Sociology*, *31*(1), 305–329.

Pearce, R. G. (2005). White lawyering: Rethinking race, lawyer identity, and rule of law. *Fordham Law Review*, *73*(94), 2081.

Pettigrew, A. M. (1990). Longitudinal field research on change: Theory and practice. *Organization Science*, *1*(3), 267–292.

Quintana, S. M. (2007). Racial and ethnic identity: Developmental perspectives and research. *Journal of Counseling Psychology*, *54*(3), 259–270.

Ram, M., & Carter, S. (2003). Paving professional futures ethnic minority accountants in the United Kingdom. *International Small Business Journal*, *21*(1), 55–71.

Ramarajan, L., & Reid, E. (2013). Shattering the myth of separate worlds: Negotiating nonwork identities at work. *Academy of Management Review*, *38*(4), 621–644.

Richardson, A. J. (1997). Social closure in dynamic markets: The incomplete professional project in accountancy. *Critical Perspectives on Accounting*, *8*, 635–653.

Riege, A. M. (2003). Validity and reliability tests in case study research: A literature review with "hands-on" applications for each research phase. *Qualitative Market Research: An International Journal*, *6*(2), 75–86.

Rollock, N., Gillborn, D., Vincent, C., & Ball, S. J. (2015). *The colour of class: The educational strategies of the Black middle classes*. Routledge.

Rollock, N., Vincent, C., Gillborn, D., & Ball, S. (2012). "Middle class by profession": Class status and identification amongst the Black middle classes. *Ethnicities*, *13*(3), 253–275.

Sommerlad, H. (2008). "What are you doing here? You should be working in a hair salon or something": Outsider status and professional socialization in the solicitors' profession. *Web Journal of Current Legal Issues*, *2*(1), 1–15.

Wellman, D. T. (2001). *Portraits of white racism* (2nd ed.). Cambridge University Press.

Chapter 4

The Railroad Connection: The Liners, the Muckers, and Me

Adam J. Saatkamp

Illinois Central College, USA

Introduction

As a new white male hire at a Big 4 firm, I was often asked to assist with inventory auditing procedures. Our firm had engagement teams across the country who would select one of their client's locations and – if our firm had an office nearby – they would ask a local associate, like me, to observe and test the inventory counts conducted by their client's employees. On these assignments, I counted everything from barbed wire to bulldozers, including windows, microchips, seeds, and steel. The most unique inventory I was assigned, however, was at a railroad.

Even though I grew up in a town bisected by tracks, and despite the fact that I received a model train for Christmas in 1986, I knew very little – almost nothing – about the operation of a railroad. As a kid, I spent my fair share of time watching trains through the window of our family's Astro van, as my parents and I waited for a freighter to pass and for those flashing red lights to stop and for the red and white gate to return to its upright position. That was about the entirety of my experience. And so, when I arrived at the address for the railroad company, I felt the discouraging effects of imposter syndrome something fierce.

I stepped out of my pickup truck, clipboard in hand, my obligatory steel-toed boots shifting in the gravel lot as I made my way toward the building. I was there to meet some folks who would show me around, take me to the materials I'd been asked to count. Winter was approaching in the Midwest and my outfit was far from the sophisticated, "professional" attire most accounting students expect to wear while on the job. I strode up the path in jeans, boots, and a flannel coat, rocks crunching beneath my feet. I took a deep breath, did my best to shake off the imposter syndrome as I wiped my boots on the welcome mat, and opened the office door. Inside I was greeted by three men, one of whom was to be my guide for the day. He tossed me a bright orange stocking cap and a pair of winter gloves, each emblazoned with the railroad's logo. Then, he said, "Let's go find some frogs."

Voices of Change, 47–58

Published under exclusive licence by Emerald Publishing Limited
doi:10.1108/978-1-83753-030-420251012

Like any rational person not versed in railroad lingo, I instantly pictured the two of us knee-deep in a bog, searching for slimy, green amphibians. It goes without saying that I had no intention of verbalizing my vision. If I did, if I had asked the railroad man about Kermit's relatives, the title on my business card should have been *ignorant-dumb-dumb-man* instead of *auditor*. Instead, I simply nodded and allowed the man to lead the way. A few minutes later, we were standing among a giant pile of frogs – not the green ones, the ones made of steel. Yes, dear reader, apparently, there's more than one type of frog. If you're just as surprised as I was, then what follows is for you.

In my brief career as an auditor, and now as an academic, I've often had to admit my benightedness – that's a fancy word for being in the dark, which is another way of saying *ignorant* or *unenlightened*. Early on in my career, I'd often say to myself, "I didn't know that" or "Seriously?" Now, with a few gray hairs in my beard, I'm more likely to think, "*Why* didn't I know that?" or "*Why* wasn't I taught this?" Standing among the steel frogs – the parts of a railroad that allow a train's wheels to switch from one track to another – I simply acknowledged my *benightedness* and started counting. Today, however, when I'm faced with my own ignorance, I want to know why. Sometimes the answer is easy. Sometimes it's not.

Why didn't I know about steel frogs? That's easy. I studied accounting, not railroad construction. But there are more difficult questions, too. Who are we as accountants, and where did we come from? That's a more difficult question to answer, but it's one some folks, like Baladouni (1979), think we should be asking. I think so, too. The question of who we are and where we came from must be asked for several reasons, one of which might just explain, or, at minimum, partially illuminate, why inclusivity has been so elusive.

Problem

In her recent research, Peralta (2022) identified the accounting profession as one of the least diverse industries. While such a finding is far from shocking given previous research on the topic, Peralta did identify a much more disturbing characteristic of the profession. Of those surveyed, accountants were "the least likely to say that DEI is important" (p. 14) and had the highest percentage of purely negative reactions to DEI initiatives. Why? The answer, I argue, is tied to the difficult question posed above – who are we and where did we come from? In this chapter, I analyze how the profession's common storied narrative regarding the railroad reinforces white, professional virtue, and how such virtue derails progress toward genuine inclusivity. I make my argument using Baldwin's (1965) zoomorphic conceptualization of the impaled butterfly as a theoretical frame to analyze key aspects of our historiography. I conclude by exploring the meaning and value of releasing our hold on innocence, extracting the pin that impales us.

Theoretical Framework

In 1965, the renowned novelist, essayist, and activist, James Baldwin, published a piece in *Ebony* magazine, in which he laid out the reason for the persistent separation between white America and Black America. He writes principally of his observations of white Americans. As he sees it, the majority of white Americans believe in a "history that flatters them" (p. 723). This, according to Baldwin, while not surprising – given the racial background of most historians – is particularly problematic. As humans, we underestimate the role history plays in our daily lives. Baldwin argues that "the great force of history comes from the fact that we carry it within us, are unconsciously controlled by it in many ways" (p. 723). Further, he maintains that "it is to history that we owe our frames of reference, our identities, and our aspirations" (p. 723). In other words, the stories we tell ourselves about the past are very much with us in the present.

Consequently, in the stern songfulness that sets him apart, Baldwin charges his reader to confront history. To achieve personal maturity and freedom, one must be willing to "assess the history which has placed one where one is and formed one's point of view" (p. 723). Unfortunately, white Americans are generally unwilling to do this; they "are impaled on their history like a butterfly on a pin" and are "incapable of seeing or changing themselves, or the world" (p. 723). Those on the pinning board hold tightly to their innocence, a position Baldwin perceives as inimical to maturity. Their constant refrain is: "Do not blame *me*, I was not there. I did not do it" (p. 723, emphasis in original).[1] Similarly, Feagin (2020) describes this as "accenting white virtuousness," particularly in response to calls for racial justice (p. 30). Put another way, the impaled butterfly clings to his innocence and "remains proud of that history for which he does not wish to pay, and from which, materially, he has profited so much" (p. 724). Ultimately, for Baldwin, the unwillingness of white Americans to read and accept recorded history "hideously menaces this country" (p. 722) because it stands in the way of true and honest dialogue.

Is, then, the profession full of impaled butterflies? Are such butterflies the cause behind Peralta's (2022) findings – that accountants are the professionals least interested in DEI? Two questions that are understandably difficult to answer. And yet, one *can* confront the profession's history, as Baldwin encourages, and consider whether our historiography encourages pin-pulling or whether it simply affirms our innocence. Take, for example, the railroad. I started this chapter with a railroad story because many believe that's where our story – the story of American accountants – begins. Sure, we've all heard of Pacioli and the birth of double-entry, a product of the Crusade crockpot – a crucible in which religious tensions simmered like soup in a slow cooker for hundreds of years. But Pacioli was Italian, and the Crusades were a long time ago. The American accounting profession, like all the others, has its own beginning. While the Italians got their start transporting soldiers and spices (Littleton, 1933/1966; Gleeson-White, 2011)

---

[1]In *Black Skin, White Masks*, Frantz Fanon uses similar imagery to Baldwin, but instead refers to the dehumanizing white gaze which dehumanizes the Black Other, pinning them like a butterfly being for display. This is then a question of agency between the white and Black subject. It is whites' unwillingness to confront their own history, particularly in relation to racism that pins them to the board. But for the Black social actor, it is the white racist gaze which pins Blacks irrespective of any action taken (Fanon, 1967).

and the British profession sprang, in part, from the shipping of slaves (Rosenthal, 2018), in America, or so we're often told, the profession was birthed by the railroad.

While we rightfully lament the Middle Passage and suck our teeth at the Crusades, we have nary a complaint about the incredible iron horse. Was the railroad truly an unsullied indicator of American industrial ingenuity, of its capitalistic prowess? Or should we believe, as a 19th century British banker noted of the English profession, that American accountants simply made "their fortunes by the misfortunes of others" (Worthington, 1895/1978, p. 67)? One's first step, then, in such an evaluative endeavor, is to hit the books – to absorb what it is we tell ourselves about our relationship to the railroad. Having acquired a sense of the story we tell ourselves, one can then widen the search and weigh our story against the broader narrative.

Conceptual Analysis

Our Story

If an aspiring accountant or university student were to seek information about our connection to the railroad, they might begin with King (2006) – a concise, readable introduction to select aspects of our history. One might then reach for Previts and Merino's (1998) more comprehensive work or crack the spine of Littleton's (1933/1966) seminal text. From there, they might gain insight from Carey (1969), glean a social view from Miranti (1990), or gain a political perspective from Soll (2014). While I am greatly indebted to all of these books, on the whole, these historical texts claim the American profession owes its ascendancy to three specific social changes brought about by the railroad: foreign investment, financial innovation, and fiscal accountability.

Foreign Investment

In his 1915 textbook on railway accounting, William E. Hooper maintains that accounting becomes more important the farther the user is from the action. Accordingly, he writes, "The man who lives in Europe and invests his money in securities of a great American railroad system…must demand from a railroad corporation a very perfect system of accounting" (p. 2). After construction began on the Baltimore and Ohio in 1828 – then the nation's most significant railroad – the nation's railway system expanded rapidly. Between 1840 and 1870, the United States built more miles of track than any other country. And yet, this was not solely an American accomplishment. As Soll (2014) notes, "This unprecedented growth needed to be funded by investors, and there was simply not enough American capital to fund investment in the American railroad" (p. 168). As a result, railroad companies sought foreign investment.

This reality is confirmed by Previts and Merino (1998) who describe how "every new burst of railway construction was met by a corresponding burst of investment from abroad" (p. 110). Likewise, Carey (1969) highlights how "large amounts of

British capital were invested in the industries of the United States" during this time (p. 21). Much of this financing was obtained without detailed financial statements. In fact, selling American railroad bonds to Europeans required a measure of persuasive hornswoggling, then a specialty of bankers at J.P. Morgan (King, 2006). From 1870–1900, European investment in America increased 150%, reaching $3.3 billion by the turn of the century (Miranti, 1990), a feat made possible via the convertible mortgage bond and the 38 railroad stocks trading on the New York Stock Exchange in 1869 (Soll, 2014). Thus, the expansion of the American railroad system was fueled, in part, by financial innovation.

Financial Innovation

Much of our modern-day finance infrastructure owes its existence and evolution to the American railroad. To underscore this reality, King (2006) points to the work of noted business historian, Alfred D. Chandler, Jr, who argues, in his work *Scale and Scope: The Dynamics of Industrial Capitalism* (1990), "nearly all the instruments and techniques of modern finance in the United States were perfected in order to fund the construction of railroads" (p. 58). One instrument of particular importance was the corporate form of organization. Previts and Merino (1998) maintain that "the corporate form of business served as the essential vehicle for railroad capital formation" (p. 67). Corporations were attractive due to the ease with which one could transfer ownership and the limited liability one assumed after investing.

Significant foreign investment also resulted in an evolving capital market. Chandler (1954) elsewhere elaborates on the evolution of railroad finance from 1830 to 1850, wherein he describes the shifting center of importance across those decades. In the 1830s, railroad companies sold bonds to Europe either directly or through banks in Philadelphia. The City of Brotherly Love eventually lost its power as the center of railroad finance due to the aftereffects of the Panic of 1837. Having relied more heavily on stocks than bonds, New England railroads were better able to weather the storm of the late 1830s and successfully shifted the center of railroad finance to Boston in the 1840s. Later on, however, another financial crisis, the bursting of Britain's railroad bubble in 1847, shifted the center of railroad finance once again, from Boston to New York City.

As America's leading port, New York benefited from increasing international trade during the latter half of the 1840s, allowing it to be the city best positioned to weather the approaching economic storm. By 1850, only New York had funds for ambitious railroad projects. Between 1850 and 1860, New York financed the expansion of the American railway system, which had grown from 7,000 to 30,000 miles. According to Chandler, Wall Street and the mortgage bond carried the railroad south and west and solidified New York as the financial center of America. As the railroad grew, so did the complexity of American business. Soll (2014) argues, "the advent of railroads not only brought great industrial innovation but also brought new and quicker avenues of financial complexity and corruption" (p. 168).

Fiscal Accountability

In the 1880s, British accountants began making the transatlantic voyage in order to verify railroad financial statements. One British firm went so far as to establish an office in the United States, a move soon followed by others. According to King (2006), this firm – Barrow, Wade, Guthrie & Company – provided the first audit of an American railroad, the New York, Ontario, and Western Railway. It was during this period that the American accounting profession began to emerge. Miranti (1990) writes, "Initially organized in Britain more than a generation earlier, the profession of public accountancy first flourished in America during the 1880s as a result of the growing need among businessmen and investors for objective economic data" (p. 25). While British firms may have been the first on the scene, American accountants weren't far behind.

In 1895, Elijah Watt Sells and Charles Waldo Haskins, two former railroad accountants, opened Haskins & Sells, the first auditing firm established by American accountants. Two years later, the University of Chicago offered a course in railway accounts (Van Wyhe, 1994); such was the need for industry-specific expertise. As explained by Previts and Merino (1998), "railroading also created a demand for new business management skills, including the services of an emerging class of accountants and auditors" (p. 72) – gentlemen who would come to view themselves as the protectors of capitalism.

As the profession evolved, so did its self-image. The profession's identity and the force driving its ascendancy – the railroad – were linked. According to Soll (2014), "If railroads collapsed or swallowed investors, capitalism – and indeed governments and nations – could not function. Oversight was needed, and accountants now stepped up as the official regulators of modern capitalism" (p. 171). Similarly, Carey (1969) describes how the rapid industrialization brought about by the railroad "was marred by financial abuses" that became "a national scandal" (p. 23). In other words, accountants would step in and step up to meet the public demand for fiscal accountability.

The Broader Narrative

If an aspiring accountant or university student were indeed to seek information about our past – about who we are or where we came from – in the above referenced works, those most readily available to such an inquirer, they would, if my summarization is correct, certainly find a "history that flatters them" (Baldwin, 1965/1998, p. 723). Our story portrays us as gentlemen who assumed responsibility for the protection of American capital markets, knocked about by corruption and malfeasance during the 19th century railroad boom. We were, as Keister (1896, as cited in Previts & Merino, 1998) put it, "the foes of deceit and champions of honesty" (p. 21). And yet, the broader story of the American railroad – the industry to which we owe our present prominence – has much for us to consider. If we are indeed "champions of honesty," we must account for the broader narrative, one of racial exploitation, ruthless imperialism, and rapacious greed.

Racial Exploitation

If the flattering tale we tell ourselves is tested for completeness – examined to determine whether all has been considered that should be considered – a number of pieces would be found missing. Most importantly, the story of our ascendancy fails to acknowledge the men and women whose hands, backs, and blood built the railroad, whose exploitation served as the foundation for the profession's elevation. While the first consequential railroad in America, the Baltimore & Ohio, had a Quaker at the helm who banned the use of slave labor, that policy was the very definition of an exception. According to Arnesen (2001), the history of railroading in America was "predicated upon racial divisions of labor. From its beginnings in the late 1820s and early 1830s, the American railway labor force was sharply segmented along ethnic and racial lines" (p. 5). Each region in the country relied heavily upon an exploitable workforce, one whose labor lined the pockets of American and British businessmen as it lined the tracks of America's railway.

In the south, prior to emancipation, railroad work was primarily assigned to those who were enslaved. Kornweibel (2010) writes, "Railroads meant progress to white southerners. But railroad construction, operation, and maintenance depended upon slaves. Thus, advancement rested on exploitation" (p. 28). The work necessary for such advancement was significantly more dangerous than agriculture. Since most railroads preferred not to own slaves – though many, like the North and South Carolina railroads, the Mississippi railroad, the Montgomery and West Point railroad, and the New Orleans, Jackson, and Great Northern railroad, did (Arnesen, 2001) – they rented help from slave owners, some of whom "took out insurance policies or insisted on contracts that excluded their slaves from the most dangerous tasks" (Kornweibel, 2010, p. 15). In other words, even slave owners recognized the perils of building a railroad. Perils aside, Arnesen (2001) notes that approximately 20,000 enslaved people were working for southern railroads when the Civil War began. At its conclusion, things began to change.

Emancipation presented a serious problem for southern railroads. Their cheap source of labor was no longer abundantly available. In response, railroad contractors in Georgia began what would come to be known as convict leasing (Arnesen, 2001). Instead of renting enslaved people, they began to rent convicts. The need for exploitable labor also led to a drastic change in the demographics of prison populations, most antebellum prisoners were white and most postbellum prisoners were Black. Kornweibel (2010) argues that convict leasing "replicated slavery, but with an earlier death sentence" (p. 44). As one example, Nelson (2006) maintains that approximately one-third of the roughly 400 convicts leased to the Chesapeake & Ohio Railroad between 1871 and 1872 died. One of the men leased out to the railroad in December 1868, was a twenty-one-year-old Black man named John Henry.

While his arrest may have been questionable – it occurred under Virginia's Black Codes – he was nevertheless arrested for stealing from a grocery store and sentenced to 10 years in prison (Nelson, 2006). Far from the fabled tales, prison records mark Henry's height at five feet one inches tall. As the C&O attempted to tunnel its way through the Allegheny Mountains, "John Henry and the dozens of others shipped to the mountains would have begun as unskilled laborers for the C&O. They worked as 'muckers', loading the broken rock and muck onto railway cars" (Nelson, 2006, p. 77). Eventually, however, evidence suggests that Henry may indeed have raced a steam drill and died sometime in 1873 at the age of 26.

Henry was by no means the lone victim of the railroads. In the 1870s, railroads like the Greenwood & Augusta showed little interest in the well-being of leased convicts. According to Kornweibel (2010), the convicts on the G&A "labored in chains and were underfed, poorly housed, and medically neglected. Almost half of the 265 prisoners died" (p. 45). Ultimately, the 19th century expansion of the railroad in the southern states depended on the exploitation of enslaved and incarcerated African Americans. Elsewhere in the country, railroads exploited other racial and ethnic groups in order to expand westward. Arnesen (2001) acknowledges that "for much of the 19th century, it was African Americans and immigrants from Europe, Asia, and Mexico who graded the roadbeds, laid the track, and ensured their upkeep over rail networks that extended tens of thousands of miles" (p. 6). In other words, the railroad crews were comprised of the "inferior" members of society.

In the southwest, trackliners were largely Mexican and Mexican American. In the west, the Central Pacific and other railroads exploited cheap Chinese labor. According to Ambrose (2000), the state of California acted on its determination of Chinese "inferiority" by doing "all it could to degrade and deny them a decent livelihood" (p. 150). The Chinese suffered said discrimination while doing the railroad work everyone else refused to do, blasting through the Sierra Nevada with black powder and nitroglycerin. Importantly, Ambrose (2000) reminds us that "white men despised the Chinese even as they used them" (p. 151). To the north, railroads used Japanese labor to build the Great Northern and Oregon short lines. Put simply, American railroads exploited numerous racial and ethnic groups to connect east and west, north and south. As Arnesen (2001) states, "By the turn of the century, Italians and other new immigrants from eastern and southern Europe, along with blacks and Mexicans, made up the section gangs on many northern and midwestern railroads" (p. 6). Ultimately, it was the exploitation of "inferior" racial and ethnic groups – groups the accounting profession actively excluded due to "suspect" morality (Miranti, 1990) – that shoveled coal into the economic engine that powered the profession.

Ruthless Imperialism

Not only did railroads exploit "inferior" racial and ethnic groups, ones "beneath" the Anglo-Saxo majority, they did so for empire-making purposes. On July 1, 1862, former railroad lawyer and then President, Abraham Lincoln, signed the Pacific Railroad Act, giving Native American land to railroad companies intent on building the first transcontinental railroad, connecting the east to the west. The Union Pacific built westward from Iowa, the Central Pacific from California to the east. As progress ensued, folks began moving west, claiming land along the railroad. This encroachment, according to Ambrose (2000), "meant doom for the [Native American] way of life. No longer could they be free and independent...They could either follow the way of the Pawnee and live on reservations, cared for by the white man, or get killed" (p. 173). Likewise, Jensen (1975) notes that Native American claims to land "were, in the cavalier phrase of the white man's law, 'extinguished'" (p. 106). Put simply, the Central Pacific and Union Pacific drove their section gangs through the homelands of at least 15 Native American tribes, justified in their actions by racial and societal "superiority."

This imperial attitude was often met with resistance. Specifically, Ambrose (2000) recounts how, west of Nebraska, the "Sioux and Cheyenne were predominant, and decidedly hostile. They despised the iron rail" and wanted railroad men "out of their country" (p. 173). As a result, the transcontinental railroad needed the protection of the US military. According to historian Walter Johnson, "The US Army and the railroad men worked together to build the western empire" (p. 164). Leading the US Army's protective efforts was General William Tecumseh Sherman, who wrote of said efforts, "We are not going to let a few thieving, ragged Indians stop the progress of the railroad," and "We must act with vindictive eagerness against the Sioux, even to their extermination, men, women, and children" (Johnson, 2020, p. 165). In other words, no level of violence was too much if it served to protect the all-important railroad. Put simply, Johnson (2020) writes, "the pathway to freedom in the late nineteenth-century United States was through Indian killing" (p. 167).

Rapacious Greed

Like chattel slavery, the exploitation of railroad workers was motivated by greed, an unquenchable desire for more – more land, more money, more power. Writing on the construction of the transcontinental railroad, Jensen (1975) describes how there was "wealth for some and poverty and death for others" and that rewards were "not necessarily given to the deserving, as is the habit of history" (p. 84). In other words, those crushed under the weight of the iron horse – the men and women who cut through the earth and tunneled the mountains – gave their lives and others made money. Jensen (1975) highlights the many railroads that were built with a "generous amount of double dealing" (p. 105): the Northern Pacific, Denver & Rio Grande, Texas & Pacific, Santa Fe, Southern Pacific, likely many more.

Both lines tasked with building the transcontinental railroad would also be included in the above list. The Central Pacific charged the mountain rate of $48,000 per mile for flat land that should have been billed at $16,000. Similarly, the leadership of the Union Pacific arranged the financing structure to enrich themselves, billing $60,000 per mile, double the estimated cost of construction, ensuring the extra funds found their way into management pockets (Jensen, 1975). To sweeten the deal and increase profits, management at the Union Pacific pitted the different racial and ethnic section gangs against each other to keep the cost of laying track as small as possible (Roediger & Esch, 2012). Put simply, greed motivated the business decisions of many railroad men and, in addition, created numerous conflicts of interest which were present in "the building of nearly all great railroads in the mid-19th century" (Jensen, 1975, p. 88).

In the antebellum south, slave owners renting their "property" to the railroad "profited handsomely from such transactions" (Kornweibel, 2010, p. 11). During the convict leasing era, states freed themselves of the "financial burden of maintaining a penitentiary, instead making money on each individual leased" (Arnesen, 2001, p. 10). If a convict died, the railroad simply asked for another. In the west, greed and racism were intertwined. One contractor on the Central Pacific refused to pay Chinese workers individually because, like his view of Native Americans, it was "impossible to tell the Chinese apart" (Ambrose, 2000, p. 153) and he was concerned about paying someone twice. As a result, he paid them as a collective, and a Chinese worker distributed the wages. These few examples only shine a partial light on the greed of those who were asked to make the railroad a reality. Those who bought and sold railroad stocks and bonds engaged in their own avaricious activities. If the profession's path to prosperity was lined by the tracks of the American railroad, then exploitation, imperialism, and greed were the ties buried underneath.

Conclusion

This brief comparison of the profession's narrative with the broader narrative is far from an omnibus assessment. And yet, even this quick glance at the two stories by an average armchair historian reveals important differences. Naturally, objections will be raised. Some may use said brevity to dismiss the analysis wholesale or excuse the omitted, unflattering bits as a mere delimitation. Like recent pushback (Sweet, 2022), others, of the historical ilk, might call it out as presentism – their label for a supposedly misguided approach to history. Objections aside, a simple reading of these two narratives exposes the flattery found in the profession's story.

Given the profession's historiography and acknowledging Baldwin's (1965) argument, that history shapes our frames of reference, naturally, when presented with the broader narrative of exploitation, imperialism, and greed, one would expect the collective refrain Baldwin critiques, "Do not blame [*us*]. [We] were not there. [We] did not do it" (p. 723) – the modern equivalent evidenced in the profession's largely negative reactions to DEI (Peralta, 2022). In other words, "We bear no guilt. We owe no debt. We are *innocent*" – the pin that secures us firmly to the board and restricts our ability to engage in honest dialogue.

Currently, the predominant philosophy of accounting education is to reflect practice, not to shape it. To produce graduates that fit the current mold, to reproduce the status quo. This view, though presently accepted, was apparently less so in decades past. At one point in time, prior to the second half of the 20th century, accounting academia served as the conscience of the profession (Van Wyhe, 1994). To produce graduates and professionals who value DEI, accounting academia must reprise that role, to accept and teach the unflattering parts of our history, to give up our claims to innocence and help our students and ourselves start the pin-pulling process. This is a challenging task, to be sure – one that takes a fair amount of courage. At least, that has been my experience attempting to extract the pin from my own chest.

References

Ambrose, S. E. (2000). *Nothing like it in the world: The men who built the transcontinental railroad 1863-1869*. Simon & Schuster.

Arnesen, E. (2001). *Brotherhoods of color: Black railroad workers and the struggle for equality*. Harvard University Press.

Baladouni, V. (1979). The study of accounting history. In E. N. Coffman (Ed.), *The academy of accounting historians: Working paper series* (Vol. 1, pp. 318–327). The Academy of Accounting Historians.

Baldwin, J. (1998). The white man's guilt. In T. Morrison (Ed.), *Collected essays*. The Library of America. (Original work published 1965).

Carey, J. L. (1969). *The rise of the accounting profession: From technician to professional 1896–1936*. American Institute of Certified Public Accountants.

Chandler, A. D., Jr. (1954). Patterns of American railroad finance, 1830-50. *Business History Review*, *28*(3), 248–263.

Chandler, A. D., Jr. (1990). *Scale and scope: The dynamics of industrial capitalism*. Harvard University Press.

Fanon, F. (1967). *Black skins. White masks*. Grove Press.

Feagin, J. R. (2020). *The white racial frame: Centuries of racial framing and counter-framing* (3rd ed.). Routledge.

Gleeson-White, J. (2011). *Double-entry: How the merchants of Venice created modern finance*. W.W. Norton & Company.

Hooper, W. E. (1915). *Railroad accounting*. D. Appleton and Company.

Jensen, O. (1975). *The American heritage history of railroads in America*. American Heritage Publishing Co., Inc.

Johnson, W. (2020). *The broken heart of America: St. Louis and the violent history of the United States*. Basic Books.

King, T. A. (2006). *More than a numbers game: A brief history of accounting*. Wiley.

Kornweibel, T., Jr. (2010). *Railroads in the African American experience: A photographic journey*. The Johns Hopkins University Press.

Littleton, A. C. (1966). *Accounting evolution to 1900*. American Institute Publishing Co. (Original work published 1933).

Miranti, P. J., Jr. (1990). *Accountancy comes of age: The development of an American profession, 1886–1940*. The University of North Carolina Press.

Nelson, S. R. (2006). *Steel drivin' man: John Henry, the untold story of an American legend*. Oxford University Press.

Peralta, P. (2022). *The ROI on DEI*. Arizent Research.

Previts, G. J., & Merino, B. D. (1998). *A history of accountancy in the United States: The cultural significance of accounting*. Ohio State University Press.

Roediger, D. R., & Esch, E. D. (2012). *The production of difference: Race and the management of labor in U.S. history*. Oxford University Press.

Rosenthal, C. (2018). *Accounting for slavery: Masters and management*. Harvard University Press.

Soll, J. (2014). *The reckoning: Financial accountability and the rise and fall of nations*. Basic Books.

Sweet, J. H. (2022, August 17). Is history history? Identity politics and teleologies of the present. *Perspectives on History*. American Historical Association. https://www.historians.org/research-and-publications/perspectives-on-history/september-2022/is-history-history-identity-politics-and-teleologies-of-the-present

Van Wyhe, G. (1994). *The struggle for status: A history of accounting education*. Garland Publishing, Inc.

Worthington, B. (1978). *Professional accountants: An historical sketch*. Arno Press. (Original work published 1895).

Chapter 5

Accounting Practices in the Public Sector in the Eastern Caribbean: Do They Reflect Caribbean Realities?

Cleopatra Gittens

University of the West Indies, Five Island Campus, Antigua

Introduction

This chapter delves into the evolutionary trajectory of financial reporting within the public sector in the Eastern Caribbean, tracing its evolution from manual procedures and ambiguous accounting standards to the contemporary realm of electronic reporting. In contrast to their larger counterparts, such as Trinidad and Tobago, Jamaica, and Guyana which gained independence from Britain in the 1960s, the smaller islands in the Eastern Caribbean, such as Antigua and Barbuda, have been more reliant on the developed world and donor agencies. This dependence underscores a critical need to assess the implications and challenges associated with the adoption of international public sector standards in these small developing Caribbean nations.

International organizations like the International Monetary Fund (IMF) and the World Bank targeted the islands of the Eastern Caribbean for technical assistance due to challenges in public sector accounting systems. However, the islands, which either are or were colonies of Britain, inherited their public sector accounting structure and systems from the structures and processes handed down from their colonial masters. This has been well established in the literature in the context of the private sector which has implications on the accounting profession and as a default education and training for the Commonwealth Caribbean (Bakre, 2006). This chapter focuses more specifically on the public sector.

Public sector accounting in the Caribbean is underpinned by legislation via appropriations acts passed annually in parliaments across the Caribbean which

Voices of Change, 59–70

doi:10.1108/978-1-83753-030-420251014

also includes financial instructions, stores rules and the imprest.[1,2] As early as the mid-1800s, accounting reports were prepared by the Treasurer and presented in the House of Assembly (House of Assembly Minutes Antigua, 1849). These records were often limited to taxation and government expenditures with little focus on economic development or financial reporting. The system of journals and ledgers was in manual books of account, ledgers, and cash books and still in place in some islands up to the early 2000s. Prior to independence, these countries had limited accounting practices since the financial records were primarily kept by the colonial powers.

Over time, small developing countries (SDCs) developed their accounting systems relying on the processes and procedures handed down to them from the colonial period. For the most part, they used a cash accounting system. Budget allocations and actual expenditures and revenue were required to be accounted for in the year incurred and all payments had to be made within the year (Colony of Antigua, 1956). The practice was for there to be no payables or receivables on the books at the end of the financial year. But now, SDCs are being encouraged to implement new standards driven by the donor institutions similar to countries like Nigeria as highlighted by Bakre et al. (2022).

The smaller islands of the region, most of which are situated in the Eastern Caribbean and form part of the Organisation of Eastern Caribbean States (OECS), lagged behind their bigger brothers and sisters in Trinidad, Tobago, Jamaica, and Guyana who had gained independence from Britain in the 1960s. All of the islands including the larger ones became reliant on the developed world and the donor agencies, which has placed the islands in a situation much like their African counterparts as highlighted by Bakre et al. (2022).

The aim of the research presented here is to provide background information on the research context and review existing literature on public accounting structures and processes in SDCs with particular emphasis on the Caribbean and Antigua and Barbuda. This chapter will conclude with a discussion on the implications of the implementation of first-world standards on the public sector in SDCs.

Background

Caribbean islands stretch from the Bahamas and Turks and Caicos Islands in the North to Trinidad and Tobago in the South. Guyana is considered to be part of the Caribbean although it is on the mainland of South America. The population of the islands is predominantly Black with a mixture of ethnicities present. The English-speaking countries form a block that is named the Caribbean Common Market (CARICOM).[3] The OECS is a subgroup of eight islands stretching from

[1]The legislation that authorizes government expenditure for a specified period of time usually one year.

[2]An account assigned to a government department under the authorization of the minister of finance.

[3]https://caricom.org. Accessed on July 11, 2024.

Grenada in the south to St. Kitts and Nevis in the north. The members of the OECS are Antigua and Barbuda, the Commonwealth of Dominica, St. Kitts and Nevis, St. Lucia, St. Vincent and the Grenadines, Grenada, Cariacou and Petit Martinque, and Montserrat.[4] These groupings have developed structures and policies designed to benefit its members in areas of integration, development, and foreign policy coordination.

The governance structures in many Caribbean territories closely resemble the British system featuring upper and lower houses of parliament with the British Monarch serving as the ceremonial head (Campbell, 2018). Although a few countries have transitioned to republics, such as Trinidad and Tobago, Guyana, Dominica, and more recently Barbados, the fundamental government structure remains largely consistent with a president as the head of state replacing the British monarch. This British influence in governance has led to the continued adherence to British standards and structures in the laws and systems inherited from the colonial era.

In English-speaking Caribbean nations, the authority for government revenue accounting and management of government expenditures is vested initially in the Constitution and subsequently in the Finance and Administration Act or Finance Act of the respective territories. The majority of Caribbean governments have historically referred to their financial legislation as the Finance and Audit Act, Finance Administration Act, or similar variations.[5] Although many of these acts were repealed following independence from Britain, they have retained consistent requirements for a specified list of financial statements over the years.

These legislative acts also grant authority to ministers to establish regulations governing the financial aspects of government operations. These regulations, considered statutory instruments, define the procedures and tools for revenue collection, recording, expense authorization, and payment. Notably, the crafting and amendment of these acts have often been led by individuals working for international agencies providing technical assistance and training to residents of the various islands.

International institutions and donor countries have played a key role in shaping public sector accounting. The IMF extends concessional and non-concessional loans to its member countries, with these loans coming with specific conditions. IMF loans are approved by the IMF Executive Board to support countries facing economic challenges with limited alternative financing options. Conditionality is a key aspect of IMF assistance, wherein governments agree to adjust their economic policies to address the issues that necessitated financial assistance (IMF, 2016). These policy adjustments are crucial for developing robust fiscal policies, improving balance of payments, and safeguarding IMF resources.

---

[4]https://oecs.org/en/who-we-are/history. Accessed on July 11, 2024.

[5]Non-English-speaking countries, namely Martinique, Guadeloupe, Les Saints, and St. Martin, follow the French system due to their status as departments of France.

Numerous Caribbean countries, including Trinidad, Jamaica, Guyana, Grenada, Dominica, Antigua and Barbuda, and Barbados, have entered into standby arrangements with the IMF due to their economic and financial difficulties. These are chronicled by Fontaine (2021) as well as the structural adjustment loans and Extended Fund Facility (EFF) agreements that several Caribbean countries engaged in with the IMF from 1979 to the late 1990s. These engagements have significantly influenced the economies and financial landscapes of these nations, particularly those that were heavily dependent on the IMF for financial support. Fontaine (2021) also highlights the historical and socioeconomic factors contributing to the dependency of these countries on developed nations and institutions like the IMF.

The World Bank, akin to the IMF, provides grants and financial support to countries while setting financial management rules for development projects. The Bank's approach relies on existing institutions and systems within the borrower's country, considering their capacity. To benefit from financing and technical assistance, SDCs in the Caribbean must ensure that their systems meet World Bank standards. Diagnostic tests, such as the Public Expenditure and Financial Accountability (PEFA) assessment, are used to evaluate the strength of public financial management frameworks. PEFA assessments have been conducted in most SDCs in the Caribbean and serve as a key tool for donors to assess the suitability of investing in a particular country. It is described by the World Bank (2019) as a multi-donor partnership which assesses the condition of country public expenditure, procurement and financial accountability systems, and develops a practical sequence for reform and capacity-building actions. It utilizes seven pillars which include (1) policy-based fiscal strategy and budgeting, (2) predictability and control in budget execution, (3), accounting, recording, and reporting, (4) external scrutiny and audit, (5) transparency of public finance, (6) management of assets and liabilities, and (7) budget reliability (World Bank, 2019).

The Canadian International Development Agency (CIDA) has supported the Caribbean region based on geographical proximity, historical ties, tourism, and border security. CIDA's initiatives in the region encompassed regional integration, institutional strengthening, human resource development, education and economic development. The agency primarily directed its support to the Commonwealth Caribbean composed of countries formerly under British colonial rule. CIDA's contributions to the region amounted to $355.4 million between 1993 and 2003 (CIDA, 2004).

The Eastern Caribbean Economic Management Programme II (ECEMPII) played a pivotal role in enhancing financial systems in the Eastern Caribbean, focusing on economic and financial planning and management. In collaboration with the Caribbean Regional Technical Assistance Centre (CARTAC), CIDA implemented financial management systems, including revenue management, across several Eastern Caribbean countries. This initiative promoted regional solutions to economic management and financial systems challenges while enhancing cooperation among key financial officials. Remnants of these countries' colonial past remain; this understanding requires further examination for paths forward.

Review of the Literature

The accounting literature pertaining to accounting structures and processes within the public sector of SDCs in the Caribbean is notably sparse with much of the existing research primarily focused on African nations. Notably, studies such as Lassou et al. (2019) and Alawattage and Azure (2021) have explored the impact of both colonial powers and international financial institutions on accounting structures in African countries revealing substantial influence from both sources. Accounting structures and processes in SDCs have also evolved from colonial-era systems with subsequent modifications and influences over time. The remainder of this chapter presents a discussion of the literature and secondary data of Eastern Caribbean countries with particular focus on Antigua and Barbuda. Secondary sources reviewed include public financial management legislation and statutory instruments, the minutes of the house of assembly in Antigua and Barbuda, and reports from donor agencies.

Preindependence Era

Before independence, the Governments in the SDCs in the Caribbean had limited accounting practices as observed in how government's revenue and expenditure were reported. The Antigua and Barbuda House of Assembly minutes from 1840 to 1849 reflect the nature of the accounting reports. Their format during this era did not follow any particular accounting standard. The information was recorded as receipts and expenditure under line items such as wages and receipts from "harbour masters." Tawiah et al. (2022) note that during the colonial era in the former British colonies, accounting focused on tax reporting with no evidence of accrual accounting. Bissessar (2010) also notes that the system in the British colonies was a simple system focused on accounting for collection of taxes along with wages and salaries.

Early Postindependence Era

In the early postindependence era, Caribbean SDCs began to develop their own accounting practices which were influenced by their social and economic conditions. According to Bissessar (2010), these practices originated from the line-item budgeting and monitoring handed down by the British as well as the realities of the countries after independence. At this time, they had to focus on the promotion of economic development and putting in place the necessary structures, budgetary controls, and monitoring mechanisms to ensure economic growth.

The transition to independent accounting systems has been challenging for many SDCs in terms of implementing effective regulatory frameworks and building the necessary infrastructure to support accounting systems. But it also presented the opportunity for SDCs to develop accounting systems that were tailored to their unique needs.

Despite the efforts to develop budgeting and accounting systems to support the thrust of economic development, SDCs still faced challenges in developing effective accounting systems. As a result, there was a growing need for accounting reforms to improve the effectiveness of accounting systems in SDCs. For example, some researchers have suggested that SDCs could benefit from adopting a more flexible approach to accounting standards allowing them to better reflect the specific economic conditions and cultural norms of their societies (Bakre, 2006).

Mid-postindependence Era

In the mid-postindependence era, SDCs began to implement accounting reforms and modernize their accounting systems to improve transparency and accountability in public finances. According to Araya-Leandro et al. (2020), these reforms included the establishment of accounting standards and the creation of regulatory bodies to oversee accounting practices. In addition, SDCs began to invest in training programs for accountants and auditors to improve their skills and knowledge.

As SDCs modernized their accounting systems, they also began to adopt new technologies to improve accounting processes. According to Lim (2013), these technologies included accounting software, electronic invoicing systems, and online payment platforms. The adoption of technology has helped to streamline accounting processes, reduce errors, and improve efficiency.

Late Postindependence Era

International Public Sector Accounting Standards (IPSAS) are issued by the International Public Sector Standards Board (IPSASB). The IPSASB states on its website that it "works to improve the public sector worldwide through the development of IPSAS, international accrual-based accounting standards, for use by governments and other public sector entities around the world."[6] IPSAS were introduced to the islands in the late 2000s when donor agencies came together to fund public financial management reform. They are seen as best practices, and governments were encouraged to adopt the standards first starting with the Cash Basis IPSAS standards.

The developed world is now encouraging Small Island Developing States of the Caribbean to implement IPSAS accrual accounting before they have even mastered Cash Basis IPSAS. CARTAC (2012) reported that it assisted Barbados in developing a "road map" for implementation of IPSAS Accrual as part of its work in the Caribbean in 2011. In this same publication, CARTAC (2012) noted that all countries were having an issue with the requirement for consolidated financial statements to include state-owned enterprises which is a requirement of IPSAS.

Bakre et al. (2022) posit that IPSAS is more suited to countries with well-developed capital markets. This is not the case in the Caribbean, and yet, governments are now moving toward the IPSAS accrual basis. In fact, the

[6]https://www.ipsasb.org/. Accessed on July 18, 2024.

IPSASB has published an implementation strategy guide on its website. The International Federation of Accountants reported that more than 60% of the Caribbean countries that were included in a study adopted IPSAS while the others were working their way toward adoption. Two-thirds of the countries will implement accrual-based standards (IFAC, 2017).

The adoption of IPSAS has been seen as an important step in improving accounting practices in SDCs. According to Atuilik and Salia (2019), IPSAS provides a common set of accounting standards that can be applied across different countries improving transparency and accountability in public finances. Financed by the IMF, the World Bank, the Government of Canada, and the European Union, the islands implemented electronic systems at various stages of their development as part of the general thrust of public financial management reform (CARTAC, 2012). CARTAC (2014) reported providing assistance to more than six Caribbean countries in reformatting their financial statements with the IPSAS standards. CARTAC (2014) also noted that two Caribbean countries were well on their way to implementing IPSAS Accrual standards as well. Jamaica embarked on the project in 2004 and expected to implement it over a 10-year period (Jamaica Information Service, 2023). Subsequent reports suggest that some government-owned agencies have transitioned to accrual accounting. The government of Barbados has also embarked on the implementation of accrual accounting (CARTAC, 2014).

The electronic systems developed in SDCs of the Caribbean in the early to mid-2000s were still cash accounting systems in most islands. Technical assistance was provided to the governments to bring their financial management and reporting in line with international standards with an emphasis on transparency, effective fiscal management, and accountability (CARTAC, 2012; CIDA, 2004). The literature suggests that the first-world accounting standards in both the private sector and the public sector are the gold standard for all even though they are issued by the international bodies for international organizations and first-world governments. However, the literature also revealed that SDCs have their unique circumstances such as high debt, poor economic growth, and small populations due to their small size which is not taken into consideration by the international standards.

Discussion

Efforts made by Caribbean countries to strengthen their accounting frameworks and regulatory bodies have not been without challenges. These systems were often not well-suited to the needs of SDCs who possessed limited resources, small economies, and underdeveloped institutional frameworks. Many of the countries within the region have limited resources, and therefore, the implementation of new accounting frameworks and regulatory requirements has been slow. Furthermore, there has been a shortage of qualified accountants which has made it difficult to enforce the new regulatory requirements.

Preindependence, the accounting processes and standards used by the government more specifically of Antigua and Barbuda and other territories in the Leeward Islands were based on the processes and standards handed down by Britain. They were outlined in the laws that governed the territories. After independence, the personnel, processes, and standards were embodied in the law. In Antigua and Barbuda, the Finance and Audit Act of 1965 was repealed and replaced by the Finance and Audit Act of 1967. It was in 1967 that Antigua's status was changed to an associated state of Britain. The Finance and Audit Act of 1985 (CAP168) replaced the 1967 Act and utilized the Financial Instructions of 1956 (also referenced by Bissessar, 2010) that continued to be used until the Financial Regulations 2010 were passed by parliament and gazetted.[7] These regulations repeat many of the rules from 1956. However, they reflect a more modern accounting structure with electronic accounting systems and electronic forms of payment and revenue collection.

After independence, all of the islands embarked on reforms to improve their public financial management systems (CARTAC, 2012; World Bank, 2019). The fiscal imbalances and high debt burdens of these countries make implementing the international accounting standards including accrual accounting difficult. Collaboration among donor agencies has streamlined efforts and reduced duplication in improving these systems although countries are not uniformly advanced in system development. Additionally, documentation of updated processes and procedures may not have kept pace with system implementation, and legislation has not always accommodated specific reporting requirements reflecting remnants of the colonial system.

The eventual adoption of IPSAS accounting standards will be very costly for the cash-strapped governments due to moving from cash-based reporting to accrual. The financial realities of these small islands could derail any efforts to adopt these standards. Ironically, the high debt burdens, low economic growth, high unemployment, and fiscal challenges are among the reasons that the small Black and Brown island governments remain beholden to the governments of the developed world, the IMF, the World Bank, and other international institutions that influence the accounting structures and systems. The English-speaking islands are also supported by the Commonwealth Secretariat which has held several workshops for developing states on the public financial management improvement which promote the development of strong accounting systems and supporting structures.

The progress in implementing the standards was slow despite the reform efforts and technical assistance led by CARTAC and other agencies. Additionally, there are still deficiencies in financial reporting. This demonstrates similar issues identified by Saleh et al. (2021). Some of the barriers noted were resources both human and information technology and cost. Similar issues arose in developing countries in Africa as noted by Bakre et al. (2022). The lack of resources both technical and financial also contributes to the slowness of implementation of

[7]https://laws.gov.ag/wp-content/uploads/2018/08/cap-168.pdf. Accessed on July 15, 2024.

international accounting standards throughout the regional public sector. As noted previously, the larger islands appear to be further ahead. This is due to the islands taking full responsibility for governance much earlier than the smaller countries which gained independence from Britain in the late 1970s and early 1980s.

Given the issues identified in the implementation of standards set by external agencies, SDCs could develop their own flexible approach to accounting standards. If there is more flexibility in the development of accounting standards rather than automatic implementation of standards developed for first-world countries with different realities, SDCs will be able to identify those aspects of international standards that can be applied without adjustment and modify other standards to reflect the peculiarities and realities of SDCs. Saleh et al. (2021) notes that Malaysia developed its local public accounting standards by tailoring IPSAS to the local context. The single statement requirement for Cash Basis IPSAS is a cash flow statement. However, the legislation in islands like Antigua and Barbuda and Grenada requires asset and liability statements and several other statements which report on how the budget was executed. This is significantly more onerous than what is required by Cash Basis IPSAS which has served the islands well. IPSAS accrual standards have requirements that have proven to be difficult to meet in Antigua and Barbuda in particular due to the cost of implementation. For example, the requirement to value all assets on a particular schedule will be at a significant cost to SDC governments due to the number and size of historical assets to be valued and the cost of resources.

The success of implementing accounting standards, international or otherwise, requires collaboration between private and public sector accounting professionals and policymakers to develop public sector standards and place them in a mainstream regulatory body. The existing regulatory bodies in the region should collaborate on reviewing standards specifically for the public sector in the region. Taking it a step further, they are encouraged to lobby their African and South Pacific counterparts and take the opportunity to contribute to the further development of IPSAS to reflect the voice of SDCs.

However, the practice of using accounting certifications of the developed world as the de facto standard for certifying accountants in developing regions must stop. The Caribbean has sufficient qualified practitioners along with The University of the West Indies, known for its research, quality education, and lettered faculty to develop accounting certification and standards tailored to the needs of the region's public and private sectors which also take into consideration the size and other characteristics of indigenous businesses.[8] The effect of globalization on businesses is acknowledged, but much like India and Australia, the region can adapt the basic standards of the developed world and add to or subtract from them to create its own standards. The cost to companies to implement some of the

[8]The University of the West Indies was established in 1948 as a university college of London in Jamaica. It now has four landed campuses and an online global campus: www.uwi.edu

international financial reporting standards can significantly erode their bottom line while not providing any real benefits to their shareholders, governments, or customers. Continuing to utilize external certification to exclude your own people from the accounting practice is a form of social closure. It also perpetuates neocolonialism experienced across the private and public sector by relying on financing and foreign direct investment to fuel economic growth.

Conclusion

The chronology of activities that occurred along the journey of developing accounting structures and processes for best practices and meeting international accounting standards has been an interesting, bumpy winding road. Unfortunately, Caribbean islands have remained tied to vestiges of the colonial past. Island governments, instead of being able to design their own systems and structures at a speed comfortable to them and choosing what is best for their island states, are often placed on a schedule by international external bodies. Given their peculiarities, not just as Small Island Developing States but as states that have developed their systems and structures on a schedule not necessarily of their own choosing, the ministries of finance and the treasuries could end up with gaps in their systems or a system that is not tailored to suit their needs.

Similar to the findings of Bakre (2014), Bakre et al. (2022), and Alawattage and Azure (2021), I suggest the work of international organizations like the IMF and the World Bank in the SDCs of the Caribbean has used a big brother approach. The standards and practices being transferred are from the same colonial powers that shaped our destiny two centuries ago. Politicians in the SDCs appear to adopt structures used in foreign government ministries and departments since the advice they receive originates from the developed world, and it is they who fund projects to build structures and implement electronic systems. The imposition of accounting standards such as IPSAS comes with the guidance of the IMF, the World Bank, and the Commonwealth Secretariat which SDC governments are happy to accept because it is being paid for by these powers. International bodies select the consultants who work with SDC countries – consultants trained by and who work in western international institutions. They know little apart from what they have learned there. What about our Caribbean realities? Their ethos is inherited from the pillage of our former colonial masters who, after their "pots of gold" were filled, left the territories barren and broken for the descendants of slavery to pick up the pieces and try to form governments to manage the affairs of their countries. But the practices of the colonialists are still perpetuated in our systems of government, the adoption of their culture in the halls of parliament, the halls of justice, the departments of government, and in the boardroom continues. Hence, the standards of accounting and governance are adopted and not adapted to the detriment of developing Caribbean nations, who now more than ever must fight for the right of self-determination to create beneficial accounting standards of their own.

References

Alawattage, A., & Azure, J. D. (2021). Behind the world bank's ringing declarations of "social accountability" and Ghana's public financial management reform. *Critical Perspectives on Accounting*, *78*.

Araya-Leandro, C. E., del Carmen Caba-Perez, M., & López-Hernández, A. M. (2020). The process of modernization of the public accounting systems in Central American countries. In G. Azevedo, J. Oliveira, R. P. Marques, & A. Ferreira (Eds.), *Tools, strategies and practices for modern and accountable public sector-management* (pp. 97–122). IGI Global.

Atuilik, W. A., & Salia, H. (2019). Impact of IPSAS adoption on transparency and accountability in managing public funds in developing countries: Evidence from Liberia. *Journal of Accounting and Taxation*, *11*(6), 99–110.

Bakre, O. (2006). Accounting education, training and the profession in the Commonwealth Caribbean: Integration or internationalisation? *Accounting Forum*, *30*, 285–313.

Bakre, O. (2014). Imperialism and the integration of accountancy in the Commonwealth Caribbean. *Critical Perspectives on Accounting*, *25*(7), 558–575.

Bakre, O., McCartney, S., & Fayemi, S. O. (2022). Accounting as a technology of neoliberalism: The accountability role of IPSAS in Nigeria. *Critical Perspectives on Accounting*, *87*.

Bissessar, A. (2010). An institutional review of planning, budgeting and monitoring in the Caribbean: Challenges of transformation. *International Journal of Public Sector Management*, *23*(1), 22–37.

Campbell, M. (2018). The structure of government. *Jamaica Gleaner*. https://www.pressreader.com/jamaica/jamaica-gleaner/20180220/282291025711600

Canadian International Development Agency (CIDA). (2004). *Caribbean Regional Evaluation Program Evaluation Synthesis Report: Performance Review Branch 2004*. https://publications.gc.ca/collections/collection_2017/amc-gac/CD4-96-2004-eng.pdf

CARTAC. (2012). *Caribbean Regional Technical Assistance Center Annual Report*. https://www.cartac.org/content/dam/CARTAC/AnnualReports/CARTAC_Annual_Report_FY_2011_-_FINAL_PDF_for_Web.pdf

CARTAC. (2014). *Caribbean Regional Technical Assistance Center Annual Report*. https://www.cartac.org/content/dam/CARTAC/AnnualReports/CARTAC_Annual_Report_FY_2014_Webready.pdf

Colony of Antigua. (1956). *Minutes of the Legislative Council*. Archival records National Archives Antigua.

Fontaine, T. (2021). Caribbean country experiences with IMF stabilization programs within the context of globalization. https://www.thedominican.net/articles/stabilization.pdf

House of Assembly Minutes Antigua. (1840–1849). *National Archives Antigua*. Archival record CO352.

IFAC. (2017). Most Caribbean countries have adopted or are in the process of implementing IPSAS. https://www.ifac.org/news-events/2017-03/most-caribbean-countries-have-adopted-or-are-process-implementing-ipsas-according-new-study-ifac-and

International Monetary Fund (IMF). (2016). *IMF conditionality*. www.imf.org/en/About/Factsheets/Sheets/2016/08/02/21/28/IMF-Conditionality

Jamaica Information Service (JIS). (2023). *Government introduces more efficient accounting system*. https://jis.gov.jm/government-introduces-more-efficient-accounting-system/

Lassou, P. J., Hopper, T., Tsamenyi, M., & Murinde, V. (2019). Varieties of neo-colonialism: Government accounting reforms in Anglophone and Francophone Africa–Benin and Ghana compared. *Critical Perspectives on Accounting*, *65*.

Lim, F. P. C. (2013). Impact of information technology on accounting systems. *Asia-pacific Journal of Multimedia Services Convergent with Art Humanities and Sociology*, *3*(2), 93–106.

Saleh, Z., Isa, C. R., & Hasan, H. A. (2021). Issues and challenges in implementing international public sector accounting standards (IPSAS). *IPN Journal of Research and Practice in Public Sector Accounting and Management*, *11*(1), 1–14.

Tawiah, V., Oyewo, B. M., Doorgakunt, L. D. B., & Zakari, A. (2022). Colonisation and accounting development in sub-Saharan Africa. *Cogent Business & Management*, *9*(1).

World Bank. (2019). *PEFA, public financial management, and good governance*. https://www.pefa.org/sites/pefa/files/resources/downloads/9781464814662.pdf

Chapter 6

The Evolution of Accounting Science: COVID-19 Pandemic Lessons on Anti-Black Racism

Akolisa Ufodike

York University, Canada

Introduction

The COVID-19 pandemic, which arrived in North America in the winter of 2019–2020, taught humankind four lessons. Two of these are business lessons: first, supply chains matter (Morrow & Walsh, 2021); and second, people can work from home and still be productive.[1] The other two are basic social or life lessons: wash your hands and do not be racist. This chapter is about the last lesson; I look specifically at how my scholarly body of work in accounting science evolved in response to anti-Black racism, exemplified by the murder of George Floyd by police officers in broad daylight, and the accompanying revival of equity, diversity, and inclusion (EDI), exemplified by the visibility of the social justice movement and Black Lives Matter thereafter.[2]

The events that occurred in the aftermath of Floyd's murder led to a scholarly awakening for me. In 2020, at the time George Floyd was murdered, I was a Black pretenure assistant professor in the accounting discipline, where Black people are underrepresented, but I had never written about discrimination or racism in accounting (or business) – partly because I believed that, to the accounting academy, issues of social justice were not research worthy, or "science." After the murder of Floyd, however, I could not stay on the sidelines any longer. Floyd was

[1]The United States adopted a US-first vaccine policy and withheld vaccines from Canada – its most important trade and foreign partner. Human instinct in its most primal form is insular and tribal.

[2]EDI is the terminology used in Canada. In the United States, EDI is referred to as diversity, equity, and inclusion (DEI).

Voices of Change, 71–82

doi:10.1108/978-1-83753-030-420251017

born in the United States on October 14, 1973, the week after I was born in Nigeria. We were essentially born at the same time, in different places. I conduct research at the intersection of business and racism, and he lost his life at the intersection of business (he allegedly passed a counterfeit $20 bill) and racism. My social awakening led me to a research program on discrimination – particularly anti-Black racism but also racism more broadly as well as sexism, and nameism.

Coincidentally, in fall 2019, along with three other Black scholars, I had commenced a structured literature review (SLR) titled "A Knowledge Synthesis of Anti-Black Racism in Accounting Research" (Ufodike et al., 2023) for a special issue of *Accounting Perspectives* on literature reviews. We had no idea what was coming in the spring, but by May 25, 2020, when Floyd was murdered, the relevance of our study became more apparent and easier to situate in the literature. Our study, published in summer 2023, is the first knowledge synthesis on anti-Black racism in accounting literature of which I am aware. Our objectives were to identify and summarize extant accounting studies on anti-Black racism and to propose avenues for future research. We found only 25 related studies, including work from Anton Lewis (2015, 2016), Theresa Hammond (1997, 2003), Cheryl Lehman (Lehman et al., 2016), and Ida Robinson-Backmon (Robinson-Backmon et al., 1997). The scarcity of accounting studies on anti-Black racism is partly the result of the torturous path to tenure for those who undertake this work, and perceptions in accounting that the issue of racism belongs elsewhere, such as in human resources (Lewis, 2016). Prior to 2020, my body of research focused primarily on public accountability (Ufodike, 2017, 2020), network accountability (Ufodike et al., 2021, 2022), and public sector finance – specifically P3s (Opara et al., 2021, 2022). Floyd's murder – an explicit example of anti-Black racism exacerbated by the COVID-19 pandemic – marked a turning point in my research, and I started studying race and discrimination in and by accounting.

The SLR was my first project on race and discrimination in and by accounting. During the SLR study, I observed that the United States and South Africa were the primary sources of the literature – an unintended but notable consequence of both countries' ugly pasts with anti-Black racism. In Canada, the literature was nonexistent, as was racial data collection by universities and the accountancy profession (CPA Canada) (Ufodike et al., 2023). The limited works that remotely concerned the Black experience mainly examined labor market integration of immigrant accountants more broadly (primarily from India) and were conducted by the duos Kelly Thomson and Joanne Jones (2016) and Marcia Annisette (2003) and Umashanker Trivedi (Annisette & Trivedi, 2013).

Having demonstrated the gaps in the accounting literature (Ufodike et al., 2023), I then also responded our own call for future research and decided to expand the study to a comprehensive project – once again, the first of its kind in Canada, perhaps in any of the Organisation for Economic Co-operation and Development (OECD) countries – to investigate the barriers and challenges that prevent Black people from entering or thriving in the accountancy (and any business) profession. In fall 2021, I applied for a grant to the Social Sciences and

Humanities Research Council (SSHRC) Race and Gender Initiative. In April 2022, I was awarded approximately $450,000 for a three-year project, with Oliver Okafor as my coinvestigator. The project, titled "A Practice Theory Approach to Diversity on Boards and in Business Professions," has resulted in several publications, including Ufodike (2025), Ufodike and Ally (2023), and Ufodike et al. (2023). For context, Toronto – where I work – has three major universities with a combined student population of over 160,000: York University, Toronto Metropolitan University, and the University of Toronto. Toronto is Canada's (if not the world's) most diverse city, yet Oliver and I constitute 50% or two of the only four (the others being Marcia Annisette and Nelson Waweru) Black accounting professors in accounting departments in the Greater Toronto Area.

This chapter documents the evolution of my research as influenced by what I learned as an individual during the COVID-19 pandemic; the revival of EDI, influenced by what society learned during the pandemic; and the resistance to EDI. Lastly, I provide evidence that racism is still alive and well across generations and discuss why it is essential to remain steadfast in normalizing EDI. Understanding resistance to initiatives aimed at combating anti-Black racism is critical if Black people are to ever achieve substantive equality. As the Government of Canada puts it:

> substantive equality is the recognition that not all people start off from the same position and that these unequal opportunities make it more difficult for some to be successful. Treating everyone the same is only fair if they are starting from the same position. (Canada, n.d.)

The Evolution of Accounting Science

As an accounting academic starting to work toward tenure just before the COVID-19 pandemic, I had learned what the path to tenure looks like for accounting academics in highly regarded (AACSB) schools. We should publish our work in Financial Times (FT) 40 journals (ideally) and/or in a journal on the university's list (which usually includes FT 40 journals and A*- and A-ranked journals from the Australian Business Deans Council [ABDC] list).[3] With the notable exception of Marcia Annisette and Joanne Jones, accounting faculty in Canada were not writing about discrimination in the accounting profession or about the labor market integration challenges faced by racialized immigrants to Canada.

In August 2020, I coauthored a piece published in *The Conversation (Canada)* that called for targets as a mechanism to achieve the representation of Black

---

[3]Globally, top business schools refer to journal rankings lists, such as the Financial Times (FT) 40 and Australian Business Deans Council (ABDC), to evaluate the quality of the publications of untenured professors seeking tenure.

directors on boards (Ufodike & Vredenburg, 2020). The article discusses how public companies used targets to achieve gender diversity on their boards between 2005 and 2021. The ensuing debate about the article focused on nomenclature and semantics (e.g., use of the more nuanced "targets" vs "quotas"). By fall 2020, however, many corporations and public companies had normalized targets and signed pledges to appoint Black people to their boards or leadership roles. Most had failed to fulfill the pledge by 2023. A report by the law firm Osler argued that "a survey conducted by the newspaper [*Globe and Mail*] of the original signatories to the pledge found that few companies had shown tangible progress in meeting the goals of the pledge" (MacDougall et al., 2021, p. 11). The signatories to the pledge did not contemplate the availability of Black directors and executives.

Later in the fall of 2020, along with three coauthors (Inya Egbe, Bridget Ogharanduku, and Tope Akinyemi), I commenced the aforementioned SLR project on discrimination in business, which resulted in the publication of two papers in *Accounting Perspectives*: one on anti-Black racism (Ufodike et al., 2023) and the other on colonialism, postcolonialism, and the marginalization of Indigenous people (Ufodike, 2025).

Following the SLR and *The Conversation* article, I developed a three-year research project that examines diversity across the continuum of business professions: the entry point (high school, undergraduate, and graduate students), mid-point (early career professionals), and apex (partners of accounting firms and corporate boards). My objective was to propose practical ways to address supply-side issues where they exist. This ongoing project also explores the most common justifications for the absence of diversity in the accounting profession and the ways in which resistance to diversity initiatives manifests.

I complimented my literature reviews by conducting interviews, having informal conversations with professionals of all backgrounds, and reading and reviewing angry comments posted on articles I wrote advocating for targets to accelerate diversity. While my article in *The Conversation* was initially considered heresy, several Canadian universities, including York University, McMaster University, University of Calgary, and University of Alberta, have since implemented targeted Black (postdoctoral and faculty) cohort hiring.[4] Furthermore, since Floyd's death, several have announced Black deans in their business schools (Queen's University) and vice-president-level (or higher) Black hires (York University, Mount Royal University, University of Toronto, University of Guelph, and Bow Valley College). While the adoption of cohort hiring or diversity targets in hiring by some organizations appears to vindicate my arguments in *The Conversation* article, there are still many people who do not see value in EDI initiatives and seek to resist or usurp them. In June 2023, the Supreme Court of the United States, for example, overturned affirmative action, which had been in

[4]The Institute of Corporate Directors, of which I am a member, wrote a letter to the editor pushing back on observations in the article that it had failed to lead on the issue of racial diversity on boards and had a definition of diversity that trivialized race by treating gender as distinct (requiring aspirations for equality), while grouping race and Indigenous status with business experience and place of residence.

place for over 40 years, effectively eliminating EDI-based admissions in US universities and colleges.

Public Interest, Equity, Supply-side, Temporal, and Spatial (PESTS): "Die DEI, Die"

> DEI is just another word for racism… –Elon Musk

Elon Musk and the United Supreme Court of Justice are just a handful of examples of the anti-EDI movement. In the aftermath of COVID, there has been an all-out assault against EDI (Ellis & Thorbecke, 2024; Keeanga-Yamahtta, 2024).

During the pandemic, healthcare workers, the police and other emergency responders, grocery store employees, and truck drivers were celebrated. I would like to add project managers (e.g., systems implementation managers, developers, business analysts, program managers, and change managers) to the list of COVID-19 heroes. Although I worked as a project manager early in my career in Canada, it is still mindboggling to contemplate the system changes that were required to allow billions of employees to continue to work remotely during COVID-19 and for billions of students to continue to study virtually. My spouse worked for the Law Society of Alberta, a regulator of the legal profession. Even the legal profession – a profession steeped in tradition and extremely resistant to change – permitted systemic changes during the pandemic to allow for practical changes to everything from how documents were notarized to how cases were heard. System implementations are necessary for the effective production of goods and services by organizations. Sometimes system implementations are informed by internal factors (e.g., growth and process improvements) and sometimes they are foisted upon organizations by external factors – as was the case during the COVID-19 pandemic. Approximately 50% of all organizational change initiatives fail (Miller, 2020), and one of the most common reasons for these failures is human irrationality. New systems mean mandatory change; change is difficult to implement and has a significant impact on people. Change demands new ways of knowing and new ways of doing. Systemic change is even more difficult because the fear of the unfamiliar, and attachments to legacy systems result in passive or active resistance. Resistance to systemic change can manifest in various forms along a resistance continuum, from indifference to opposition to sabotage.

When assessing a control environment, accountants evaluate the tone at the top management level. Tone at the top is also important when it comes to systems; for this reason, projects require project sponsors, decision-makers who have bought into the required system implementation or change and are fully committed cheerleaders of the project. In practice, these project sponsors are sometimes just as indifferent or opposed to a project as the rest of the organization. While all these elements are true for information-technology-related system implementations, they are also true for the systemic changes required to overcome anti-Black racism.

Practical approaches such as setting diversity goals (Shook, 2021) and using targets or quotas, the less nuanced cousin of targets, for hiring racialized people (Ufodike & Vredenburg, 2020) have been proposed by scholars who believe that the diversity – racial and otherwise – found at the individual level (micro) of society needs to be reflected at the organizational (meso) level and the societal (macro) level as a whole in the interest of equity and inclusion. However, as is the case for any form of systemic overhaul, there is often resistance. The five most cited rationales for resistance to systemic changes related to anti-Black racism are PESTS. Brief descriptions of these five rationales are presented below and are analyzed in depth in a second chapter in this book (see "Rebutting PESTS: The Five Most Common Rationales against Equity, Diversity, and Inclusion").

Simply put, the public interest rationale aims to protect the public from inferior foreign trained professionals. Immigration is the primary source of labor market growth in many G8 countries; however, many immigrants, upon arrival, are gatekept from joining their professions – evidence that colonial and post-colonial discriminatory practices are sustained by actors such as professional bodies under the guise of professionalization (Ashraf & Ghani, 2005; Poullaos, 2016). In the Commonwealth, substantial equivalency is granted by Canada, the United Kingdom, Ireland, Australia, and New Zealand (countries known as the Old Commonwealth and perceived as white countries) to each other, even though the education and professional training systems elsewhere in the racialized Commonwealth – for example, Nigeria, Jamaica, and India – are based on the same curriculum as they were developed and implemented by the British.

The equity rationale argues that EDI initiatives are inappropriate, create competition between equity-seeking groups, and, consequently, will be opposed by members of other equity-seeking groups that may not be beneficiaries of said EDI initiatives (or even by the members of the benefiting equity-seeking group for which the initiative was designed).

The supply-side rationale argues that there are not enough Black people in the pipeline to achieve the desired diversity goal. The boards of public companies or other agencies may argue that they want to appoint more Black directors but there simply are not enough Black directors available. This logic assumes that qualified Black people who can be appointed do not exist; in reality, a significant number of qualified Black candidates are ignored or sidestepped.

The temporal rationale includes three main arguments: that EDI initiatives are ineffective and hence not worth pursuing; equity initiatives have been achieved or gained "too much," or Black people have bigger problems, such as crime and poverty; and members of the equity-seeking group should simply "get over it." All of these arguments are temporal in that they claim that, although society may have failed Black people in the past or failed to provide EDI initiatives to ameliorate inequitable social outcomes (and consequently sustain discrimination), these issues are in the past and society needs to move on.

The spatial rationalization applies when distinctions are made about the Black experience in one country versus another. It is deferral, not denial. Simply put, anti-Black racism is worse somewhere other than the subject society, institution, or organization. In a hypothetical hierarchy of racist societies, if Society A is less racist than Society B, Society A believes it has the moral high ground, which becomes a rationalization for inaction by Society A to combat racism or to strive for a more inclusive society.

Since COVID, the resistance against diversity, equity and inclusion (DEI) has morphed into an all-out assault on DEI, with (some very powerful) opponents of EDI keen on belittling or reversing any gains made in the preceding years.[5] This reality is what makes this book and the work of the dedicated group of scholars who conduct research in this space noteworthy and relevant. The academy has a moral obligation, to continue to illuminate the forms of resistance and opposition to EDI – subtle to blatant if any of the gains of the pre-COVID era are to be preserved, because sadly – racism is still very alive and well.

Racism Is Alive and Well: *A Luta Continua*

The return to some form of post-COVID-19 normalcy provides another opportune time for reflection and action to overcome anti-Black racism. This is also particularly relevant in the current (2024/2025) anti-EDI climate. Humans are quick to forget crucial life and societal lessons which appears to be the case today as societies do away with all the COVID era anti-racism gains. We need to understand what form the assault on DEI takes in order to resist them. My reflections since 2020 suggest that the most common rationale for resistance toward EDI initiatives aimed at resisting and ending anti-Black racism are PESTS – public interest, equity, supply-side, temporal, and spatial rationales. Understanding these forms of resistance is important because anti-Black racism is not a thing of the past; it is still prevalent in Canada and across the world. In Canada, COVID-19-related news was widely aired on the Canadian Broadcasting Corporation (CBC), Canada's publicly funded media outlet. In October 2021, the Black employees of CBC alleged systemic racism against the broadcaster. In March 2023, the Canadian Human Rights Commission – the very agency empowered to address systemic racism – was indicted for being discriminatory toward Black employees (Thurton, 2023). Canadians criticized Donald Trump for referring to African countries as "shithole countries" at a time when Canadian immigration staffers labeled a group of African countries "the dirty 30."

Canada and the United States were not alone. China, where COVID-19 originated and whose citizens were the subject of an exponential increase in anti-Asian racism (Huang et al., 2023) in North America, was responsible for significant anti-Black racism in the guise of COVID-19 preventive measures

[5] I've used US nomenclature here (DEI rather than EDI) because some of the most visible instances of assault on DEI or reversal of previous gains have been in the United States, however examples also exist in Canada such as the University of Alberta announcing it was doing away with DEI. https://nationalpost.com/opinion/jamie-sarkonak-the-university-of-alberta-said-it-was-ending-dei-that-was-a-lie

(Cahlan & Lee, 2020; Jin, 2021; Wang, 2021). The Russian invasion of Ukraine exposed the same mistreatment of Black people as millions of people sought to evacuate Ukraine (Dovi, 2022; Osei-Opare & Loyd, 2022): Black people were refused at border crossings, and "videos show Black people being pushed off trains and Black drivers being reprimanded and stalled by Ukrainians as they try to flee" (Ray, 2022). Such anti-Black racism was condemned and left many surprised. In many ways, it feels as though there is a hierarchy of racialized and equity-seeking groups, with Black people at the bottom. The reality is that anti-Black racism is so normal in Europe that soccer fans still throw bananas onto the soccer field to disparage Black players (PA Media, 2022). In Canada, Brian MacGillivray, a coach of an under-11 boys' hockey team, pulled his team off the ice during the third period of a game in February 2023 "after a number of players reported being called 'monkey,' 'banana,' and the N-word by opposing players on the Ridge Meadows U-11 boys team" (Larsen, 2023). If Canada and the United States have work to do, most of Europe is still in the stone ages when it comes to anti-Black racism.

I will end on a personal note. For racism to lessen in the future, there must be an observable trend line today. I have heard that Gen Z's are more equity-minded, and they will eliminate the issues of racism which society confronts globally today. However, the firsthand experience of three Black children in my life suggests something different. During the COVID-19 pandemic, a 6-year-old was told his skin is the color of poop by one of his "best" white friends. An 8-year-old was called the N-word by a white grade mate, and a 12-year-old was called the N-word by a white teammate. All these incidents were witnessed by other children and, in one instance, by the parents of other children. Before the pandemic, I had not experienced any such incidents.

There is ample evidence that racism continues to exist. Racism is learnt behavior; young racists grow into adult racists. There is no better story to illustrate this than the case of Andrew Lester, an 85-year-old white man, who shot 16-year-old Ralphy Yari twice for going to the wrong address. Klint Ludwig, one of Lester's grandsons, told CNN, "I believe he held – holds – racist tendencies and beliefs" (Yan, 2023). Ludwig added that he was disturbed by racial comments made by Lester about Black people in the past. Interestingly, Klint Ludwig's older brother, Daniel, disputed that his grandfather was racist and told *The New York Times* that Lester was "literally too nice and spoiled other relatives" (Yan, 2023). With such divergent assessments about the same individual from his two grandchildren, I can only conclude that he was a "nice racist" – nice to his grandkids and family and racist to the Black teen he shot twice – once in the head without saying a word after he answered the door and once in the chest as the teen lay on his patio bleeding out.

Let me clarify – there are racists and "nice racists" – people who treat those of their own race well – in all races. Race, is only the most visible and dominant form of a human tribe, but make no mistake – Humans, generally speaking are inherently tribal. I was born in Nigeria, where almost 100% of the country is Black, so they resort to tribalism as a way of discriminating against each other. When Nigerians are all of the same tribe, they may resort to religion as they basis of discriminating against each other. When they are of the same, tribe, and religion, they resort to religious sects as the basis for discrimination, such as Catholics versus Anglicans. As a young kid growing up, I was referred to derogatorily in a boarding school as "*nyamiri*" – a derisive way of referring to Biafrans who, during the Nigerian Civil War, would approach Nigerian soldiers begging for water in Igbo – "*nyem mmiri.*" Millions of children died in the genocide (Korieh, 2013) that occurred during the civil war, prompting John Lennon to return his Member of the British Empire (MBE) medal with a letter to the Queen stating, "Your Majesty, I am returning this in protest against Britain's involvement in the Nigeria-Biafra thing, against our support of America in Vietnam, and against Cold Turkey slipping down the charts. With love. John Lennon" (1969). The tribal tensions in Nigeria continue to this day, which is evident from attacks against Gbadebo Rhodes-Vivour, a Yoruba gubernatorial candidate, because his mother and wife were Igbo. Not much has changed in the 60 years since Nigerian independence from colonial rule. Simply put, there are racists in all races, but that does not mean that society should accept or normalize racism.

Then, how do we acknowledge our differences and celebrate multiculturalism, the cultural mosaic that is today's OECD countries, if we do not understand racism and the hurdles to practical EDI? That the current state of EDI is imperfect is not a credible reason for inaction. That many accounting researchers do not consider racism, sexism, or other types of discrimination in their work also does not mean that discrimination is not a problem. Rather, discrimination is simply not mainstream in the field or, as Lewis (2015) argued, accounting scholars may actually avoid the subject. Given the visibility of anti-Black racism during the COVID-19 pandemic, accounting scholars should contemplate their role in illuminating social issues before they prompt societal outrage. Otherwise, accounting research will always respond to, but never lead, societal change.

Dedication

> You only become a man when your father dies... –Igbo proverb

In that case, I wish I was still a boy. In loving memory of Colonel Leonard Ginikaezindu Ufodike (Onuo Ona, Nnewi) who passed away June 9, 2024 from heart break of Uche's death, to Uche Ezike-Dennis my baby sister who passed away May 13th, 2021; to George Floyd, who passed away on May 25, 2020; to the many departed between January 2020 and May 2023; and to all their loved ones left behind with a void nothing can fill.

Acknowledgment

This research is funded by the Social Sciences and Humanities Research Council of Canada (SSHRC).

References

Annisette, M. (2003). The colour of accountancy: Examining the salience of race in a professionalisation project. *Accounting, Organizations and Society*, *28*(7–8), 639–674. https://doi.org/10.1016/S0361-3682(02)00030-2

Annisette, M., & Trivedi, V. U. (2013). Globalization, paradox and the (un)making of identities: Immigrant chartered accountants of India in Canada. *Accounting, Organizations and Society*, *38*(1), 1–29. https://doi.org/10.1016/j.aos.2012.08.004

Ashraf, J., & Ghani, W. I. (2005). Accounting development in Pakistan. *International Journal of Accounting*, *40*(2), 175–201.

Cahlan, S., & Lee, J. S. (2020, June 18). Video evidence of anti-black discrimination in China over coronavirus fears. *Washington Post*. https://www.washingtonpost.com/politics/2020/06/18/video-evidence-anti-black-discrimination-china-over-coronavirus-fears/. Accessed April 19, 2023.

Canada. (n.d.). *Jordan's principle: Substantive equality principles*. https://www.sac-isc.gc.ca/eng/1583698429175/1583698455266. Accessed May 15, 2023

Dovi, V. (2022, April 1). The treatment Africans are facing in Ukraine is despicable, but why are we surprised? *Euronews*. https://www.euronews.com/2022/04/01/the-treatment-africans-are-facing-in-ukraine-is-despicable-but-why-are-we-surprised. Accessed April 19, 2023.

Ellis, N. T., & Thorbecke, C. (2024, January 11). DEI efforts are under siege. Here's what experts say is at stake. *CNN*. https://www.cnn.com/2024/01/07/us/dei-attacks-experts-warn-of-consequences-reaj/index.html. Accessed March 15, 2024.

Hammond, T. (1997). From complete exclusion to minimal inclusion: African Americans and the public accounting industry, 1965–1988. *Accounting, Organizations and Society*, *22*(1), 29–53.

Hammond, T. (2003). *A white-collar profession: African American certified public accountants since 1921*. University of North Carolina Press.

Huang, J. T., Krupenkin, M., Rothschild, D., & Cunningham, J. L. (2023). The cost of anti-Asian racism during the COVID-19 pandemic. *Nature Human Behaviour*, *7*, 682–695. https://doi.org/10.1038/s41562-022-01493-6

Jin, X. (2021, March 2). How COVID-19 exposed China's anti-Black racism. *Open Democracy*. https://www.opendemocracy.net/en/pandemic-border/how-covid-19-exposed-chinas-anti-black-racism/. Accessed April 19, 2023.

Keeanga-Yamahtta, T. (2024, January 22). The campaign against D.E.I. *The New Yorker*. https://www.newyorker.com/news/our-columnists/the-campaign-against-dei. Accessed March 15, 2024.

Korieh, C. J. (2013). Biafra and the discourse on the Igbo genocide. *Journal of Asian and African Studies*, *48*(6), 727–740. https://doi.org/10.1177/0021909613506455

Larsen, K. (2023, May 3). Surrey, B.C., hockey parents question why coach was suspended after standing up to alleged racism. *CBC News*. https://www.cbc.ca/news/canada/british-columbia/surrey-b-c-hockey-parents-question-why-coach-was-suspended-after-standing-up-to-alleged-racism-1.6830865. Accessed May 3, 2023.

Lehman, C., Annisette, M., & Agyemang, G. (2016). Immigration and neoliberalism: Three cases and counter accounts. *Accounting, Auditing & Accountability Journal*, *29*(1), 43–79. https://doi.org/10.1108/AAAJ-09-2013-1470

Lennon, J. (1969). Valued exposure: MBE. *BBC News*. http://news.bbc.co.uk/2/hi/in_depth/8378080.stm. Accessed May 15, 2023.

Lewis, A. M. (2015). 'Counting black and white beans': Why we need a critical race theory of accounting. *European Journal of Contemporary Economics and Management*, *2*(2), 1–13. https://doi.org/10.19044/elp.v2no2a1

Lewis, A. (2016). This racism stuff belongs in human resources! A critical race theory discussion of neutrality in accounting. *Advances in Public Interest Accounting*, *19*, 113–134. https://doi.org/10.1108/S1041-706020160000019005

MacDougall, A., Valley, J., & Jeffrey, J. (2021). *Diversity and leadership at Canadian public companies: Diversity disclosure practices*. https://www.osler.com/osler/media/Osler/reports/corporate-governance/Osler-Diversity-Disclosure-Practices-report-2021.pdf. Accessed October 11, 2021

Miller, K. (2020, March 19). 5 critical steps in the change management process. *Harvard Business School Online blog*. https://online.hbs.edu/blog/post/change-management-process#:~:text=Change%20management%20is%20the%20process,any%20changes%20that%20may%20occur. Accessed May 15, 2023.

Morrow, A., & Walsh, M. (2021, February 21). Biden upholds U.S.-first vaccine policy, shutting door on Canada, for now. *The Globe and Mail*. https://www.theglobeandmail.com/politics/article-biden-upholds-us-first-vaccine-policy-shutting-door-on-canada-for-now/. Accessed March 9, 2024.

Opara, M., Okafor, O. N., & Ufodike, A. (2022). Invisible actors: Understanding the micro-activities of public sector employees in the development of public–private partnerships in the United States. *Australian Journal of Public Administration*, *81*(2), 237–278. https://doi.org/10.1111/1467-8500.12502

Opara, M., Okafor, O. N., Ufodike, A., & Kalu, K. (2021). Institutional entrepreneurship: Collaborative change in a complex Canadian organization. *Accounting, Auditing & Accountability Journal*, *34*(9), 284–314. https://doi.org/10.1108/AAAJ-06-2020-4610

Osei-Opare, N., & Loyd, T. (2022, March 3). Anti-Black racism is upending easy narratives about the exodus from Ukraine. *Washington Post*. https://www.washingtonpost.com/outlook/2022/03/03/anti-black-racism-is-upending-easy-narratives-about-historic-exodus-ukraine/. Accessed April 19, 2023.

PA Media. (2022, September 27). Richarlison demands action after banana thrown at him in Brazil win. *The Guardian*. https://www.theguardian.com/football/2022/sep/27/banana-thrown-at-tottenhams-richarlison-as-brazil-beat-tunisia. Accessed April 30, 2023.

Poullaos, C. (2016). Canada vs Britain in the imperial accountancy arena, 1908–1912: Symbolic capital, symbolic violence. *Accounting, Organizations and Society*, *51*, 47–63. https://doi.org/10.1016/j.aos.2016.05.001

Ray, R. (2022, March 3). The Russian invasion of Ukraine shows racism has no boundaries. *Brookings*. https://www.brookings.edu/blog/how-we-rise/2022/03/03/the-russian-invasion-of-ukraine-shows-racism-has-no-boundaries/. Accessed April 19, 2023.

Robinson-Backmon, I., Weisenfeld, L., & Clark, G. (1997). Is it double jeopardy: The African American woman in accounting? *The Negro Educational Review*, *48*(1), 53–69.

Shook, E. (2021, June 25). How to set—and meet—your company's diversity goals. *Harvard Business Review*. https://hbr.org/2021/06/how-to-set-and-meet-your-companys-diversity-goals. Accessed May 15, 2023.

Thomson, K., & Jones, J. (2016). Colonials in camouflage: Metonymy, mimicry and the reproduction of the colonial order in the age of diversity. *Critical Perspectives on Accounting*, *35*, 58–75. https://doi.org/10.1016/j.cpa.2015.05.001

Thurton, D. (2023, March 23). Ottawa says Human Rights Commission discriminated against its Black employees. *CBC News*. https://www.cbc.ca/news/politics/canadian-human-rights-commission-black-racialized-1.6780794. Accessed March 9, 2024.

Ufodike, A. (2017). *The role of accounting in the delivery of health care to Canada's Aboriginal population* Doctoral Dissertation. University of Calgary.

Ufodike, A. (2020). Reviving austerity: Populist support for unpopular economics in Canada. *Journal of Accounting, Ethics & Public Policy*, *21*(4), 451–479. https://doi.org/10.2139/ssrn.3720355

Ufodike, A. (2025). The sociology of exclusion: A knowledge synthesis of imperialism and post-colonialism in accounting research. *Accounting Perspectives*. https://doi.org/10.1111/1911-3838.12378

Ufodike, A., & Ally, S. (2023). Enhancing gender-responsive financing in Africa: A sustainable development perspective. In F. Olayele & S. Yiagadeesen (Eds.), In *Sustainable development in post-pandemic Africa: Effective strategies for resource mobilization* (pp. 48–67). Routledge, Taylor & Francis Group. https://library.oapen.org/handle/20.500.12657/85257

Ufodike, A., Egbe, I., Ogharanduku, B. E., & Akinyemi, T. E. (2023). A knowledge synthesis of anti-Black racism in accounting research. *Accounting Perspectives*, *22*(3), 375–401. https://doi.org/10.1111/1911-3838.12336

Ufodike, A., Okafor, O. N., & Opara, M. (2021). First Nations gatekeepers as a common pool health care institution: Evidence from Canada. *Financial Accountability and Management*, *39*(3), 731–752. https://doi.org/10.1111/faam.12309

Ufodike, A., Okafor, O. N., & Opara, M. (2022). Network accountability in healthcare: A perspective from a First Nations community in Canada. *Accounting Perspectives*, *21*(1), 101–129. https://doi.org/10.1111/1911-3838.12283

Ufodike, A., & Vredenburg, H. (2020, August 24). Corporate diversity targets could help dismantle systemic racism. *The Conversation*. https://doi.org/10.17613/ ahsm5-bg628

Wang, Y. (2021, February 18). From Covid to blackface on TV, China's racism problem runs deep. *Human Rights Watch*. https://www.hrw.org/news/2021/02/18/covid-blackface-tv-chinas-racism-problem-runs-deep. Accessed March 17, 2023.

Yan, H. (2023, April 21). Grandson of White homeowner who shot a Black teen who rang his doorbell said he 'wasn't shocked' by the news. His brother has a different take. *CNN*. https://www.cnn.com/2023/04/20/us/ralph-yarl-shooting-andrew-lester-grandson/index.html. Accessed October 31, 2023.

Chapter 7

Does Fraud Risk in the Charter School Industry Disproportionately Affect Minority Students?

Chevonne Alston

Governors State University, USA

Introduction

The United States' charter school (CS) industry is a growing alternative to traditional public-school education that is governmentally funded, but are often able to operate independently of the state school system and can be managed by for-profit organizations. This privatization of public education continues to raise questions regarding fraud risk including its negative impact on under-represented minorities (URMs).[1] It is noted that when compared with traditional public schools (TPS), CSs serve significantly different demographics. A National Center for Education Statistics (NCES) study reports 35.9% of CS students were classified as high-poverty schools for the 2016–2017 academic year, with more than 75% of their students eligible for free or reduced lunch (U.S. Department of Education, 2019a). Comparatively, just 23.9% of TPS met the same requirements. Additionally, CSs have a higher proportion of English language learners than all US public schools. The placement of CSs greatly influences these factors, since in most states, CSs are able to choose their locations. According to the same NCES study, 56% of CS students are from urban city areas, followed by 26.2% from suburban locations (U.S. Department of Education, 2019a). Racial demographics more specifically will be addressed later in this chapter.

In 2016, the Department of Education's (DOE) Office of Inspector General (OIG) performed an assessment of current and emerging risks of CS relationships with management organizations "concerning conflicts of interest, related-party

[1]For purposes of this study, under-represented minorities (URMs) will be used to refer to Black, Hispanic/LatinX, and Native Americans who are under-represented relative to their proportion of the American population.

Voices of Change, 83–96

Published under exclusive licence by Emerald Publishing Limited
doi:10.1108/978-1-83753-030-420251019

transactions, and insufficient segregation of duties" (OIG, 2016, p. 29).[2] The audit period covered July 1, 2011 through March 31, 2013, to assess the current and emerging risk that CS relationships with management organizations pose to federally funded grants and overall program objectives. Additionally, the audit was an evaluation of internal controls to mitigate the risk. The OIG judgmentally selected six states (California, Texas, Michigan, Florida, Pennsylvania, and New York) based on the number of management organization relationships during the 2010–2011 school year. Thirty-three CSs were selected from the six states based on Internal Revenue Service (IRS) Form 990 information, previous audit findings, and news article searches regarding Education Management Organizations/Charter Management Organizations (EMO/CMO) relationships, and management/operational characteristics.[3] The study revealed internal control weaknesses in 66% percent of the sample.[4] While the OIG DOE audit noted limitations that the sample was judgmentally selected and the results cannot be generalized to the universe of CSs because it was not statistically drawn, OIG concluded that increased oversight is necessary to monitor risk to Federal programs (OIG, 2016). For this study, I selected the same six states used in the 2016 OIG DOE study. It is significant that the OIG's judgmentally drawn sample includes several of the nation's largest public-school districts that serve a large portion of URMs. This study also includes three additional states of Illinois, Minnesota, and Ohio due to the important roles that they play.

While it is extremely challenging to quantify the severity of fraudulent instances, this study will highlight key fraudulent events in the states sampled which also contain a high URM CS population. For example, I highlight two CS advocates, Paul Vallas and Betsy DeVos, that have swindled URM communities throughout the nation. I posit the fraud diamond which offers a model including (1) incentive, (2) capability, (3) opportunity, and (4) rationalization is relevant for the CS model that has a history of fraudulent activities (Greene, 2022). Prior CS studies use surveys, academic performance data, or individual school assessment data (U.S. Department of Education, 2004a; Miron et al., 2012; OIG, 2016).

[2]Charter schools operate in one of the following three categories: (1) Independent/freestanding, meaning school operations are managed internally, (2) Charter Management Organizations (CMOs) are nonprofit management organizations and (3) Education Management Organizations (EMOs) are for profit management organizations. Management Organizations are external organizations that contract with charter schools to provide management-related services that could include, but are not limited to, staffing, curriculum implementation, services for students with disabilities. There is a broad variation of the services provided to different schools.

[3]The OIG judgmentally selected 33 of 758 charter schools identified with for-profit or nonprofit management organization relationships. The universal population (758) was identified using Common Core Data (CCD) in the National Center for Education Statistics (NCES) matched with the independent for-profit and nonprofit organizational form study performed by the National Education Policy Center (NEPC).

[4]The OIG found 22 of the 33 schools examined had Internal Control Weaknesses (ICW). In total, the deficient schools had 36 ICWs including (1) Potential Conflicts of Interest, (2) Related-Party Transactions, and (3) Insufficient Segregation of Duties.

However, this is the first study to examine the CS model through a lens of how fraud effects the minority population.

Background

The public education industry represents a significant portion of the nonprofit sector; however, it is unique because its primary activities do not include fund-raising as is the case with many other nonprofits. Public elementary, middle, and high schools are a nonprofit industry that account for $995.7 billion in revenue (Ayers, 2023). The education revenue volatility is very low because it primarily comes from the state, local, and federal government tax dollars. A stable public education is a service that citizens expect the government to offer. However, recent years have seen a downward shift with the introduction of CSs and the privatization of public-school education.

A CS is a publicly funded school operating under a CS contract entered into between the school and its authorizing agency (Squire et al., 2014). The charter contract allows the school significant educational autonomy to pursue specific educational objectives. CSs have been authorized by school districts, colleges and universities, state education agencies, teachers, EMO, and CMO (Baker et al., 2012; Squire et al., 2014). While several advocates argue that a market-based, for-profit business environment is appropriate in education, opponents purport those management organizations with a profit-motive further strain limited public education resources (OIG, 2016; Miron et al., 2012).

Minnesota led the nation with the first CS and accompanying legislation in 1991 when City Academy in St. Paul became the first CS in the United States (Knaak & Knaak, 2013; Noguera, 2014). State senator and CS advocate, Ember Reichgott, was the principal author of Minnesota's CS law which is currently ranked number four by the National Alliance for Public Charter Schools (NAPCS) (National Alliance for Public Charter Schools, 2023).[5] There is great debate though over CS accountability and the associated regulatory environment. While some advocates embrace strong state and federal accountability, others posit that a heightened regulatory environment stifles creativity (Noguera, 2014; Raymond, 2014).

Current CS Environment

The industry is comprised of government-funded elementary and secondary schools that offer free education to community and district children and largely operates on a nonprofit basis. Within the past decade, IBISworld began to publish a report for the CS industry specifically, based on the industry's growth

[5]The National Alliance for Public Charter Schools ranks charter schools annually based on what they have established as the "21 essential components of a strong charter school law". https://publiccharters.org/news/measuring-up-to-the-model-a-ranking-of-state-public-charter-school-laws-2022/. Accessed on August 18, 2024.

in "public education" (Ayers, 2023). In 2022, it accounts for $53 billion in revenue, and there were approximately 7,800 CSs across the country, accounting for an estimated 7.4% of all American public schools (Le, 2023). Thirty-four percent of students are classified as high poverty, and 56.6% of CS students are from urban areas. Currently, 46 states along with Washington D.C., Puerto Rico, and Guam have passed CS legislation (Le, 2023). This movement is the widest reaching school reform initiative in the United States.

While CSs began as a concept serving as the poster child for school reform, they have now become well established with several state and national associations and with lobbyists and public relations staff and support from media, politicians, and well-funded foundations (Knaak & Knaak, 2013). There is no national definition that applies to all CSs because the schools operate under state law. CSs primarily operate independently of the school district, but they have been chartered by a public entity or a publicly appointed entity that qualifies them for local, state, and federal taxpayer funds. Their funding process is similar to the funding process for public district schools (Miron et al., 2012). Many taxpayers support the private management of district schools based on a belief that "private business models are more efficient and effective than nonprofit, government-operated institutions" (Miron et al., 2012). However, charters lack financial transparency and a strong internal control environment (Noguera, 2014; Petrovits et al., 2011). While public schools disclose their operating information, CSs are not required to release details regarding how funds are raised and used which permits charters to operate in a "black box" (Noguera, 2014). Approximately 65% of the states with CSs offer transparency in per-pupil funding.[6] With little structure and an inherent lack of accountability, CSs are an open target for mismanagement and fraud.

Fraud and the Fraud Diamond

CSs have a problem with corruption and financial malfeasance particularly in states that provide the weakest regulatory oversight (Casey, 2014). The Securities and Exchange Commission (SEC) charged UNO, a Chicago CS operator, with defrauding investors (U.S. SEC, 2014). In April 2015, the Center for Popular Democracy (CPD) published a report highlighting more than $100 million in reported fraud, abuse, and waste over time from 15 states (CPD, 2015).[7]

Unfortunately, this occurrence is not something new to the nonprofit arena. While many operate under the misguided assumption that nonprofit employees and volunteers operate in a substantially benevolent and altruistic manner, accountants and auditors recognize that this assumption enables nonprofits as a breeding ground for fraudulent activity (Buckhoff & Parham, 2009). Several studies document countless case examples in the nonprofit sector which include embezzling, mail and wire fraud, forging checks, computer fraud, contract fraud,

[6]https://data.publiccharters.org/knowledge-base/4-how-are-charter-schools-funded/ (data pulled December 2023).

[7]All nine states in this sample were featured in report.

and tax evasion. While the nonprofit industry continues to develop rules and structures to aide in fraud detection, the CS industry should be a step ahead of the rest based on education's institutional background. Since the industry operates under the umbrella of the public school system, one might logically conclude that they would operate as an extension, adopting existing controls and structure in place. However, in several states, this has not been the case, leaving public funds vulnerable to mismanagement. This is a significant risk particularly in minority communities as the schools are under-resourced and easy targets.

The fraud diamond is a useful tool in understanding and managing fraud risks and takes into account incentive, opportunity, and rationalization similar to the widely used fraud triangle. It adds a fourth element which is capability in the form of personal traits and abilities. In other words, some fraudulent activity could not happen if not for the right person with the right abilities who can find an opportunity and turn it into reality which is the focus in the next section.

Application of Fraud Diamond

Incentive

Based on the sheer dollar amount of tax dollars devoted to education, an incentive for fraud exists. Following the 2016 OIG study, California, Texas, Michigan, Florida, Pennsylvania, and New York were six of the key states used for additional analysis. With the exception of Michigan, all these states encompass the largest school districts in the nation. While Michigan does not have the largest school district, it has a disproportionately high number of CSs. The sample includes Illinois because it is the third largest school district in the nation, Minnesota because it is the seminal CS state, and Ohio since it has a large number of CSs and subsequent CS closures. These nine states represent a significant component of CS funding over the years as represented by Table 7.1. They collectively received more than 50% of Charter School Program's (CSP) federal DOE funding between 2001 and 2019.

The federal government overall has spent over $3.3 billion dollars stimulating the CS industry since inception and more than $200 million dollars have been tied to waste and fraudulent uses over the past decade (Persson, 2015). It is also commonplace for these schools to close. During the 2012–2013 school year, there were more than 2,280,000 students enrolled in 6,004 CSs (Levine & Levine, 2014). However, more than 2,200 CSs affecting 288,000 students have closed between 2001 and 2013 (Persson, 2015). Based on a preliminary review of the charter schools that have closed between 2000 and 2013, Ohio has the greatest number of closures. This number of closed schools is alarming and much higher than TPS.[8] This disproportionate closure rate is often motivated by financial gain along with manipulation of the traditional

[8]This study notes a sample of closed charter schools by state and notes that the school closure percentage, calculated by using the number of closed charter schools divided by the total number of charter schools in the state, ranges from 7% to 38%.

Table 7.1. Charter School Funding.[a]

State	Amount in $
California	406,871,257.67
Florida	174,013,658.89
Illinois	39,160,695.50
Michigan	77,827,086.00
Minnesota	63,545,270.62
New York	168,704,434.78
Ohio	51,534,110.20
Pennsylvania	40,593,920.34
Texas	170,337,633.81
Total	*1,192,588,067.80*

[a]Beginning with SY 2006–2007, the Department of Education collects subgrant award information from Charter Schools Program (CSP) grantees, including State Educational Agencies (SEAs) and Non-SEA grantees that receive funding directly from the Department, and began collecting subrecipient award information from charter management organizations (CMOs) in 2012 (U.S. Department of Education, 2019b).

public-school structure where fraudsters typically close without mandates to deliver services or repay funds.

Opportunity

A good system of internal controls includes three primary objectives: (1) safeguarding organization assets, (2) ensuring accuracy and timeliness of financial information, and (3) encouraging compliance with organizational policies, procedures, laws, and regulations (Buckhoff & Parham, 2009). Based on CS headlines and documented fraud losses, it appears that a number of schools have shortcomings in this area. CSs have been likened to a second coming of Enron with dangerous related party transactions (Green et al., 2018). CSs are deregulated from the traditional public-school model and frequently have philanthropic private investors with a promise of improving "educational options in low-income and minority neighborhoods" (Green et al., 2018). While CSs have been around for close to three decades, there is little standardization in their accountability and reporting across states.

Rationalization

This system lacks a well-designed accountability structure which creates a culture for fraud to flourish. Administrations promoted CSs as a tool to improve school choice and education outcomes (U. S. Department of Education, 1991, 2004b). As an attempt to promote sharing of information, the US DOE launched the Office of Innovation and Improvement homepage including CS grant information along with state and nonstate education agencies.[9] The website offers links to grants and guidance resources. However, there are no comprehensive reports offering trends on enrollment, funding, and the overall state of CSs. When the initiative took on full steam in 2000, there was a federal review offering information on charter trends, enrollment, and accountability with the last federal review of CSs released in 2022 (OIG, 2022). However, there is a need for the federal government along with states to review the level of financial control, organization compliance, procedural, legal, and regulatory structure in place for CSs as compared to public schools.

Capability

The CS industry has been dominated by key players that have been able to exercise significant influence across the nation in the privatization of public education. Two in particular, Paul Vallas and Betsy DeVos, have held positions as strong advocates of "school choice" treating education as a service to be secured in a free-market environment.

Paul Vallas, a former candidate for mayor for the City of Chicago, was the first Chicago Public Schools (CPS) CEO. In 1995, the legislature granted Mayor Richard M. Daley mayoral control over the school district. In an unprecedented move, Daley appointed his budget director, Paul Vallas, CPS CEO. While Vallas had no background in education, he pushed standardized testing and promoted opening CSs as a new education business model in the city. He also encouraged opening militarized schools for urban and impoverished students.[10]

Vallas moved on to travel the nation pushing CSs and his "school choice" agenda. In Little Rock, New Orleans, and Philadelphia, he set up CSs with rigid policies without answering to anyone (Daley, 2023) and has destabilized majority-Black schools across the country in the process. While he has referred to the purpose of his life's work to fix the educational system, his moves devastate communities with his business model tactics. In Vallas' bid for Chicago Mayor in 2023, his campaign was endorsed by a political action committee (PAC) founded by Betsy Devos who was appointed the 11th Secretary of Education in 2017 and claims to be "fighting for freedom in education."[11]

Betsy Devos is from Michigan and prior to her appointment "personally invested in K12, the largest for-profit charter school management organization in the nation" (Alston, 2020; Darling-Hammond, 2017). She has always been a stark

---

[9]http://www2.ed.gov/about/offices/list/oii/csp/index.html?exp=2 is the website for the Department of Education's Charter School Program.

[10]Militarized schools include explicit efforts to expand and legitimate military training in public schools.

[11]https://betsydevos.com/. Accessed on August 18, 2024.

advocate of "school choice" and was a driving force behind the CS expansion in Michigan (Strauss, 2016) particularly in Detroit.

Recently, Devos said she believes the federal DOE should not exist and instead education decisions should be left to state and local boards (Cassels, 2022). Interestingly, a report revealed the "oversight of federal charter school funds by the Education Department was lax and the state with the most charter schools that received public funding but never opened was Michigan, Devos's home state" (Strauss, 2020). DeVos was also responsible for lobbying against legislation in Michigan that would establish accountability for the CSs along with closing those that were failing. Her overall agenda was to "keep tax low and restrict regulation in order to maximize profit" (English, 2022).

Devos and Vallas are both strong advocates of "school choice" which has been acutely described as segregation (Anderson, 2017; MacLean, 2021; Pierce, 2021). It promotes an interest in privatizing public education and removing its funding. While Devos and Vallas are highlighted in this section, they are part of a broader population whose goals are to abolish public education. Although neither party has been explicitly convicted of fraud, each has the capability to increase the risk of fraud. Each promotes weakening public education which ultimately harms URM students.

The Negative Impact on URMs

While advocated as a public school of school choice, CSs overwhelmingly serve URM communities in urban areas. Table 7.2 – Panel A provides the CS demographics in comparison to the overall school district in the state. When comparing the Black and Hispanic columns between the charter and district/TPS, the majority of the state charters have a combined URM % total that is at least double the district/TPS with the exception of California, Florida, and Texas.

A consequence then of the elevated risk of fraud and serving URM communities is school closures in these areas. Refer to Table 7.3 for an example of school closings during a high growth period for CSs in the selected states (2002 – 2013). For comparison, Table 7.4 highlights the overall school closings between the same period across the United States between CSs and TPS. The average TPS closure over this period is 1.72% compared to 4.15% for CS. The states chosen in this sample are all greater than both sets of benchmarks.

Focusing on Ohio more specifically, a study notes that 418 of the 2,200-plus CSs closed from 2000 to 2013 were in that state (Persson, 2015). In June 2015, *The Washington Post* published an article entitled "Troubled Ohio charter schools have become a joke – literally" (Strauss, 2015). The article goes on to highlight audit reports since 2001 that uncovered $27.3 million in missing funds due to the schools being allowed to "open and operate with virtually no transparency" (Strauss, 2015). The Ohio CS Industry is a billion dollar industry that has come under fire due to the severely lenient and relaxed CS sponsor ratings where sponsors with significant deficiencies were awarded an "exemplary" rating (O'Donnell, 2015). Additionally, the state was awarded $32.6 million, the largest

Table 7.2. Student Race/Ethnicity Demographics by State and Type of School, 2020–2021.

Panel A

State	Charter-Asian	Charter-Black	Charter-Hispanic	Charter-White	Charter-Other	District-Asian	District-Black	District-Hispanic	District-White	District-Other
CA	7%	7%	52%	27%	7.00%	12.50%	4.90%	55.90%	21.00%	5.70%
FL	3%	19%	44%	30%	3.60%	2.80%	21.80%	33.60%	37.30%	4.40%
IL	1%	51%	43%	3%	1.50%	5.60%	15.20%	26.40%	48.40%	4.40%
MI	3%	48%	10%	33%	5.50%	3.60%	14.00%	8.20%	68.80%	5.30%
MN	16%	29%	11%	38%	6.30%	6.30%	10.20%	10.00%	65.80%	7.70%
NY	3%	51%	37%	6%	3.10%	10.30%	14.00%	27.80%	43.80%	4.00%
OH	1%	45%	9%	37%	7.40%	2.80%	14.60%	6.40%	70.30%	5.90%
PA	3%	39%	18%	35%	5.50%	4.50%	11.90%	12.50%	66.40%	4.80%
TX	4%	18%	63%	13%	2.30%	4.80%	12.30%	52.00%	27.70%	3.30%

Panel B

State	CMO	EMO	Freestanding	URM	FRPL Eligible	Urban	Schools	Students	% of Schools	% of District	Charter Law
New York	47.50%	3.40%	49.10%	90%	79.4%	94.1%	341	170,509	6.87%	13.40%	1998
California	22.60%	2.50%	74.90%	61%	57.7%	54.4%	1,334	692,783	12.50%	27.30%	1992
Illinois	67.70%	0.00%	32.30%	96%	n/a	95.5%	137	62,765	3.10%	16.60%	1996
Florida	7.70%	44.70%	47.50%	65%	47.5%	29.4%	690	341,045	16.87%	21.90%	1996
Texas	62.60%	2.50%	34.90%	82%	71.5%	70.4%	983	435,854	11.09%	21.90%	1995
Michigan	13.40%	54.40%	32.20%	60%	76.1%	48.9%	368	149,317	10.57%	40.50%	1993
Pennsylvania	16.20%	12.70%	71.10%	59%	70.5%	74.3%	188	169,135	6.09%	36.10%	1997
Minnesota	3.30%	6.90%	89.80%	42%	51.2%	53.7%	257	65,987	10.45%	32.30%	1991
Ohio	25.80%	40.00%	34.30%	55%	n/a	80.2%	318	119,100	10.45%	32.30%	1997

Source: NAPCS (2023).

Table 7.3. Charter School Failures 2002–2013.[a]

State	# of Charter Schools	# of Charter School Failures by State	% of Charter School Failures by State
CA	462	74	16%
FL	304	66	22%
IL	54	9	17%
MI	18	2	11%
MN	129	27	21%
NY	257	18	7%
OH	179	20	11%
TX	92	35	38%
PA	181	14	8%

[a]Sample from National Center of Charitable Statistics (NCCS) data. Form 990 data were collected from the NCCS Core Files between 2002 and 2013 to obtain the education observations based on NTEE Classification.

DOE grant in the 2015 competition for federal funding. When Ohio submitted an application in July 2015, the CS Chief, David Hansen, intentionally excluded online and other CSs with poor performance. He resigned two days after submitting the grant request to the feds and several days after admitting that he broke the law by excluding 51 failing schools (Beilke, 2016). In 2015, the state auditor released a report that contained the results from unannounced inspector visits to 30 CSs. In approximately 50% of the schools, the observed headcount varied significantly from the reported attendance. This discrepancy cost the state approximately $5.7 million dollars (Democracy, 2015).

What make these school closures even more disturbing is their negative impact on URM and poor communities. According to Table 7.2 – Panel B, Ohio shows one of the largest variances, second to Michigan, between URM and majority attendance in CSs compared to traditional district public schools. Regarding Michigan, a US DOE Department found that Detroit was one of the poorest cities in the country and had a higher rate of CS closures in addition to the cities of Tuscan and Milwaukee (Strauss, 2020). It is notable in Table 7.2 – Panel B that across the states, the majority of the CSs are in urban areas with students eligible for free/reduced price lunch (FRPL eligibility), yet another indication of low income and poverty in under-resourced URM communities.

Conclusion

Despite its growth in the market, CSs remain a controversial topic. Based on the removal of public dollars from education, there are still several questions that need to be addressed. Charter supporters celebrate the CS movement as reform to

Table 7.4. Number of Educational Institutions, by Level and Control of Institution: Selected Years, 2002–2003 Through 2012–2013.

	2002–2003	2003–2004	2004–2005	2005–2006	2006–2007	2007–2008	2008–2009	2009–2010	2010–2011	2011–2012	2012–2013
% CS closed	4.26%	2.49%	5.71%	5.70%	6.60%	3.03%	3.43%	3.82%	4.10%	3.55%	3.01%
% TPS closed	1.37%	2.26%	1.86%	1.44%	1.70%	2.10%	1.44%	1.74%	1.83%	1.77%	1.42%

Source: Data retrieved from Table 216.95 from NCES (2016).

the public education system; however, the numbers do not reflect this. This chapter has shown that an elevated risk of fraud in the CS industry continues to devastate the URM community despite the industry existence for three decades.

Additional research is needed around CS management organizations, internal controls, and how to improve internal controls for the betterment of URMs. For example, fraud prevention and detection practices are essential to reduce losses and improve ongoing operations. Nonprofit entities have the potential to prevent approximately 80% of workplace fraud by effectively screening prospective employees and volunteers (Buckhoff & Parham, 2009). This screening should include conducting employee and volunteer background checks. While nonprofit entities often skip this step due to the cost, the education industry should be more willing to include this based on current screenings in place that address positions that interface with children. Beyond employee and volunteer screening, the entity can further reduce fraud by minimizing opportunities for internal theft using a stronger system of internal controls (Buckhoff & Parham, 2009; Petrovits et al., 2011).

There is a great need to protect public resources in URM areas rather than redirect them to a business model. "School choice" narratives continue to be used by wealthy populations that promote school privatization to the detriment of URM students. As citizens, parents, and (or) taxpayers, we are stakeholders that must highlight the urgency of transparency and accountability of these public funds.

References

Alston, C. (2020). *Charter schools: How does organizational quality differ between for-profit and non-profit organizational forms?* (Doctoral dissertation). University of Mississippi, Patterson School of Accountancy.

Anderson, M. (2017, May). *School choice: Segregation by another name*. San Diego Free Press. https://sandiegofreepress.org/2017/05/school-choice-segregation-by-another-name/

Ayers, J. (2023). *61111A public schools in the US*. IBISWorld.

Baker, B., Libby, K., & Wiley, K. (2012). *Spending by the major charter management organizations* edited by N. E. P. Center (p 63).

Beilke, D. (2016, February). Ohio charter school scandal grows as Kasich ascends national stage. *PR Watch*. https://www.prwatch.org/news/2016/02/13045/ohio-charter-school-scandal-grows-while-john-kasich-ascends-national-stage

Buckhoff, T., & Parham, A. G. (2009). Fraud in the nonprofit sector? You bet. *Strategic Finance*, 53–56.

Casey, L. (2014). The charter school challenge. *New Labor Forum*, *24*(1), 22–30. https://doi.org/10.1177/1095796014562861

Cassels, L. (2022, July). Betsy DeVos calls for abolition of federal Education Department she once led. *Florida Phoenix*. https://floridaphoenix.com/briefs/betsy-devos-calls-for-abolition-of-federal-education-department-she-once-led/

CPD. (2015). The tip of the iceberg: Charter school vulnerabilities to waste, fraud, and abuse. https://www.populardemocracy.org/news/tip-iceberg-charter-school-vulnerabilities-waste-fraud-and-abuse

Daley, J. (2023, March). Paul Vallas's trail of school privatization. *The Tribe*. https://thetriibe.com/2023/03/paul-vallas-trail-of-school-privatization-chicago/

Darling-Hammond, L. (2017, March). Education for sale? *The Nation*. https://www.thenation.com/article/archive/can-the-education-system-survive-betsy-devoss-extreme-school-choice-agenda/

Democracy, T. C. f. P. (2015). Charter school black hole: CMD special investigation reveals huge info gap on charter spending. https://populardemocracy.org/news-and-publications/

English, F. (2022). The Scream and the 'Dependent Beauty' of Betsy DeVos. In E. A. Samier (Ed.), *Existential crisis in educational administration and leadership: Existential anxiety and loss of meaning in the gaze of 'The Scream'* (pp. 150–169). Routledge Press.

Green, P. C., Baker, B. D., & Oluwole, J. O. (2018). Are charter schools the second coming of Enron? An examination of the gatekeepers that protect against dangerous related-party transactions in the charter school sector. *Indiana Law Journal*, *93*, 1121–1140.

Greene, P. (2022, November). Four ways charter schools undermine good educational policy. *Forbes*. https://www.forbes.com/sites/petergreene/2022/11/10/four-ways-charter-schools-undermine-good-education-policy/

Knaak, J. T. & W. C., Knaak. (2013). Charter schools: Educational reform or failed initiative? *The Delta Kappa Gamma Bulletin*, *79*(4), 45–53.

Le, T. (2023). *OD4993 Charter Schools Industry Report*. IBISWorld.

Levine, M., & Levine, A. (2014). Charters and foundations: Are we losing control of our public schools? *American Journal of Orthopsychiatry*, *84*(1), 1–6. https://doi.org/10.1037/h0098942

MacLean, N. (2021, September). 'School choice' developed as a way to protect segregation and abolish public schools. *Washington Post*. https://www.washingtonpost.com/outlook/2021/09/27/school-choice-developed-way-protect-segregation-abolish-public-schools/

Miron, G., Urschel, J. L., Aguilar, M. A. Y., & Dailey, B. (2012). *Profiles of for-profit and nonprofit education management organizations*. National Education Policy Center. https://nepc.colorado.edu/publication/EMO-profiles-10-11?utm_source=search&utm_campaign=nepc_visitors

NAPCS. (2023). *NAPCS-demographic-details*. https://data.publiccharters.org/knowledge-base/2-who-attends-charter-schools/

NCES. (2016). *Digest of Education Statistics 2014*. https://files.eric.ed.gov/fulltext/ED565675.pdf

Noguera, P. (2014, October). *Charter schools as black boxes*. The Nation.

O'Donnell, P. (2015, June). Ohio ignores online school F's as it evaluates charter school overseers. *Cleveland*. https://www.cleveland.com/metro/2015/06/ohio_ignores_online_school_fs_as_it_evaluates_charter_school_overseers.html

OIG, U.S. Department of Education. (2016). *Nationwide Assessment of Charter and Education Management Organization – Final Audit Report*. U.S. Department of Education.

OIG, U.S. Department of Education. (2022). *Effectiveness of Charter School Program in Increasing the Number of Charter Schools*. ED-OIG/A21IL0034. https://oig.ed.gov/sites/default/files/reports/2024-05/FY22A21IL0034020724v100SECURED.pdf

Persson, J. (2015). The Education Dep't let charter schools off the hook. Accountability? How overseers let charters off the hook; $3.3 billion spent (Part 4). *PR Watch*. https://www.prwatch.org/news/2015/05/12837/accountability-how-overseers-let-charters-hook-33-billion-spent-part-4

Petrovits, C., Shakespeare, C., & Shih, A. (2011). The causes and consequences of internal control problems in nonprofit organizations. *The Accounting Review*, *86*(1), 325–357.

Pierce, R. (2021, May). The racist history of "school choice". *Forbes*. https://www.forbes.com/sites/raymondpierce/2021/05/06/the-racist-history-of-school-choice/

Raymond, M. E. (2014, February). To no avail, A critical look at the charter school debate. *Phi Delta Kappan*, *95*(5). https://kappanonline.org/critical-look-charter-school-debate-raymond/

Squire, J., Robson, K., & Smarick, A. (2014). *The road to redemption: 10 policy recommendations for Ohio's charter schools*. Bellwether Education Partners. https://files.eric.ed.gov/fulltext/ED553704.pdf

Strauss, V. (2015, June). Troubled Ohio charter schools have become a joke – Literally. *Washington Post*. https://www.washingtonpost.com/news/answer-sheet/wp/2015/06/12/troubled-ohio-charter-schools-have-become-a-joke-literally/

Strauss, V. (2016, December). A sobering look at what Betty Devos did to education in Michigan – and what she might do as secretary of education. *Washington Post*. https://www.washingtonpost.com/news/answer-sheet/wp/2016/12/08/a-sobering-look-at-what-betsy-devos-did-to-education-in-michigan-and-what-she-might-do-as-secretary-of-education/

Strauss, V. (2020, August). New report finds high closure rates for charter schools over time. *Washington Post*. https://www.washingtonpost.com/education/2020/08/06/new-report-finds-high-closure-rates-charter-schools-over-time/

U.S. Department of Education. (1991). *America 2000: An education strategy*. https://eric.ed.gov/?id=ED327009

U.S. Department of Education. (2004a). *Public Charter School Program Evaluation Final Report*. https://www2.ed.gov/rschstat/eval/choice/pcsp-final/finalreport.pdf

U.S. Department of Education. (2004b). *A guide to education and no child left behind*. https://files.eric.ed.gov/fulltext/ED483055.pdf

U.S. Department of Education. (2019a). *National Center for Education Statistics, Common Core of Data (CCD), "Public Elementary/Secondary School Universe Survey," 2000-01 through 2016-17*. (This table was prepared February 2019.) https://nces.ed.gov/programs/digest/d18/tables/dt18_216.30.asp

U.S. Department of Education. (2019b). *CSP Awards Database*. https://www.ed.gov/media/document/csp-awards-database-july-2019xls-5549.xls

U.S. Securities and Exchange Commission (SEC). (2014). *SEC charges charter school operator in Chicago with defrauding bond investors*. https://www.sec.gov/newsroom/press-releases/2014-110

Chapter 8

From "Civilized" to "Professional": A Critique of Accounting Education and the Business Case for Diversity

Adam J. Saatkamp

Illinois Central College, USA

Roughly four months after a five-year trek through an accounting program, having successfully passed all four sections of the CPA exam, I began my career as an assurance associate at a Big 4 firm. Externally, I was a properly attired white male—crisp shirt, fancy tie, shiny shoes. Internally, my mind was conformed to the mold of the profession. It would not be unreasonable to say that I was mulish; such was the depth of my belief in the virtues of shareholder capitalism, the meritocratic nature of American society, and the purity of the profession's place within it. These convictions had ossified in my mind, rendering it impervious to intellectual challenges and soothing away the discomfort that comes with doubt.

Engagement after engagement, bedecked in the raiment of the profession, I dutifully undertook my responsibilities—tasks that achieved the modern equivalent of holler and tick. If I had made a vision board during my time at university, the post-it notes and pictures it would have contained representing my goals and dreams could have been taken down, marked as *accomplished*. One would have read "Big 4." On another, I certainly would have scrawled "audit." In other words, I had acquired my dream job and delighted in days and nights spent looking at ledgers on my laptop, fully convinced of the moral rightness of my efforts and the superiority of American society—that the propositions in the Pledge of Allegiance were present realities rather than aspirations, "justice for all" and thus and such.

Not altogether dissimilar to the fierceness of my professional devotion, my academic and life experience had imbued me with an implicit, instinctive belief in what Citron (1969) termed the "rightness of whiteness"—wherein white cultural norms are considered natural and set the standard by which other ways of being are to be judged. Even though I was raised to treat others with respect, regardless of skin color, and in spite of my sincere desire to do so, I nevertheless believed that the present disadvantages suffered by people of color were largely self-inflicted—that

Voices of Change, 97–110

Published under exclusive licence by Emerald Publishing Limited
doi:10.1108/978-1-83753-030-420251022

any and all disadvantages would simply disappear upon the adoption of white norms. My naïve perspective on race had been shaped, almost entirely, by popular media. My primary school and secondary school were almost exclusively white and, as best I can recall, my university accounting program was, too. And though the accounting curriculum prepared me for certification, it did not provide me with an understanding of the social dynamics of the profession.

I entered public accounting roughly 40 years after the creation of the Minority Initiatives Committee. And yet, I entered lacking any knowledge of the under-representation of Black accountants, entirely unaware that it was even a problem. In fact, it was only after entering academia that I began to ask more challenging questions of the profession—questions that could not be answered with *accept* or *reject*. I had, after all, assumed responsibility for preparing the next generation of accountants. How was I to prepare them? Who was I preparing them to be? My two accounting degrees left me understandably ill prepared for answering such questions. I was, in Tinker's (1985) words, a social ignoramus. That said, my inability to answer challenging social questions did not prevent them from consuming my thoughts. One question, in particular, began to consume the majority of my mental energy: While my campus was relatively diverse, my classes were not. Enrolling in a doctoral program was the first of many steps in a six-year quest to understand why.

For 40 odd years, the profession has espoused—with no shortage of eagerness—a desire for greater diversity. However, in spite of the profession's many programs and publications, and its purported devotion to the cause, Black accountants continue to represent a mere 2% of CPAs at American firms (AICPA, 2019). While it is true that this percentage is higher than it was in the mid-20th century—when Black CPAs represented approximately 0.1% of the profession (Hammond, 1997)—it pales in comparison to the profession's inclusion of women, which rose from 1% in 1940 to 42% in 2019 (AICPA, 2019; Gow & Kells, 2018).

Today, women make up approximately 50.5% of the US population (U.S. Census Bureau, 2021). If women do indeed represent 42% (279,300) of the 665,000 actively licensed CPAs in the United States (NASBA, 2022), the profession is roughly 83% of the way toward achieving the equivalent of women's demographic representation in society. Applying this same logic to Black CPAs, however, reveals that the profession is a mere 15% of the way toward achieving full representation. Why the disparity? Why has the profession experienced such different results pursuing gender and racial diversity?

In this chapter, I analyze the discourse regarding the history of the accounting profession using Feagin's (2010) white racial frame and Halbwachs' (1950/1980) conceptualization of collective memory, in order to show how public accounting continues to be influenced by its historic self-portrait—that of a "civilized gentleman"—and how this contributes to the profession's persistent racial imperviousness. I begin by defining Feagin's (2010) white racial frame and Halbwachs' (1950/1980) theorization of collective memory. Then, I use these concepts as my lens to critically examine the relationship between the profession's historic portrait and its present diversity efforts. I conclude by exploring the value of revising the undergraduate accounting curriculum.

What follows also serves as a form of counterstory, as called for in the Critical Race Theory literature (Delgado, 2013; Twyford et al., 2022). While I write from within the dominant—or dominating—group, the story I am about to tell seeks to challenge the status quo, the dominant "story"—the shared reality—of our in-group identity.

Theoretical Framework

The White Racial Frame

In his book *The White Racial Frame: Centuries of Racial Framing and Counter-Framing*, Feagin (2010) maintains that the majority of white people in the United States are aware of the negative views they hold regarding people of color, which was certainly my experience. He argues that "implicit" or "unconscious" bias is a rarity, and that the prototypical racial perspective of white Americans, what he (2010) terms the "white racial frame," includes beliefs, interpretations, language, images, and emotions that shape behavior and attitudes. According to Feagin, this frame includes, at its core, anti-Black stereotypes, images, and narratives as well as emotions and inclinations that have historic roots. Feagin argues that three key elements of the modern white racial frame date back to the 17th and 18th centuries. He writes:

> Among the important ingredients of this frame are: (1) the recurring use of certain physical characteristics, such as skin color and facial features, to regularly differentiate social groups; (2) the constant linking of physical characteristics to cultural characteristics; and (3) the regular use of physical and linked cultural distinctions to differentiate socially "superior" and "inferior" groups in a social hierarchy. (pp. 53–54)

Early European American colonists made use of these three ingredients in their framing of Native Americans and Africans who were stereotyped as uncivilized, unintelligent, dangerous, and savage—stereotypes that were codified by European social scientists who adapted the Great Chain of Being or Elizabethan worldview (Tillyard, 1943/1959) to create a hierarchy of human beings. In the 1700s, according to Feagin (2020), "white North American and European scientific and philosophical traditions were insistently grounded in influential racial ideas about whites' biological, cultural, and social superiority" (p. 81). The idea of white superiority or *supremacy* was made a "scientific reality" by men like English anatomist, Sir William Petty (in the 1670s), Swedish botanist, Carl Linnaeus (in the 1730s), and German medical professor, Johann Blumenbach (in the 1770s) (Smedley, 2007). Consequently, these socially constructed racial categorizations were "designed to rationalize the subordination of indigenous and African peoples" (Feagin, 2020, p. 63)—confirmation of Coates' (2015) argument that "race is the child of racism, not the father" (p. 7).

Feagin (2020) contends that the stereotypes present in the colonial period of American history—that people of African descent were uncivilized, unintelligent, immoral, lazy, and dangerous—are directly tied to the modern anti-Black stereotypes of Black criminality, family disorganization, and lack of work ethic. Ultimately, the white racial frame provides its adherents with an unrivaled sense of moral superiority that is evident even in the Declaration of Independence, wherein indigenous Americans are labeled "merciless Indian Savages" who kill women and children. These historic anti-Black stereotypes and images continue to shape the racial frame of many white Americans, including CPAs like myself.

In 2018, an off-duty law enforcement officer mistakenly entered the wrong unit in her apartment building and shot its occupant, Botham Jean, a Black accountant, who was eating ice cream and watching television. The officer killed Botham because she claimed to fear for her life (Ortiz & Johnson, 2019). Anti-Black stereotypes of criminality and violence embed fear into the racial framing of white Americans leading to consequences that are inescapable, even for successful Black CPAs like Botham Jean. In short, the white racial frame with its anti-Black ideology and belief in white virtue is a present reality—whether or not people wish to acknowledge it. It certainly shaped the way I saw the world.

If someone were to scan the list of books I was asked to read during the 18 years of schooling I completed prior to my doctoral studies, they would be hard pressed to find a Black author. There might be one, but not that I remember. I do remember E.B. White, Lowis Lowry, Harper Lee, and The Bridge to Terabithia—and I certainly read my fair share of Chaucer, Twain, Dickens, and Shakespeare. It was only recently, a few years before my 40th birthday, that I encountered, for the first time, James Baldwin (1963/1992), Carter G. Woodson (1934), bell hooks (2000), and Ta-Nahisi Coates (2015)—not to mention Isabel Wilkerson (2010), Chancellor Williams (1987), and W.E.B. Du Bois (1903/1994). Engaging with these and other Black authors allowed me to deconstruct some of the white racial frame in my view of the world, a process that continues.

Collective Memory

My failure to understand the extent to which I had been influenced by the white racial frame and my ignorance of the issues faced by Black accountants made my time at university and as an auditor particularly effective at maintaining the status quo. My understanding of public accounting had been delimited by the profession's collective memory, a concept developed by French sociologist, Maurice Halbwachs. According to Halbwachs (1925/1992), memory is a collective act. For example, from time to time, I am approached by a former student who tells me a story about a classroom event of which I have little memory. And yet, the student's memory aids my own, and, collectively, we reconstruct a memory of the event that is distinct from either of our own recollections. In his book *On Collective Memory*, Halbwachs (1925/1992) argues that "we can understand each memory as it occurs in individual thought only if we locate each within the thought of the corresponding group" (p. 53). In other words, the ideas expressed in discourse emanate from an individual's beliefs which have been informed by the beliefs of the group or groups to which they belong.

Halbwachs (1950/1980) theorizes that "each [individual] is immersed successively and simultaneously in several groups—all of which possess distinct collective memories". A group's collective memory is constructed over time as certain people and events are remembered and others are forgotten. In the end, the collective memory of a social group "provides the group a self-portrait that unfolds through time, since it is an image of the past, and allows the group to recognize itself" (Halbwachs, 1950/1980, p. 86). Similarly, building on Halbwachs' foundational work, Wertsch and Roediger (2008) argue that "collective remembering inevitably involves some identity project—remembering in the service of constructing what kind of people we are—and hence is resistant to change even in the face of contradictory evidence" (p. 320). This resistance is revealed in the language and culture of social groups as well as the common narrative filters group members use to interpret the past.

In Halbwachs' (1950/1980) conceptualization, memories of the past can be grouped into one of two categories: historical and autobiographical. The former relates to dates and events of the past in which the remembering party has not participated, while the latter are memories from one's own personal experience. One develops historical memories by reading historical records and participating in commemorative events. For example, since Americans today lack personal memories of the Civil War, their memories of the War Between the States are constructed via historical documents, monuments, works of art, and commemorative events. Autobiographical memories, on the other hand, are refined as group members discuss, and thereby reconstruct, past shared experiences. While Americans lack autobiographical memories of the Civil War, many personally experienced or witnessed the events of 9/11. When reconnected to those with whom a person witnessed or experienced the tragedy, an individual's memory is aided by the memory of others in reconstructing the event. In essence, Halbwachs argues that group members select and construct both historical and autobiographical memories, and that these memories paint the group's self-portrait, the image that informs group identity and shapes the actions and perspectives of group members.

The accounting profession's historical collective memory is partially passed down to students through the accounting curriculum as students read textbooks and partake in discussions of accounting history. Like other social groups, accountants collectively remember—or reconstruct—the past in order to paint the profession's self-portrait. For accountants, collective remembering has produced an almost cubist self-portrait with hard, rigid, white lines delimiting professional identity, epistemology, and ontology. After six years of study, attempting to understand the racial imperviousness of the profession, I found this theoretical framework—the white racial frame and collective memory—best explained the profession's problems and my personal experience.

Conceptual Analysis

While the earliest forms of accounting can be traced back to the continent of Africa, people of African descent have long been excluded from and alienated by the American accounting profession. Even though some of the greatest civilizations in the ancient world were built by African people, their descendants would later be accounted for as animals in the books of empire-making men, and empire men would go on to establish the profession of accountancy in Britain and the United States. The establishment of the profession at the end of the 19th century must not be viewed as a creation ex nihilo. Though it bloomed at this time, the stem of the profession had long since emerged from the soil of white supremacy, in which it had been firmly rooted in typical geotropic fashion.

The "Gentlemanly" Profession

After failed attempts to forcibly colonize Ireland in the 15th and 16th centuries, the English found a new focus for their imperial efforts. The people of Ireland had been deemed "wild" and "savage"—terms which then meant uncivilized, dangerous, and criminal (Feagin, 2020; Smedley, 2007). The savage was subhuman, and therefore, colonization for wealth-building and empire-building purposes was justified. In the 17th century, this empire justifying ideology was exported to the New World, a place whose native peoples became "savages" and the "inferior" people imported and forced to work the land became "savages," too.

The classification of people into "superior" and "inferior" groups, the savage and the civilized—the third component in Feagin's (2020) theorization of the early white racial frame—grew to become the underlying ideology of the accounting profession at the turn of the 20th century. Richard Brown, in his 1905 work, *A History of Accounting and Accountants*, contends that the origins of numbering "can only be conjectured from the habits of those lower races who are still uncivilized" (p. 3). Furthermore, he writes, "It is abundantly evident from the narratives of travellers that the majority of savage races learned to make use of their fingers and toes in helping them to count" (p. 4). The social dichotomy of wildness/savagery and civilization/humanity was created by empire-making men to "designate an area of subhumanity that was characterized by everything they hoped they were not"—a political move White (1978) refers to as "self-definition by negation" (p. 152). The accounting profession inherited this ideology, and it was the wash that set the tone for the self-portrait it would paint.

The profession's desire for accountancy to be comprised of "civilized" people has never waivered and whiteness has always defined the characteristics of the "superior" practitioner—one who embodies the profession's "gentlemanly" nature. This is underscored by Gow and Kells (2018) who describe early professional firms as "gentlemen's clubs in their atmosphere and décor" (p. 88)—an appropriate aura given white men's "wish to have their money. . .dealt with by [white] gentlemen" (Macdonald, 1995, p. 31). To this end, much was done to ensure that only "gentlemen"—men of reputable race and respectable class—i.e., wealthy Anglo

Saxons—were accepted into the profession (Miranti, 1990). This was exemplified at an event Carey (1969) describes as the "outstanding event of the first 20 years" of the profession—the first International Congress of Accountants (p. 49).

In 1904, Arthur Lowes Dickinson, partner with London-based Price Waterhouse, proposed that the first International Congress of Accountants be held "as part of the Louisiana Purchase exposition being organized in St. Louis by one of his firm's clients" (Miranti, 1990, p. 65). According to historian Walter Johnson (2020a), the whole exposition—perhaps better known as the St. Louis World's Fair—was a spectacle that spoke of the "character of imperial whiteness" (p. 210). It was fitting then that the president of the fair, in his opening address to the congress, emphasized the presence of "every civilized country on the globe" and the fair's representation of "many primitive races" or "savages" that were displayed in what was the equivalent of a human zoo (Johnson, 2020b; Samuels, 1985). One presenter even made sure to emphasize how the Anglo-Saxon race, unlike others, was "honest and straightforward in its dealings" (Samuels, 1985, p. 102). In other words, a particular silhouette had been sketched as the underpainting for the profession's self-portrait. Atop the silhouette, the fine lines of the portrait—that of a "civilized" white gentleman—were undoubtedly painted with certain figures in mind, likely using as reference men like Robert H. Montgomery, Elijah Watt Sells, and George O. May, among others. Even though the significance of their accomplishments goes largely untaught in accounting education, the portrait painted in their image still hangs in the halls of academia, shaping student perceptions of what it means to be an accountant.

While the portrait of a white "gentlemanly" profession still serves as the profession's self-image, there are a few cracks in the canvas. The first measurable cracks appeared as a consequence of two world wars. These wars resulted in a slight shift in the makeup of the profession but did little to alter its self-portrait. Many men became soldiers during the first three decades of the 20th century, creating a void in the accounting profession. This void presented an opportunity for women, albeit out of necessity rather than choice (Carey, 1970). Previously, the entrance of women into the profession had been considered, by men like Worthington (1985/1978) and Brown (1905/2004), to be an "invasion"—a word chosen and deployed with intention, to identify and circumscribe one's enemy, achieving "the negative representation of the Others" (van Dijk, 1993, p. 263). And yet, even though wartime necessity widened the opening for white women, it did not go so far as to paint over the profession's self-portrait. In fact, merely extending greater opportunity to white women kept the profession's whiteness intact and preserved it for decades to come.

When I entered the profession, I could not see and did not question its whiteness, since, as whiteness epitomized, I lacked racial self-awareness, had minimal understanding of the societal privileges of being white, and possessed a heightened belief in individualistic, meritocratic ideology. Only after studying America's racial history did I begin to understand the profession's imperviousness. The study of history proved to be a Matrixian red pill, opening my eyes to the realities of racialized society. Studying the history of race in America alongside the history of the accounting profession was a revelatory endeavor. In addition to learning about the profession's early ties to Anglo-Saxon "superiority" at the 1904 World's Fair, the study of history revealed the ever-present influence of the white racial frame.

Since its earliest days at the beginning of the 20th century, the accounting profession has prized conformity over diversity. Accountants were expected to conform in dress (Toffler, 2003), social behavior, and politics (Montagna, 1974)—and conservatism governed all three. The 1960s saw the publication of Roy and MacNeill's (1967) *Horizons for a Profession*—an AICPA-commissioned report on the future of the profession and its common body of knowledge. In line with the historic self-portrait, Roy and MacNeill (1967) maintained that the accounting profession should be comprised of "civilized" people. They expressed "the hope that tomorrow's CPAs will be cultivated"—i.e., "civilized"—people who possess knowledge of literature, music, and art, which were the "[hallmark] of cultivated men and women" (p. 14). They painted a picture of an accountant as sophisticated, gentlemanly, and cultured. Historically, these qualities were attributed to "civilized" white men, but over time, they came to epitomize what is expected of the "professional" accountant.

The mentality of cultural superiority infused within the terms "civilized"/"cultivated"/"professional" can be traced back through history, from Supreme Court decisions in 1857, *Scott v. Sanford* , and 1823, *Johnson v. McIntosh*, to the Declaration of Independence, and all the way back to the Doctrine of Discovery in 1493. As Cooper and Robson (2009) argue, accountants have long maintained elitist values that are upheld as "gentlemanly, aristocratic, and paternalistic" (p. 288)—conformity to which is still the order of the day. In the 1980s, seasoned accountants continued to maintain that the accounting profession was "a gentleman's business" (Stevens, 1981, p. 22) and was being "invaded" by "uncivilized" people. At present, roughly 40 years later, our collective memory continues to produce a self-portrait recognizable to elite, "civilized," or "professional" white society.

While it may seem like the profession's modern-day self-portrait—in which accountants are depicted simply as business professionals—is that of a profession open and welcoming to all, the historic portrait underlies everything and still calls for conformity. According to Baladouni (1979), "historical understanding can and does help us to know who we are as accountants because it tells us from where we came and how we got here" (p. 319). Unfortunately, most accounting graduates exit their programs without historical understanding, without knowing "how we got here." As a result, graduates are expected to conform to a professional identity, the origins of which they know nothing about. Moreover, such conformity to the profession's historic portrait also requires the unquestioning use of its wayfinding device.

The "Neutral" Compass

Shortly after World War II (WWII), 10 men, who had contributed mathematical muscle to Allied military efforts, endeavored to apply the same strict rationalism to corporate America. These men—later known as the "Whiz Kids"—used numbers to maximize the profitability of American business in the 1950s and 1960s. For these men, "numbers became the one true moral compass, the deciding point in every decision" (Byrne, 1993, p. 8). While many considered this a revolutionary approach to business, it certainly was not. Numbers have always been the predominant moral compass for accountants.

Numbers were the moral compass for colonial bookkeepers who used accounting to extract every ounce of productivity possible from enslaved people and report the results to absentee owners across the Atlantic—an evolution in financial reporting foundational to British racial capitalism (Rosenthal, 2018). Numbers were the moral compass for German accountants during WWII when they "used a cost-benefit analysis to compare the cost of killing children with gas and then burning their bodies, to the alternative of burning the children to death" (Lippman & Wilson, 2007, p. 288). Americans are no exception. From Japanese concentration camps—where people were converted into numbers (Tyson & Fleischman, 2006)—to the veneration of profit maximization, American accountants have long worshiped numbers and their utility for the control and valuation of people and things.

In truth, the American accounting profession grew out of soil that was fertilized by British racial capitalism—a form of capitalism where one racial identity group extracts economic value from another (Robinson, 1983/2021). Plantations provided the most significant proving grounds for the growth of accounting and reporting. While Yamey (1949/1978) and Baxter (1956/1978) both question the prevalence of double-entry in colonial America, neither addresses plantation accounting. Instead, Baxter argues that colonial bookkeeping merely facilitated barter—transactions "apt to call up mental pictures of a savage trying to swap a pig for a spear" (p. 273). And yet, it was accounting that served as the underlying administrative apparatus of Britain's violent colonial efforts (Rosenthal, 2018).

The "neutrality" demonstrated by plantation bookkeepers as they accounted for the productivity and value of violently enslaved people foreshadowed what it would later mean to "think like an accountant"—to remain "neutral" regarding exploitation and accumulation, to maximize both efficiency and profit, to be morally silent regarding that for which one is accounting. Bookkeepers were to be "respectable" gentlemen whose primary duty was to the numbers. In the mid-1700s, many of these bookkeepers traveled the triangle of the slave trade. According to Previts and Merino (1998), "rum shipped out of New England was traded for slaves on the African coast; slaves were in turn traded for molasses and gold in the West Indies; molasses was taken home for use in distilling rum" (p. 14). Rosenthal (2018) states, "Many young men migrated from Europe to the islands and from the islands to North America, bringing the experience of West Indian slavery with them" (p. 75).

Later, in the 1800s, accounting evolved once again with the emergence of the railroad. However, like the slave-based economy that came before, the prosperity of railroads was largely dependent upon the exploitation of people of color. Roediger and Esch (2012) describe how there could be "no separation between the race to lay track and the racial management of those laying it" (p. 73). Not only did railroads like the Central Pacific exploit Chinese workers, freedmen-turned-sharecroppers were financially exploited by the Freedman's bank which invested customer deposits in risky railroad bonds (Garrett-Scott, 2019; Levy, 2012). While a good deal of attention is given to railroads in most histories of accounting, the confluence of accounting, racial exploitation, and railroads appears to have been collectively forgotten.

Most accounting students are given only a glimpse into the historical collective memory of accountants when they progress through the undergraduate curriculum. I remember hearing about Luca Pacioli, the "father" of accounting, in my first accounting class. It was more myth than history, given that Pacioli did not "father" double-entry accounting (Gleeson-White, 2011). While these bits of accounting lore are often passed from teacher to student, I encountered real history for the first time in Intermediate Accounting when I learned about the Securities and Exchange Commission, the Committee on Accounting Procedure, and the Accounting Principles Board. Jumping from Pacioli to the Principles Board, however, skips over approximately 400 years of accounting history that tell us a great amount about where we came from and how we got here. Without an understanding of history, students get a whitewashed, "neutral" picture of the profession.

The "neutrality" of numbers and the exclusion of history from the accounting curriculum have allowed the American accounting profession to distance itself from the exploitative events that fostered its prestige—slavery, railroads, world wars, and financial scandals—all of which have benefited the profession immensely. Indeed, to "think like an accountant," one must open the "neutral" compass and follow where it leads, even when charting a course toward diversity and inclusion.

The "neutral" compass has led the profession to repeatedly argue the "business case" for diversity. The American Institute of Certified Public Accountants (2014) suggests that the second step in overcoming organizational barriers to diversity—after obtaining buy-in from leaders—is to "build the business case" (p. 12). In other words, sadly, the profession's primary argument for diversity and inclusion is that it is "good for business." Only a short time ago, the compass pointed in the opposite direction, instructing the profession to exclude people of color because it was "good for business." When the neutral compass guides our actions, it prevents the creation of a diverse and inclusive profession. It may increase diversity, but it will never produce inclusion. If the business case is to be included in the list of arguments for diversity, it should be in a footnote on by-products, not the first bullet point. Instead, I argue for a different way forward.

Conclusion

After reading this chapter there will be some who critique my analysis—condemn even—as though I committed fraud and kicked a puppy. My younger self would have been the first to bring charges. At that time, however, my understanding of the profession was almost wholly lacking in historical context, the majority of which had been collectively forgotten in the construction of the modern self-portrait. For those, like my younger self, who object to my analysis, I maintain that acknowledging the problematic circumstances of the profession's path to prestige—its rootedness in white supremacy and its persistent racial imperviousness—is key to creating true inclusivity and belonging.

That being said, acknowledging the profession's not-so-neutral past and addressing its ties to the present racial imperviousness in no way diminishes the positive things the profession has done. Unfortunately, the normal means of teaching students to "think like an accountant" is to supply them, exclusively, with the technical knowledge required for reading the "neutral" compass, failing to provide them with an understanding of where we came from and how we got here (Baladouni, 1979). Similar to Moore's (2008) analysis of law schools, this method of teaching requires that students begin to think and reason like the "neutral" white gentlemen who established the profession and its practices—a process resulting in conversion costs for students of color and racial ignorance for students like me.

If the profession truly desires to reflect the diversity of the population it serves, then the accounting curriculum must change. If no changes are made, the "gentlemanly" portrait painted by the profession's collective memory will simply maintain the status quo. Instead, accounting education must begin producing graduates who are not only prepared to navigate our present and future challenges but who can do so with something more than a "neutral" compass. To achieve this, accounting history must become a more integral component of the accounting curriculum, which should be revised in such a way as to produce graduates who will advocate for the accountability and financial storytelling practices necessary for the flourishing of all peoples, rather than the few. Put another way, accounting education must provide students with the knowledge and skills that should be expected of those who desire to call themselves *public* accountants.

References

AICPA. (2014). *Recruitment and retention toolkit: A journey toward a more inclusive workforce*. American Institute of Certified Public Accountants. https://us.aicpa.org/content/dam/aicpa/career/diversityinitiatives/downloadabledocuments/recruitment-retention-toolkit.pdf

AICPA. (2019). *Trends in the supply of accounting graduates and the demand for public accounting recruits*. Association of International Certified Public Accountants. https://us.aicpa.org/content/dam/aicpa/interestareas/accountingeducation/newsandpublications/downloadabledocuments/2019-trends-report.pdf

Baladouni, V. (1979). The study of accounting history. In E. N. Coffman (Ed.), *The academy of accounting historians: Working paper series* (Vol. 1, pp. 318–327). The Academy of Accounting Historians.

Baldwin, J. (1992). *The fire next time*. Vintage. (Original work published 1963).

Baxter, W. T. (1978). Accounting in colonial America. In A. C. Littleton & B. S. Yamey (Eds.), *Studies in the history of accounting* (pp. 272–287). Arno Press. (Original work published 1956).

Brown, R. (Ed.) (2004). *A history of accounting and accountants*. Cosimo Books, Inc. (Original work published 1905).

Byrne, J. A. (1993). *The whiz kids: Ten founding fathers of American business-and the legacy they left us*. Doubleday.

Carey, J. L. (1969). *The rise of the accounting profession: From technician to professional 1896–1936*. American Institute of Certified Public Accountants.

Carey, J. L. (1970). *The rise of the accounting profession: To responsibility and authority 1937–1969*. American Institute of Certified Public Accountants.

Citron, A. F. (1969). *The "rightness of whiteness": The world of the white child in a segregated society*. Michigan-Ohio Regional Education Lab., Inc., Wayne State University, College of Education.

Coates, T.-N. (2015). *Between the world and me*. Spiegel & Grau.

Cooper, D. J., & Robson, K. (2009). Practitioners, work and firms. In J. R. Edwards & S. P. Walker (Eds.), *The Routledge companion to accounting history* (pp. 274–296). Routledge.

Delgado, R. (2013). Storytelling for oppositionists and others. In R. Delgado & J. Stefancic (Eds.), *Critical race theory: The cutting edge* (3rd ed., pp. 71–80). Temple University Press.

Du Bois, W. E. B. (1994). *The souls of Black folk*. Dover Publications. (Original work published 1903).

Feagin, J. R. (2010). *The white racial frame: Centuries of racial framing and counter-framing* (1st ed.). Routledge.

Feagin, J. R. (2020). *The white racial frame: Centuries of racial framing and counter-framing* (3rd ed.). Routledge.

Garrett-Scott, S. (2019). *Banking on freedom: Black women in U.S. finance before the new deal*. Columbia University Press.

Gleeson-White, J. (2011). *Double-entry: How the merchants of Venice created modern finance*. W.W. Norton & Company.

Gow, I. D., & Kells, S. (2018). *The big four: The curious past and perilous future of the global accounting monopoly*. Berrett-Koehler Publishers.

Halbwachs, M. (1980). *The collective memory*. Harper & Row, Publishers. (Original work published 1950).

Halbwachs, M. (1992). *On collective memory*. The University of Chicago Press. (Original work published 1925).

Hammond, T. A. (1997). From complete exclusion to minimal inclusion: African Americans and the public accounting industry, 1965–1988. *Accounting, Organizations and Society*, *22*(1), 29–53.

hooks, b. (2000). *Where we stand: Class matters*. Routledge.

Johnson, W. (2020a). *The broken heart of America: St. Louis and the violent history of the United States*. Basic Books.

Johnson, W. (2020b). *The largest human zoo in world history: Visiting the 1904 world's fair in St. Louis*. Lapham's Quarterly. https://www.laphamsquarterly.org/roundtable/largest-human-zoo-world-history

Levy, J. (2012). *Freaks of fortune: The emerging world of capitalism and risk in America*. Harvard University Press.

Lippman, E. J., & Wilson, P. A. (2007). The culpability of accounting in perpetuating the Holocaust. *Accounting History*, *12*(3), 283–303.

Macdonald, K. M. (1995). *The sociology of the professions*. Sage.

Miranti, P. J., Jr. (1990). *Accountancy comes of age: The development of an American profession, 1886–1940*. The University of North Carolina Press.

Montagna, P. D. (1974). *Certified public accounting: A sociological view of a profession in change*. Scholars Book Co.

Moore, W. L. (2008). *Reproducing racism: White space, elite law schools, and racial inequality*. Rowman & Littlefield.

NASBA. (2022). *How many CPAs are there?* National Association of State Boards of Accountancy. https://nasba.org/licensure/howmanycpas/

Ortiz, E., & Johnson, A. (2019, October 2). Amber Guyger sentenced to 10 years for murdering neighbor Botham Jean. *NBC News*. https://www.nbcnews.com/news/crime-courts/amber-guyger-sentencing-resumes-after-murder-conviction-death-botham-jean-n1061146

Previts, G. J., & Merino, B. D. (1998). *A history of accountancy in the United States: The cultural significance of accounting*. Ohio State University Press.

Robinson, C. (2021). *Black Marxism: The making of the Black radical tradition* (3rd ed.). The University of North Carolina Press. (Original work published 1983).

Roediger, D. R., & Esch, E. D. (2012). *The production of difference: Race and the management of labor in U.S. history*. Oxford University Press.

Rosenthal, C. (2018). *Accounting for slavery: Masters and management*. Harvard University Press.

Roy, R. H., & MacNeill, J. H. (1967). *Horizons for a profession: The common body of knowledge for certified public accountants*. American Institute of Certified Public Accountants.

Samuels, J. M. (1985). The 1904 congress of accountants: National or international? *The Accounting Historians Journal*, *12*(1), 99–105.

Smedley, A. (2007). *Race in North America: Origin and evolution of a worldview*. Westview Press.

Stevens, M. (1981). *The big eight: An incisive look behind the pinstripe curtain of the eight accounting firms whose practices affect the lives and pocketbooks of every American*. Collier Books.

Tillyard, E. M. W. (1959). *The Elizabethan world picture*. Vintage Books. (Original work published 1943).

Tinker, T. (1985). *Paper prophets: A social critique of accounting*. Praeger.

Toffler, B. L. (2003). *Final accounting: Ambition, greed, and the fall of Arthur Andersen*. Broadway Books.

Twyford, E., Tanima, F. A., & George, S. (2022). Critical race theory, counter-accounting, and the emancipatory potential of counter-stories. *Accounting, Auditing & Accountability Journal*, *35*(9), 330–358.

Tyson, T. N., & Fleischman, R. K. (2006). Accounting for interned Japanese-American civilians during World War II: Creating incentives and establishing controls for captive workers. *The Accounting Historians Journal*, *33*(1), 167–202.

U.S. Census Bureau. (2021). *Quick facts: United States*. https://www.census.gov/quickfacts/fact/table/US/LFE046221

van Dijk, T. A. (1993). Principles of critical discourse analysis. *Discourse & Society*, *4*(2), 249–283.

Wertsch, J. V., & Roediger, H. L., III (2008). Collective memory: Conceptual foundations and theoretical approaches. *Psychology Press*, *16*(3), 318–326.

White, H. (1978). *Tropics of discourse: Essays in cultural criticism*. The Johns Hopkins University Press.

Wilkerson, I. (2010). *The warmth of other suns: The epic story of America's great migration*. Random House.

Williams, C. (1987). *The destruction of Black civilization: Great issues of a race from 4500 B.C. to 2000 A.D.* Third World Press.

Woodson, C. G. (1934). *The Negro professional man and the community: With special emphasis on the physician and the lawyer*. The Association for the Study of Negro Life and History, Inc.

Worthington, B. (1978). *Professional accountants: An historical sketch*. Arno Press. (Original work published 1895).

Yamey, B. S. (1978). Scientific bookkeeping and the rise of capitalism. In B. S. Yamey (Ed.), *Essays on the history of accounting* (pp. 99–113). Arno Press. (Original work published 1949).

Section 2

Toward the Future

Chapter 9

Rebutting PESTS: The Five Most Common Rationales Against Equity, Diversity, and Inclusion

Akolisa Ufodike

York University, Canada

Introduction

This chapter builds on the work in my earlier chapter in this book, which documents some of what I have learned so far from an ongoing Social Sciences and Humanities Research Council (SSHRC) Race and Gender Initiative project, which I commenced during the COVID-19 pandemic, titled "A Practice Theory Approach to Diversity on Boards and in Business Professions." Specifically, this chapter examines the five most commonly cited justifications for a lack of diversity and inertia or rationalization against diversity initiatives: public interest, equity, supply-side, temporal, and spatial (PESTS).

As part of the project, I conducted two structured literature reviews (SLRs). The first SLR (Ufodike et al., 2023) is the first literature review on anti-Black racism research in accounting (and more broadly, business) research. The second (Ufodike, 2025) conducts a review of imperialism, colonialism, and post-colonialism studies in accounting. The literature reviews reveal that of the articles that aspire to positive, forward-looking approaches to inclusion – which I refer to as a sociology of inclusion – most of the studies propose implementing and furthering various forms of equity, diversity, and inclusion (EDI) initiatives. This chapter expands this body of work by improving our understanding of why people resist EDI initiatives in the first place. The argument that EDI initiatives are imperfect is the crux of the EDI resistance movement, and by improving our collective understanding of resistance to EDI, we can pave the way for greater acceptance and normalization of actions and programs in furtherance of EDI, even if imperfect.

Voices of Change, 113–127

doi:10.1108/978-1-83753-030-420251024

The work in this chapter is a stark departure from my scholarly work prior to COVID which focused primarily on public accountability (Ufodike, 2017, 2020), network accountability (Ufodike et al., 2021, 2022), and public sector finance (Opara et al., 2021, 2022). George Floyd's murder marked a turning point in my research and kindled my interest in racism. This is some of what I have learned about how racism is sustained through resistance to EDI initiatives.

Public Interest Rationale

"A Knowledge Synthesis of Anti-Black Racism in Accounting Research" (Ufodike et al., 2023), our SLR published in a special issue of *Accounting Perspectives* on literature reviews, found that the professionalization literature argues that Black and other racialized people are deliberately excluded from the accountancy profession (Bakre, 2008; Hammond, 2003) or at best minimally included (Hammond, 1997). Quite often, such an exclusion is disguised as public interest, which is also true of other professions such as healthcare and law. Bakre (2008) argues that in colonial times, race officially served as the basis for discrimination, but the independence of colonies did not end discriminatory practices. In postcolonial times, societal class or relevance, gender, immigration status, and ethnicity have continued as a basis for discrimination (Annisette & Trivedi, 2013; Bakre, 2008; Ufodike, 2017). These ongoing discriminatory practices are perpetuated by actors such as professional bodies under the guise of professionalization (Ashraf & Ghani, 2005; Poullaos, 2016).

Excluding racialized people from the accounting profession takes the form of protecting the public from "inferior" or "poor quality" accountants trained in foreign countries. Hence, even in 2023, it is normalized in Organisation for Economic Co-operation and Development (OECD) countries that only accountants trained in the United Kingdom, Ireland, Canada, the United States, Australia, and Western Europe are seen as equivalent. This situation is made worse by a common perception that the best Black students opt for medicine or law, leaving the "mediocre" Black students for accounting (Lewis, 2015, p. 4).

Organizations that purport to advocate for the public interest often have a conflict of interest, because the public interest they argue for advances their own superordinate goals, and may be at odds with the 'true' public interest, if ever there was one (Ufodike, 2020). In Canada, laws are passed in the name of public interest (Canada, n.d.a; Ufodike, 2020). In 1906, a time when most immigrants to Canada came from predominantly white countries in Europe, immigration laws were used to prevent the immigration of "idiots" and "epileptics" (i.e., people with disabilities), "the insane" (immigrants with mental health issues), paupers and beggars (the disadvantaged), and criminals (Canada, 1906), effectively criminalizing disability, poverty, and ill mental health. In another example specific to Black people, in 1911, Canada's prime minister signed an Order-in-Council (PC 1911-1324) that prohibited the immigration of people belonging to the "Negro race" because they were deemed unsuitable for the Canadian climate and its immigration requirements. This Order-in-Council culminated in the 1911 Black ban, a law passed in "public interest" to prevent immigration by Black people.

In recent times, however, Canada's population and workforce have been sustained by welcoming mostly racialized immigrants at a rate that outpaces all its OECD peers. Immigration impacts businesses and is deeply connected to accounting. Yet Lehman et al. (2016) found that accounting was employed as a tool for responsibilization – a device used to control immigrants to the United States, Canada, and the United Kingdom, intended to make them governable. A 2023 *Globe and Mail* article revealed that despite the exponential increase in immigration to Canada over the past 20 years, Statistics Canada reported a 40% decline in citizenship uptake since 2001 (Collington, 2023). Cost of living and job prospects are professed drivers of immigration to Canada (Collington, 2023), but a lack of Canadian experience is an accepted justification for refusing to hire a foreign-trained (mostly racialized) qualified applicant. Simply put, applicants can be screened out from a job for which they are qualified – not because of a lack of experience but because of the country in which that experience was obtained. This policy provides human resources managers across the country with a normalized way of expressing bias and discrimination.

Some jurisdictions, such as Ontario, have sought ways to curtail this discrimination. On December 2, 2021, Ontario modified the Fair Access to Regulated Professions and Compulsory Trades Act to prevent professions such as chartered accountancy from requiring Canadian experience for licensing without obtaining an exemption "in the public interest"; this exemption, however, allows the practice to continue.

As I've noted elsewhere, "at best, the public interest is used generously to refer to majority interest, and, at worst, it is a group's interest pretending to be everyone's – the public's interest" (Ufodike, 2020, p. 20). Rand et al. (1986) describe this paradox as follows: if public interest is to be "regarded as something apart from and superior to the individual good of its members, it means that the good of some men takes precedence over the good of others" (pp. 12–13). The reality is that individuals or dominant groups often mischaracterize their interests as a proxy for public interest without considering how it impacts the invisible segments of society.

Equity Rationale

The equity rationale comprises two arguments. The first is that anti-Black racism (or any race-based EDI) initiatives are inappropriate because they create competition with other equity-seeking groups or will be opposed by other equity-seeking groups (or even by the members of the equity-seeking group for which the initiative was designed). The second is that these initiatives create competition among equity-seeking groups. These arguments are meant to save society from the scourge of squabbling equity-seeking groups (competition) or to patriarchally address the concerns of members of the equity-seeking groups opposed (opposition) to the detriment of those who are in support or, worse still, to save other equity-seeking groups from Black people or to save Black people from their selves.

The same logic is used when people argue that it was Africans who sold other Africans to Europeans during slavery as a way of diminishing or sharing the responsibility of Europeans toward slavery (Nwaubani, 2019). The logic of the argument goes like this: because Africans sold other Africans into slavery, those who were sold are not owed reparations by their non-African buyers.[1] Divide and conquer was a common strategy used during the colonial era and continues as a means of delegitimizing the efforts of equity-seeking groups. Some opponents of EDI initiatives believe that it is sufficient to point to members from an equity-seeking group who are against the equity initiative as a way of delegitimizing it. Some even go a step further to make a racialized person the mouthpiece of the opposition to the equity initiative. In short, the presence of Black employees opposed to targeted Black hiring is seen as irrefutable evidence of why targeted hiring should not happen. Alternatively, opposition from another equity-seeking group is provided as evidence of why the EDI initiative is ill advised; for example, the face of the opposition to Indigenous cultural sensitivity training imposed on Alberta lawyers by the Law Society of Alberta was an Asian immigrant (Dawson, 2023).

Equity-based initiatives for nonracialized people, such as gender equity initiatives related to the representation of women directors on boards, can also help illuminate the equity rationale. Initiatives to increase the number of women on boards were effective, despite some opposition from existing women directors. In early 2015, the absence of board diversity was mainly seen as pertaining to women (McFarland, 2015). At that time, only 31 of the 722 (McFarland, 2015) Toronto Stock Exchange (TSX)–listed companies had adopted written diversity policies in response to the requirement of the Ontario Securities Commission to comply (i.e., by adopting such policies) or explain their failure to adopt diversity policies (MacDougall et al., 2019). Indeed, few companies listed on the S&P/TSX 60 Index had female board members; however, after 2015, various entities such as Osler, Women's Executive Network (a national network of professional women), and the Canadian Board Diversity Council enacted diversity initiatives focused on actively recruiting and mentoring women for boards (MacDougall et al., 2019). MacDougall et al. (2021) found that these initiatives led to an increase in women's representation in Canada. Specifically, their research showed that by 2021, 71.7% of S&P/TSX 60 companies had adopted diversity policies to recruit women and that 58.3% had adopted targets for women's representation on their boards. Moreover, 80% of S&P/TSX 60 companies had women on their boards, with 46% having more than one female board member (MacDougall et al., 2021). By contrast, only 6.8% of all board positions in Canadian firms (or 150 of 2,200) were held by visible minorities as of 2021, with just eight from Indigenous groups. Meanwhile, only an estimated 0.3% of all public company directors are Black or seven of over 2,000 directors (Diversity Institute, 2020). My SSHRC study aims to replicate the success of the

[1]While strict fidelity to the word *reparations* usually means financial compensation for slavery, reparation can take other forms of reconciliation, including affirmative action, acknowledgments, or apologies to the descendants of enslaved peoples or honoring the memories of enslaved peoples.

gender-equity initiatives for racial equity by recruiting Black directors onto boards.

Interestingly, white women were both the greatest beneficiaries of diversity initiatives/affirmative action – such as gender diversity initiatives adopted by Canadian public companies – *and* their fiercest opponents (Massie, 2016). Logically, it is a territorial human instinct to believe that if many other white women joined boards, it would diminish the achievement of current members and the challenges they overcame to become directors – without diversity initiatives. It should then come as no surprise that marginalization will result in inter (white women vs other new up-and-coming white women directors) and intra equity-seeking group competition (white women vs Black women directors). However, when the competition is between, say, a Black (fe)male director and a Black (fe)male nondirector, this phenomenon is generously referred to as crabs-in-a-bucket mentality and as justification to not pursue equity initiatives further.[2]

Perhaps many members of equity-seeking groups take pride in being the only member of that represented group (e.g., the only partner at a Big Four accounting firm). They remember their struggles and assume that targeted hiring will oversimplify the process of overcoming those challenges, diminish their accomplishment, and result in a number of unqualified people, of their own race, being hired. While this is the norm for Black people, it was also the norm for white women directors, and this mindset is common when discussing the issue of advancing equity for any equity-seeking group. Sometimes, the greatest opposition may come from the group itself or other equity-seeking groups. The reality is marginalization may result in competition. However, competition is not exclusive to racialized peoples, and more importantly, equity initiatives work – as they did for achieving gender diversity, despite opposition from white women directors. Regardless of where the opposition comes from, it does not diminish the effectiveness of affirmative action.

Lastly, there is an implicit assumption that equity-seeking groups are homogeneous. All Black people are not the same, just as all white women are not the same. There are, of course, differences in language, culture, religion, education, social status, and a myriad of other mutable or immutable traits. Therefore, it is not surprising that members of a designated equity-seeking group cannot be expected to have a homogeneous position on an issue, even if it has to do with diversity or a cause that improves their lot when aggregated as a homogeneous group.

Supply-Side Rationale

The supply-side rationale argues that there are not enough Black people in the pipeline to achieve the desired diversity goal. The boards of public companies or

[2]Crabs in a bucket will pull the crabs who are making the most successful attempts at getting out of the bucket back into the bucket; thus, crabs-in-a-bucket mentality uses this analogy to articulate the attitude “If I can’t have it, then none of us can.”

other agencies may argue that they want to appoint more Black directors, but there simply are not enough Black directors available. This logic assumes that qualified Black people who can be appointed do not exist; in reality, a significant number of qualified Black candidates are ignored or sidestepped.

Black candidates who are qualified for directorships are generally not present in the traditional circles from which these organizations recruit. The supply-side rationale is also steeped in racial undertones about the perceptions of "unqualified" or incompetent Black people. In the 1990s, it was shown that Black female accountants in the United States were more qualified than their Black male, white male, and white female counterparts; however, Black female accountants enjoyed less supervisory responsibilities than all three of those groups (Robinson-Backmon et al., 1997). Furthermore, if a Black accounting professional or company director fails, their supervisor's first instinct is to attribute that failure to incompetence. Often, in such a case, the superior may also assume that the Black person was a patronage (or token) hire. The same judgments are not necessarily made about the non-racialized chair of the Alberta Human Rights Commission, for example, who was fired within his first three months in office (Johnson, 2022) but are insinuated when it is a Black female – such as Claudine Gay for example. Stewart et al. (2011) provide supporting evidence of group-projected bias, wherein failure by a white person is viewed as an individual matter while failure by a Black person is seen as a reflection of all Black employees within the organization.

Nonracialized people have stronger networks than racialized people or immigrants. In other words, nonracialized people have greater access to the social circles where patronage appointments are made. Black and other racialized peoples simply do not have that kind of social capital. Board nominations for most public companies remain opaque and inaccessible to highly qualified Black and racialized people, but society does not assume that all public company board appointments are based on patronage. One judge was appointed to the Supreme Court of the United States during COVID-19. Judge Ketanji Brown Jackson, arguably the most qualified appointee ever in terms of scholarly and legal experience at the time of her appointment (Demand Justice, 2022) and the most popular appointee since 2005 (Enten, 2022), needed a platform commitment – by all intents the use of a quota – from President Biden to become the first Black woman appointed to the Supreme Court. She and many other Black people in leadership roles are accustomed to the question "how did you get this role?" – sometimes from their peers. It turns out that targets, goals, quotas, and social networks are used to appoint much-needed, highly qualified, and competent Black people to positions of leadership for which they would otherwise be overlooked not unqualified Black people. Therefore, an alternate fact becomes apparent: Black appointees to highly visible positions of leadership often must possess superior qualifications to their fellow non-Black appointees.

An organization I founded, the John Ware Institute, has observed just that. In the years since the George Floyd's death, the institute has recruited, mentored, and placed over 70 Black executives on various agencies, boards, and commissions in Canada. These qualified individuals were invisible to the recruitment process before our intentional efforts. The allyship of various governments, agencies, boards, and commissions seeking diverse talent made them visible to the process, which brings me to demand-side stagnation in accounting. In 2017, Black CPAs accounted for 0.3% of the partners in major firms in the United States (down from approximately 1% in 2011) (AICPA, 2019). Stewart et al. (2011) offer two reasons: first, there is a disproportionately low number of Black accountants in the management pipeline; and second, underlying economic factors influence the participation of Black accountants in major firms.

The dominant view is that Black people are under-represented in certain professions and academic fields because they are not voluntarily choosing to enter them, but there is a fallacy to this logic (Ufodike et al., 2023). In the United States in 2018, African Americans made up 13.6% of the population, 11.7% of the workforce, and only 8.8% of accountants and auditors (Data USA, n.d.). Similarly, the American Institute of Certified Public Accountants (AICPA, 2019) found that African Americans made up 12.1% of the workforce but only 8.2% of accountants and auditors. We can correlate that to employment data. In 2007, 11% of all newly graduated accountants seeking employment in US CPA firms were African Americans; however, they accounted for only 8% of new hires in the field (AICPA, 2019). By 2016, African-American graduates accounted for 9% of the supply and only 4% of the demand (AICPA, 2019). Simply put, half of the Black accounting graduates who actively sought employment at CPA firms were not accepted, which the AICPA refers to as "demand stagnation." Moreover, during that period, the percentage of Black students enrolled in Bachelor's and Master's accounting programs increased by almost 50% from approximately 6% in 2012 to 9% in 2018. These figures contradict the supply-side explanation of the lack of diversity in the profession. Unsurprisingly, the result of demand stagnation is that while 6% of all undergraduate and Master's accounting graduates are Black, only 3% of employees in US CPA firms are African American, and, worse still, only 0.3% of partners in these companies are Black (AICPA, 2019). These statistics demonstrate the supply-side fallacy – there is no suggestion that when 9% graduates are Black (assuming all those enrolled in 2018 completed their program), the percentage of Black employees would increase.

Am I suggesting that there is never a supply-side issue? No. However, supply-side issues likely exist for other groups, too, whether they are equity-seeking or not. Regardless, supply-side challenges are no justification for inaction. Furthermore, while the scarcity of Black professionals in any profession may start as a supply-side issue, it is often sustained by demand-side stagnation, providing empirical evidence of institutionalized discrimination. Thus, scholars and practitioners alike must recognize when exclusion is no longer a demand issue. The supply of Black professionals in accounting is not the issue; the reality is that Black accountants and professionals are often ignored in hiring practices even when they are qualified. In fact, for Black immigrants, being overqualified has become an acceptable, normalized criteria for being screened out.

Temporal Rationale

The temporal rationale includes three main arguments: (1) that EDI initiatives are ineffective and hence not worth pursuing; (2) equity initiatives have been achieved or gained "too much," and Black people have bigger problems, such as crime and poverty; and (3) members of the equity-seeking group should simply "get over it." All of these arguments are temporal in that they claim that, although society may have failed Black people in the past or failed to provide EDI initiatives to ameliorate inequitable social outcomes (and consequently discrimination), these issues are in the past and society needs to move on. Temporal arguments against EDI are anchored in the notion that race "is an irritating residue of a past historical moment and not a deeply embedded feature of existing social structures" (Annisette & Prasad, 2017, p. 13). Temporal arguments also treat Black people as a monolith, but, in fact, Black people face a myriad of social issues concurrently, and, as such, a plurality of concurrent initiatives are required to ameliorate these issues. EDI initiatives intended to overcome systemic racism are only one dimension of a complex solution.

In May 2021, one week to the anniversary of Floyd's death, my sister Uche Ezike-Dennis died of cancer. She never smoked a day in her life but was diagnosed with lung cancer in September 2020, just as the second COVID-19 wave hit. She started chemotherapy later that fall, completing her last treatment in December. The treatment was unsuccessful. I may logically conclude that chemotherapy does not work, and yet many people take it nonetheless, sometimes as a last resort and sometimes unsuccessfully. The reality is this: while chemotherapy did not work for Uche, it works for some people. Cancer is not a homogeneous problem and neither is the solution. Therefore, society is willing to continue to accept chemotherapy as healthcare science. The same should apply to the treatment of racism. The solution to racism cannot be a binary construct where a solution works or does not work. Despite any perceived issues with quotas, the United States now has a Black female Supreme Court justice - this is progress. In Canada, over 20 Black women now sit on agencies, boards, and commissions because of the John Ware Institute, and many Black and racialized girls can now see themselves as future business leaders – this is also progress. Fifty percent of these women are now board or committee chairs; this also is progress.

Justice is necessary action before reconciliation is possible. This is so because reconciliation inadvertently assumes that two parties were at peace with each other, one or both parties were injured, and a remedy is sought to restore the original peace. If this is what reconciliation means – peace, injury, peace – it must be brought about by some action and that action is justice. Simply put, justice must precede genuine reconciliation. These arguments also have application in Canada's reconciliation efforts with Indigenous peoples, as the example of land claim settlements illustrates. In Canada, land claim settlements have empowered Indigenous communities, as the journey to justice must also be economic. The largest land claim settlement in Canadian history, $1.3 billion, happened in June 2022 (Graveland, 2022). Countries that have benefited financially from slavery also need to contemplate repatriations as economic justice for genuine reconciliation. Substantive equality is the foundation of Jordan's Principle, used in public policy and administration in Canada to ensure that First Nations children "can access the products, services and supports they need, when they need them" (Canada, n.d.b). The principles of substantive equity can inform similar programs that aspire to achieve equality in outcomes for Black people everywhere. I have previously written about per capita defense – namely, using how much governments spend per capita (e.g., on the healthcare of First Nations peoples) – as a measure of success rather than actual outcomes (Ufodike et al., 2021, 2022), and so my comments on repatriations do not merely encourage throwing money at a problem. However, outcomes ultimately matter, and adequately funding EDI initiatives has implications for those outcomes.

Spatial Rationale

A conventional argument to support the denial of anti-Black racism at the macro level is that racism is worse elsewhere. It is not quite a denial, but this argument relies on relative morality and deflects attention from the problem of racism. In a hierarchy of racist societies, Society A is better than Society B, so let Society B deal with its issues first. It can sometimes be defended using arguments such as there was no slavery in Canada – a false assertion (McRae & McCullough, 2018) – or that Canada's history with slavery was different, with an emphasis on the fact that the underground railroad ended in Canada (Frost, 2007), which must mean that the Black experience with slavery or discrimination was better in Canada.[3]

These spatial arguments apply when distinctions are made about the Black experience at the hands of the police in Canada versus the United States. While there were isolated incidents of police brutality in Canada during the pandemic, reported incidents of police brutality were more frequent and certainly more severe in the United States. Yet these arguments ignore the fact that Canada in 1911, like the United States in 1803, also enacted laws banning the immigration of Black people. In many ways, when it comes to racism, societies do not believe that the grass is greener on the other side. Instead, they believe that the grass is greener on their side of the fence and the situation with racism is significantly darker elsewhere.

Countries with a colonial history, such as Canada, Australia, and New Zealand, have done a better job at confronting issues relating to the colonial role of accounting or accountants in dispossessing Indigenous people in their academic research than countries without a colonial past. Relatedly, countries with a history of subjugating or enslaving Black people – namely, the United States and South Africa – have done a better job confronting issues of anti-Black racism in accounting research than countries without such a history. Where the United States appears to be making progress on affirmative action for Black Americans but not so much on reconciliations for Indigenous people, the opposite may be the case in Canada.[4] Therefore, it is not surprising that several of the race-based

[3]The underground railroad was a network of routes and safe houses that aided African-American slaves escaping bondage. Slaves usually escaped north from slave states (mostly in the south). Canada was the main terminus for the underground railroad (Frost, 2007).

[4]This is no longer the case. In 2023 (while this chapter was still in the editorial process.), the Supreme Court of the United States in Students for Fair Admissions v. Harvard struck down years of normalized Affirmative Action.

affirmative action programs that exist in the United States are nonexistent in Canada.[5] In early spring 2021, during the peak of the third wave of COVID-19, as businesses engaged with anti-Black racism, CPA Ontario rejected my proposal to partner on the SSHRC project. Addressing anti-Black racism and increasing the participation of Black students in the profession was not on the radar in Canadian accounting. In rejecting our proposal, CPA Ontario pointed to work they had in the pipeline on Indigenous experience with racism. In other words, the organization inadvertently set up competition between equity-seeking groups. While they were willing to consider one form of exclusion (the consequences of colonialism on Indigenous people in Canada), anti-Black racism was a blind spot, despite making national headlines.

Rather than creating competition among equity-seeking groups, disaggregating the equity-seeking group known as "Black, Indigenous, and people of color" (BIPOC) acknowledges that the issues are not homogeneous and allows for targeted solutions. Equity initiatives are not a finite, common-pool resource that can be overconsumed if not moderated and hence require gatekeeping (Ufodike et al., 2021). We can pursue equity for multiple equity-seeking groups parallelly. This is a rudimentary but important argument. Like a wise child once said, we can walk and chew gum at the same time.

Some diversity initiatives in business such as the PhD Project, which aspires to increase the pipeline of Black and LatinX doctoral students, are nonexistent in Canada. The PhD Project is cofounded by KPMG, a Big Four accounting firm with a huge presence in Canada. The absence of a comparable program in Canada is not a reflection of KPMG; it is a reflection of Canadian accountancy. The US accountancy profession can identify demand stagnation for Black accountants because it collects relevant data. At the time of writing, no Canadian university or provincial CPA organization could tell me the number of registered Black students or members.[6]

Hence, I am only able to illuminate this phenomenon in the United States because the relevant professional bodies and researchers are willing to collect and analyze the data, even if it reveals a dismal state of affairs. This is not the case in Canada and the United Kingdom, where racial data are not collected. Accountants need data and accounting scholars need evidence. Collecting racial data on students and professions as well as part of census programs is necessary to establish a genuine, intentional commitment to diversity – just as collecting COVID case and death data by race during the pandemic was a moral imperative, which was missed by many jurisdictions for fear of what the data would reveal. The social justice movement of 2020 offers accounting researchers in Canada (and elsewhere) an opportunity to assess their discipline's commitment to diversity, as this is an ethical obligation of the profession.

---

[5]On June 29, 2023, the US Supreme Court struck down affirmative action, effectively barring colleges that considered race in admissions for equity purposes.

[6]Some universities ask for race as part of scholarship applications, but the information collected is not representative of entire student population.

Conclusions

COVID is a virus. Viruses are pests because they adapt and evolve, and although they may become dormant, they refuse to die and resurrect when the right environment presents itself. If we think racism (and other forms of discrimination, e.g., sexism) as akin to a virus, then we come to the realization that racist (or sexist) biases also evolve and can resurface and often do. Biases that are visible today can evolve and become discrete and overt in the future and, if the time permits, they re-emerge and become visible again or they may re-emerge in a different place altogether. When people forget the past, old biases are made new again. Nowhere is this more evident today than in the United States, where in June 2023, the Supreme Court of the United States (SCOTUS) of America struck down decades of precedence that allowed universities and colleges to consider race in college admissions (Panetta, 2023). An analysis of the facts of the case – which alleges reverse discrimination against Asian applicants to Harvard University – provides confirmatory evidence for the equity and public interest rationales I've made in this chapter.

In other words, old biases are made new again. When faced with the unfamiliar – such as immigrants or racialized people – it is usual for some members of the dominant group to respond by being tribal and treating the immigrants as "Others." PESTS rationalizations are excellent examples of *ex post* rationalization for being tribal. *Ex post* rationalization is the human impulse to make conclusions about an issue without evidence and then selectively find evidence to corroborate their predetermined, often biased opinions.

Equity initiatives – such as the targets adopted by many corporations in the wake of the social justice movement of 2020 (Ufodike & Vredenburg, 2020) – cannot and likely will never be perfect, but that's the case with all human decisions. Seeking perfection is a pursuit for divinity. In a world of theoria (ideas), there is a role for praxis (action) – hence the title of my current research project: "A Practice Theory Approach to Diversity on Boards and in Business Professions." Among other things, this research project summarizes extant literature on anti-Black racism in accounting (Ufodike et al., 2023) and Indigenous Peoples in accounting literature (Ufodike, 2024); both studies propose new and interesting avenues for future research that seeks positive, forward-looking solutions to address the marginalization of Black and Indigenous Peoples specifically and BIPOC more broadly. Another article, published in 2023, highlights the role of intersectionality by studying the financing challenges of women entrepreneurs in Africa (Ufodike & Ally, 2023) and discusses effective actions and government policies that have been taken in other jurisdictions in the global south to empower women entrepreneurs. Those jurisdictions without policy initiatives lag and those with policy initiatives – even imperfect ones – saw progress.

Ultimately, current inequities faced by marginalized peoples and the corresponding disparities in outcomes require action. Societal response can no longer be a binary choice between perfect action on one hand and imperfect action on the other hand. Put differently, the tradeoff may be a choice of imperfect action derived from imperfect ideas, but any action will be much more impactful than perfect ideas and no action. As we strive for collective action toward a more inclusive society, all must understand the frequent rebuttals to EDI and continue to make the case for the importance of EDI initiatives, expanding the community of allies and those willing to support and/or advocate for EDI especially in the current climate where EDI is facing an all out onslaught.

Acknowledgment

This research is funded by the Social Sciences and Humanities Research Council of Canada (SSHRC).

References

AICPA. (2019). *2019 Trends in supply of accounting graduates and the demand for public accounting recruits*. https://us.aicpa.org/content/dam/aicpa/interestareas/accountingeducation/newsandpublications/downloadabledocuments/2019-trends-report.pdf

Annisette, M., & Prasad, A. (2017). Critical accounting research in hyper-racial times. *Critical Perspectives on Accounting*, *43*, 5–19. https://doi.org/10.1016/j.cpa.2016.06.002

Annisette, M., & Trivedi, V. U. (2013). Globalization, paradox and the (un)making of identities: Immigrant chartered accountants of India in Canada. *Accounting, Organizations and Society*, *38*(1), 1–29. https://doi.org/10.1016/j.aos.2012.08.004

Ashraf, J., & Ghani, W. I. (2005). Accounting development in Pakistan. *International Journal of Accounting*, *40*(2), 175–201.

Bakre, O. M. (2008). Financial reporting as technology that supports and sustains imperial expansion, maintenance and control in the colonial and post-colonial globalization: The case of the Jamaican economy. *Critical Perspectives on Accounting*, *19*(4), 487–522. https://doi.org/10.1016/j.cpa.2006.09.002

Canada. (1906). *Immigration Act, 1906*. https://pier21.ca/research/immigration-history/immigration-act-1906. Accessed April 20, 2023.

Canada. (n.d.a). *Chapter 16: The legislative process*. https://www.ourcommons.ca/procedure/procedure-and-practice-3/ch_16_2-e.html. Accessed May 15, 2023.

Canada. (n.d.b). *Jordan's principle: Substantive equality principles*. https://www.sac-isc.gc.ca/eng/1583698429175/1583698455266. Accessed May 15, 2023.

Collington, C. (2023, February 15). Percentage of permanent residents becoming Canadian citizens in decline, Statscan data show. *Globe and Mail*. https://www.theglobeandmail.com/canada/article-percentage-of-permanent-residents-becoming-canadian-citizens-in/. Accessed April 19, 2023.

Data USA. (n.d.). *Accountants and auditors*. https://datausa.io/profile/soc/accountants-auditors#demographics. Accessed May 9, 2023.

Dawson, T. (2023, February 4). Alberta lawyers decry mandatory Indigenous cultural training imposed by law society. *National Post*. https://nationalpost.com/news/canada/alberta-lawyers-decry-mandatory-indigenous-cultural-training-imposed-by-law-society#:~:text=Fifty%2Done%20Alberta%20lawyers%20are,the%20%E2%80%9Ccultural%20competency%E2%80%9D%20training. Accessed April 24, 2023.

Demand Justice. (2022, February 4). Judge Ketanji Brown Jackson is one of the most qualified nominees for the Supreme Court ever press release. https://demandjustice.org/judge-ketanji-brown-jackson-is-one-of-the-most-qualified-nominees-for-the-supreme-court-ever/#:~:text=new%20window%20Search-,Judge%20Ketanji%20Brown%20Jackson%20is%20One%20of%20the%20Most,for%20the%20Supreme%20Court%20Ever&text=Jackson%20would%20be%20the%20most,Court%20in%20almost%20a%20century. Accessed April 19, 2023.

Diversity Institute. (2020). *Diversity leads 2020: Diverse representation in leadership: A review of eight Canadian cities*. https://www.torontomu.ca/diversity/reports/DiversityLeads_2020_Canada.pdf. Accessed May 8, 2023.

Enten, H. (2022, March 26). Ketanji Brown Jackson is the most popular Supreme Court nominee in years. *CNN*. https://www.cnn.com/2022/03/26/politics/ketanji-brown-jackson-supreme-court-biden/index.html. Accessed April 19, 2023.

Frost, K. S. (2007). *I've got a home in glory land: A lost tale of the underground railroad*. Macmillan.

Graveland, B. (2022, June 2). PM signs historic land claim settlement with Siksika First Nation. *CBC News*. https://www.cbc.ca/news/canada/calgary/siksika-trudeau-signing-ceremony-1.6475167. Accessed April 24, 2023.

Hammond, T. (1997). From complete exclusion to minimal inclusion: African Americans and the public accounting industry, 1965–1988. *Accounting, Organizations and Society*, *22*(1), 29–53.

Hammond, T. (2003). *A white-collar profession: African American certified public accountants since 1921*. University of North Carolina Press.

Johnson, L. (2022, September 16). Shandro fires chief of Alberta Human Rights Commission who refused to resign. *Edmonton Journal*. https://edmontonjournal.com/news/local-news/he-has-done-nothing-wrong-chief-of-alberta-human-rights-commission-refusing-to-resign. Accessed April 24, 2023.

Lehman, C., Annisette, M., & Agyemang, G. (2016). Immigration and neoliberalism: Three cases and counter accounts. *Accounting, Auditing & Accountability Journal*, *29*(1), 43–79. https://doi.org/10.1108/AAAJ-09-2013-1470

Lewis, A. M. (2015). 'Counting black and white beans': Why we need a critical race theory of accounting. *European Journal of Contemporary Economics and Management*, *2*(2), 1–13. http://doi.org/10.19044/elp.v2no2a1

MacDougall, A., Valley, J., & Jeffrey, J. (2021). *Diversity and leadership at Canadian public companies: Diversity disclosure practices*. https://www.osler.com/osler/media/Osler/reports/corporate-governance/Osler-Diversity-Disclosure-Practices-report-2021.pdf. Accessed October 11, 2021.

MacDougall, A., Valley, J., Jeffrey, J., Dick, M., Lastman, B., Aziz, R., & Traore, T. (2019). *2019 Diversity disclosure practices: Women in leadership roles at TSX-listed companies*. https://www.osler.com/en/resources/governance/2019/2019-diversity-disclosure-practices-report-women-in-leadership-roles-at-tsx-listed-companies. Accessed October 11, 2021.

Massie, V. M. (2016, May 25). White women benefit most from affirmative action—and are among its fiercest opponents. *Vox*. https://www.vox.com/2016/5/25/11682950/fisher-supreme-court-white-women-affirmative-action. Accessed April 20, 2023.

McFarland, J. (2015, September 28). Vast majority of Canadian firms reject gender diversity policies. *Globe and Mail*. https://www.theglobeandmail.com/report-on-business/vast-majority-of-canadian-firms-reject-gender-diversity-policies/article26567795/. Accessed October 20, 2021.

McRae, M., & McCullough, S. (2018, August 22). The story of Black slavery in Canadian history. *Canadian Museum for Human Rights*. https://humanrights.ca/story/story-black-slavery-canadian-history?gad=1&gclid=EAIaIQobChMIvZyI2_HD_gIVaidMCh2uzgS0EAAYASAAEgL0V_D_BwE. Accessed April 24, 2023.

Nwaubani, A. T. (2019, September 20). When the slave traders were African. *Wall Street Journal*. https://www.wsj.com/articles/when-the-slave-traders-were-african-11568991595. Accessed April 24, 2023.

Opara, M., Okafor, O. N., & Ufodike, A. (2022). Invisible actors: Understanding the micro-activities of public sector employees in the development of public–private partnerships in the United States. *Australian Journal of Public Administration*, *81*(2), 237–278. https://doi.org/10.1111/1467-8500.12502

Opara, M., Okafor, O. N., Ufodike, A., & Kalu, K. (2021). Institutional entrepreneurship: Collaborative change in a complex Canadian organization. *Accounting, Auditing & Accountability Journal*, *34*(9), 284–314. https://doi.org/10.1108/AAAJ-06-2020-4610

Panetta, A. (2023, June 29). U.S. court strikes severe blow to affirmative action. Here's what's next. *CBC News*. https://www.cbc.ca/news/world/us-supreme-court-colleges-affirmative-action-1.6892475. Accessed December 20, 2023.

Poullaos, C. (2016). Canada vs Britain in the imperial accountancy arena, 1908–1912: Symbolic capital, symbolic violence. *Accounting, Organizations and Society*, *51*, 47–63. https://doi.org/10.1016/j.aos.2016.05.001

Rand, A., Branden, N., Greenspan, A., & Hessen, R. (1986). *Capitalism: The unknown ideal*. Penguin.

Robinson-Backmon, I., Weisenfeld, L., & Clark, G. (1997). Is it double jeopardy: The African American woman in accounting? *The Negro Educational Review*, *48*(1), 53–69.

Stewart, L. J., Wells, J., & Ross, F. (2011). Promotion and retention of African American accountants in the 21st century US public accounting profession: A summary of findings and a call for action. *Journal of Diversity Management*, *6*(4), 9–18. https://doi.org/10.19030/jdm.v6i4.6663

Ufodike, A. (2017). *The role of accounting in the delivery of health care to Canada's Aboriginal population* Doctoral Dissertation. University of Calgary.

Ufodike, A. (2020). Reviving austerity: Populist support for unpopular economics in Canada. *Journal of Accounting, Ethics & Public Policy*, *21*(4), 451–479. https://doi.org/10.2139/ssrn.3720355

Ufodike, A. (2025). The sociology of exclusion: A knowledge synthesis of imperialism and post-colonialism in accounting research. *Accounting Perspectives*. https://doi.org/10.1111/1911-3838.12378

Ufodike, A., & Ally, S. (2023). Enhancing gender-responsive financing in Africa: A sustainable development perspective. In F. Olayele & S. Yiagadeesen (Eds.), *Sustainable development in post-pandemic Africa: Effective strategies for resource mobilization* (pp. 48–67). Routledge, Taylor & Francis Group. https://doi.org/10.4324/9781003185062-4

Ufodike, A., Egbe, I., Ogharanduku, B. E., & Akinyemi, T. E. (2023). A knowledge synthesis of anti-Black racism in accounting research. *Accounting Perspectives*, *22*(3), 375–401. https://doi.org/10.1111/1911-3838.12336

Ufodike, A., Okafor, O. N., & Opara, M. (2021). First Nations gatekeepers as a common pool health care institution: Evidence from Canada. *Financial Accountability and Management*, *39*(3), 731–752. https://doi.org/10.1111/faam.12309

Ufodike, A., Okafor, O. N., & Opara, M. (2022). Network accountability in healthcare: A perspective from a First Nations community in Canada. *Accounting Perspectives*, *21*(1), 101–129. https://doi.org/10.1111/1911-3838.12283

Ufodike, A., & Vredenburg, H. (2020, August 24). Corporate diversity targets could help dismantle systemic racism. *The Conversation*. https://doi.org/10.17613/ ahsm5-bg628

Chapter 10

Comfortably Uncomfortable: A Framework for Meaningful and Productive Race Conversations

Jina Etienne

Etienne Consulting LLC, USA

Introduction

Entrenched beliefs make discussions about equity, discrimination, and unconscious bias difficult. In an effort to raise awareness and foster dialogue, training and other programs emerged to facilitate uncomfortable discussions. While well-intentioned, these programs are unlikely to succeed until people discover how internalized beliefs subconsciously influence self-perception, self-esteem, and emotional well-being. True learning requires environments where people feel supported, not judged, offering space to grow at a pace that feels doable. Meaningful, transformational dialogue and culture change require a different approach. I offer a holistic framework that anticipates this discomfort and offers techniques to support emotional reactivity, provide psychological safety, and promote reflection and healing.

Unpacking the DEI Dilemma

The murder of George Floyd prompted an awakening, of sorts, across the United States. I say "of sorts" because issues of racial inequity, white supremacy, and the marginalization of African Americans aren't new. They simply resurfaced.[1] The national conversation sparked a dialogue across corporate America that was quickly embraced by the accounting profession. Firms with pre-existing diversity,

[1] I define White Supremacy as the belief (ideology) in the natural or innate superiority of white people, granting them the perceived right to lead, control and define people of color. This ideology is reinforced through ideas, thoughts, beliefs, and actions that manifest in social structures, systems, and behaviors designed to uphold and perpetuate white dominance.

Voices of Change, 129–144

Published under exclusive licence by Emerald Publishing Limited
doi:10.1108/978-1-83753-030-420251026

equity, and inclusion (DEI) statements reaffirmed their commitment while others, who did not, quickly pledged to do the same. Those reaffirmations and new pledges led to a surge in diversity and inclusion (D&I) training. Efforts to explore other avenues, such as launching DEI committees and examination of recruiting practices to diversify staff, would come later.

This initial wave of training focused on two things: uncomfortable conversations (UCs) and implicit bias (IB). The goal of UC training is to offer employees tools to better manage conversations around sensitive topics relating to diversity. The goal of IB training is to raise awareness of hidden beliefs, stereotypes and preferences that influence thinking and decision-making in the workplace. This wave of training often focused on race, either explicitly (i.e., supporting conversations about the murder of George Floyd) or implicitly (e.g., examining how systemic bias perpetuates discrimination and marginalization of African Americans). Even when race wasn't the primary focus, it was often included as a core issue.

Over the next 18–24 months, as the national discussion on racial injustice faded, there were calls to move beyond race and address other marginalized groups, particularly people with disabilities and members of the LTBGQ+ community. By its very nature, inclusion should be inclusive of all groups. However, this transition inadvertently diverted time and resources away from the anti-racist foundations that shaped much of IB and UC, particularly as they related to the Black experience. Given all this, the question remains, does DEI training really work? If so, how and where does it work best?

Binary Thinking

Arguably, given its potential ineffectiveness, where will DEI training get the "biggest bang" for its buck in professional spaces? Even if firms are determined to add DEI training to the annual schedule for staff, research on the efficacy of IB training suggests that it might not simply be ineffective, it could be harmful (Gino & Coffman, 2021). One study found that training might actually activate bias rather than reduce it. It may even increase resistance to DEI efforts or negatively impact performance and/or promotion of minorities (Kalev et al., 2006).

As a CPA with over 26+ years of practice in public accounting, I know first hand that professional success isn't just about technical skills. It also comes from social or "soft" skills, such as leadership development programs, which are often seen as a pathway to partnership.[2] From a DEI perspective, these programs add value by emphasizing people skills, marrying well with the idea that at the C-Suite

[2]Nearly 24% of respondents in ICPAs 2022 report "A CPA Diversity Report: Uncovering Barriers to Success" (https://www.icpas.org/information/professional-issues/cpa-diversity) cited a lack of professional development opportunities as a barrier to advancement for people of color. Although there has been an increased focus on mentorship as a key component of leadership development programs (https://www.aicpa-cima.com/resources/article/mentoring-at-cpa-firms-fosters-strong-leaders), only 40% of firms have meaningful mentorships in place (https://clutejournals.com/index.php/JDM/article/download/6663/6738).

level, senior colleagues will have to deal with diverse clients, both nationally and internationally. It is a de facto proxy, signaling to the "right" people one's suitability for and progress on the partner track.

Further, a DEI perspective argues for firmwide involvement, as people of all types facilitate business transactions, and sensitivity is required when doing so. But the accounting profession takes an opposite stance, a binary view of training, splitting it into technical areas and soft skills. Technical training is highly regarded due to the necessity of maintaining the practical skills required to provide services. The opposite is true of soft skills, covering a broad range of training tangential to the central function of accounting (financial reporting), but by no means less necessary. This one up, one down dichotomy privileges technical skill over soft. DEI training – everywhere other than leadership training – falls into the soft skills camp, meaning its value remains questionable irrespective of public pronouncements about bolstering DEI. Binary thinking around DEI training presents a unique barrier. Since it is not required for promotion, its "usefulness" in an already crowded field of training opportunities rapidly diminishes.

Perhaps this conversation is moot. DEI programs, though well-intentioned, cannot easily teach people how to be unbiased or inclusive, failing to create more equitable accounting organizations. I argue, along with a number of critical accounting scholars, achieving such a goal – inclusive accounting organizations – requires a deep understanding of institutionalized inequities such as racism and its intersection with other categories of subjugation, their impact on institutional culture, professionalism, and what constitutes a genuine determination to dismantle those systems within firms (Annisette & Prasad, 2017; Lewis, 2015; Twyford et al., 2022). Even if the binary problem mentioned is addressed and organizations become successful at designing more equitable policies, systemic barriers still exist and cannot be "fixed" through traditional DEI training, leaving the profession with a problem.

If Training Doesn't Work, What Then?

Diversity, inclusion, and cultural change are uniquely challenging because they impact the entire workplace ecosystem: executive leadership, management, employees, customers, vendors, and the public. It requires a collective willingness to examine racial and societal constructs and understand how they manifest in organizational systems, policies, practices, and business norms. I argue that lasting equity and inclusion in accounting firms require an accounting-specific critical education that examines race, racism, and other inequities within the profession. A number of critical accounting scholars agree, including Alston et al. (2023), who call to "transform the classroom" in accounting.

Just as they argue accounting instructors should not leap into teaching debits and credits at the introductory level because it turns students off from accounting, I argue that leaping into surface-level, standard DEI training on white privilege, IB, and colorblindness similarly turns off white professionals. This is how white guilt in DEI training is fostered, failing to produce empathy for the Other and instead causing white professionals to feel they are experiencing DEI persecution. At best, traditional DEI training teaches the *how* of discrimination, not the *why*, which is a critical educational approach, one that is sorely needed. It is one advocated by Saatkamp (2022), who notes that:

> accounting courses must include a greater emphasis on the history of the profession (particularly critical examination of accounting's roots), the social nature of accounting, and the many ways in which removing deficit-thinking from accounting could lead to a more just and equitable society. (p. 64)

However, until we can all agree on *why* and agree on its fundamental importance to the profession, finding long-term solutions will be difficult. Well-intentioned, meaningful, transformational dialogue and culture change requires a different approach. Efforts to be inclusive are often well-meaning, but they are almost always framed as efforts to help minorities *feel* included. This is the wrong approach.

The behaviors intended to foster inclusion are typically rooted in a belief that the existing culture is ideal, tweaks simply need to be made for everyone to feel comfortable in the current environment. This patronizing view positions minorities as people to be mollified. The question is not how to make people comfortable *here*. Rather than training the majority to create inclusive spaces where the minority will feel comfortable, a change in basic assumptions is needed. The focus must change from a "them" to "we" mindset. It starts with imagining a culture that reflects everyone and is rooted in the principles of intersectionality, equity, and holistic diversity.

In my proposed framework, I differentiate inclusivity as uniquely individual behaviors and equity as organizational action. This approach positions belonging as an outcome, where members of marginalized communities are not treated as people to be soothed. Instead, organizational culture is a reflection of the diversity in the firm, where minorities are integral, not integrated, members of the whole. When everyone can see themselves, as they are, as a part of the organization, it creates space for aspiring Black accountants and CPAs to seek genuine opportunities for advancement. This approach requires taking a step back to look at the history of race in the profession. By understanding how we got here, we can reimagine the construction of an inclusive culture built via a radically different approach.

Color-Coded Accounting

Like other white-collar professions in the United States, African Americans were largely excluded from accounting in three ways: denial of access to accounting education, inability to gain practice (in white firms), and rejection of licensure where possible. The lack of racial diversity in the profession was compounded by a number of factors, all rooted in the systemic barriers facing Black Americans.

In her seminal book, *A White-Collar Profession*, Hammond (2002) explains that closure to accounting was nigh on complete, "for most of the 20th century, virtually no whites would hire and train an African American to be come a CPA, justifying this by claiming that clients would not tolerate an African American's involvement in their financial affairs" (P3, Hammond, 2002). Yet after years of being kept on the margins of the profession, when African Americans were able to overcome these obstacles, Black CPAs were still reliant on the limited demand for accounting services from Black businesses serving the Black economy, which was insufficient to support large numbers of Black CPAs.

The barriers facing African Americans across society were mirrored in the accounting profession: little generational wealth, lack of access to education, lack of access to jobs. Although John Cromwell became the first Black CPA in 1927, 13 years later, out of 27,000 CPAs, only eight were Black (Hammond, 2002). It would take 38 years to achieve the milestone of 100 Black CPAs when Bert Mitchell became a CPA in 1956. Against this backdrop, it should come as no surprise that the profession still struggles to attract African Americans to accounting. The lack of representation at the leadership level in public accounting is a visible reminder of the barriers facing Black people. The disparities start at graduation. The AICPA's Trends Report revealed 65% of new graduates hired into CPA firms are white, yet they make up only 47% of graduates (AICPA, 2021). By the time they get to the partner level, only 2% are Black.

The situation is exasperated by the dwindling number of Black students pursuing accounting degrees. But diversity is only part of the story. Even if the pipeline were to expand significantly, CPA firms, promising to be more inclusive, would still struggle to hire Black CPAs. Why? Because diversity statements and DEI strategies do not drive change. They are nonperformative, at best, designed to artifact rather than enact DEI (Ahmed, 2012). This is why retaining Black CPAs will continue to be difficult – the promise of inclusivity does not align with what it feels like to exist while Black in accounting. As Hammond and others have documented, the profession does not have the cultural competency to recognize issues in the accounting workplace and why they need to change.

Myth of Postracial Workplace Culture

I align myself with other race critical accounting scholars, who challenge the assumption that accounting is a neutral, merit based, technical profession. In this view, only "ability" counts. For many, this is absolute. The inherently rigorous technical nature of the field leaves little space for bias. I argue, because of this view, accounting as a profession has silently adopted the belief that it is a postracial environment.[3] The election of Barack Obama as the 44th President of the United States was a watershed moment for postraciality. African Americans were

[3]Postraciality proclaims racism has contracted in our modern era, believing it to be aberrant and personal, as opposed to systemic and institutionalized within society (https://www.humanities.uci.edu/news/are-we-all-post-racial-yet-1).

elated. Reactions among other minority groups were varied but mostly positive. For many white Americans, Obama's presidency represented clear evidence of the fall of racism and the nation's inevitable march toward a society where race was no longer a barrier to opportunity.

Unfortunately, supposed progress often muddies the water where DEI is concerned. Take Millennials, for example, who make up the majority of the workforce today. They were born decades after the passage of the Civil Rights Act. As a result, I argue their perception of racism is influenced more strongly by media rather than firsthand experience. As a result, they could unwittingly perpetuate racial bias. Many identify as allies fighting racism and systemic injustice, and to suggest they might have some part to play triggers defensiveness, pushback and denial. Here, accusations of racism cause white people to take immediate self-protective actions to mitigate feelings of distress, feelings that arise when others challenge them to address racial actions in which they may be complicit (DiAngelo, 2018).

Perhaps, in some instances, this is an understandable reaction, an injury to ones's self-perception as an anti-racist, making the problem more difficult to tackle. Discussions around race and discrimination can feel accusatory and unjust. Many whites feel persecuted, as if they are being accused or unfairly implicated in discrimination. This stymies DEI dialogue – a resistance rooted in the belief that "good intentions" cannot lead to racist actions. Those racist behaviors are not part of their present-day reality. Efforts to address this through IB and UC training were destined to fail.

These beliefs and constructs are woven into the very culture of our societal DNA. They form the unconscious beliefs that lie beneath the perceptions and assumptions that drive our thinking, behaviors, and actions moment by moment, day to day. While overt racism may be on the decline, unconscious bias perpetuates the stereotypes and barriers that continue to marginalize African Americans in the workplace. Left unaddressed, it signals the permanence of society's racialized status quo. DEI training must address the issue at hand, and right now, it is falling short.

The Partner Archetype

The myth of the postracial workplace conceals a deeper issue and more ingrained problem. If postraciality is the profession's first article of faith, the second is held in equal esteem: meritocracy. Yet, as several critical accounting scholars have noted, a shadow structure exists (Lewis, 2012), where one's conformity to the partner archetype is the true determinate of success. This directly impacts the advancement of Black people in the workplace due to the (mostly) unspoken "culture fit" expectation when identifying top talent. That unspoken element being "pale and male," as the best fit of course. Humans have a natural affinity for familiar things, people, and environments. A generous reading would simply label this affinity bias, which is our inherent tendency to favor individuals like us.

But a less generous reading says that this affinity is a function of an institutionally racist and gendered profession; either way, proving this link, is nearly impossible.

The partner archetype is further complicated by attribution bias, the tendency to attribute one's own actions to external circumstances and the actions of others to inherent abilities and characteristics. This plays out in two ways: first, successes and achievement of Black employees may be attributed to luck or affirmative action rather than competency and skill; second, this bias can heighten the misperception that mistakes are an indication of incompetence or lack of skill. The circular nature of this challenge can be particularly frustrating, leaving those stigmatized as Other with a feeling that leadership will forever remain white and male. And yet, affinity bias remains a core driver in the profession, making unconscious preference when evaluating talent seem unremarkable. As a result, those who look "like me" are logically a "good fit" for the firm. And as a result, the lack of representation in the leadership pipeline continues to persist, as noted in research conducted by McKinsey & Company (2021). Black employees are less likely to get promoted, receive support to advance, or have a sponsor in companies with a sponsorship program. Although Black employees make up 12% of entry-level workers, representation drops to 5% at the senior manager and vice president levels, and 5% at the senior vice president level. In public accounting firms, Black CPAs at the partner level from 2016 to 2020 only increased 1.7% despite widespread educational efforts to increase awareness of under-representation in the partner pipeline.[4] Furthermore, only 31% of Black employees report having access to senior leaders at work (Coqual, 2019).

White, cisgender, heteronormative men have always shaped workplace culture. Their beliefs, traditions, and historical privileges shape the archetype of the successful business leader – one who embodies white male norms regarding communication style, dress, beliefs, body language, expression, assertiveness, and individualism. This mindset is further reinforced by white privilege, the advantages and opportunities afforded white people because organization cultures, systems, and practices are rooted in white male norms. White privilege doesn't imply that every white individual has had a smooth journey in their career. Instead, it simply means they have not encountered the specific challenges, barriers, and workplace experiences of their Black colleagues. This privilege often goes unnoticed, which further reinforces these workplace norms, leading to the implicit belief that they are above reproach. Over time, this mix of white, male norms and white privilege have defined the partner archetype and what workplace culture should look like and feel like.

These biases influence perceptions and decision-making and have far reaching implications in the workplace. They unconsciously dictate perceptions and expectations that either lead to or perpetuate workplace barriers for people of color. Here are just a few examples:

---

[4]Change in CPA Firm Partner demographics reported in the 2017 and 2021 AICPA Trends Reports.

- Resumes with white-sounding names are nearly twice as likely to get a call-back than Black-sounding names (Bertrand & Mullainathan, 2023).
- Self-promotion by Black employees results in less favorable perceptions of job performance and culture "fit" than white, Hispanic, and Asian employees (Asare, 2022).
- Black employees make up less than 5% of executive leadership positions versus 14% of all employees (McKinsey & Company, 2021).

Companies often claim that they reward employees based purely on performance and contributions, without any bias. Yet, white privilege challenges this ideal, leading to disparities in opportunities and outcomes that are unrelated to merit. All too often, the entrenched "good intentions can't be racist" mindset results in disbelief (that racism does exist), dismissal (that racism is pervasive), or denial (that racism does happen here) whenever people are provided with examples of mindset and systemic barriers. Taken as a whole, the successful partner archetype and white privilege – influenced by our natural affinity toward people who are similar to us and compounded by the potential negative effects of the attribution bias – create an environment generally not conducive to DEI.

The Elephant in the Room

In the years since George Floyd's murder, a number of movements, campaigns, and other efforts have gained momentum and have significantly changed the tone and tenor of engagement with DEI. Many of these were either directly or indirectly tied to race, such as:

- Black Lives Matter (BLM) saw a massive resurgence and gained worldwide momentum.
- Defund the police campaigns popped up across the country, raising fear on the part of some white people about the risk of heightened violence by Black people.
- Stop Asian Hate was sparked in part due to the negative rhetoric around the origins of the COVID-19 virus.
- Critical Race Theory (CRT) became a hotly contested issue to the point where it has been reduced to a catchall term for any line of racial inquiry deemed a threat to white-washed history and white identity, ultimately leading to campaigns seeking to ban Black history in K-12 classrooms across the United States.
- The rise in "patriotic" education and messaging in response to perceived efforts to reframe American history in ways that would overemphasize the negative aspects of slavery, treatment of indigenous peoples, and civil rights abuses.
- #SayHerName aimed at raising the awareness of police brutality on Black women.
- Blue Lives Matter, a counter movement to BLM to raise awareness of the challenges and dangers police face in their line of duty, seen by many as defending police brutality, reinforcing the status quo, and denying claims of racism in policing – a historical fact dating back to racist policing policies and race patrols following the emancipation of slaves.

- Claims of election and voter fraud that disproportionately affect people of color and low-income communities were quickly followed by or paired with redistricting efforts and other tactics (such as voter ID laws, limiting early and mail-in voting, reducing polling locations, etc.) to disenfranchise people living in these communities.

This mix of campaigns resulted in increased polarization across a number of issues tied either directly or indirectly to race. Social media amplified fractious national discourse with mixed results. While raising awareness, it also gave rise to fear of retribution. And with good reason. There is no shortage of people who have lost jobs speaking truth to power. An innocent tweet or social media comment can go viral, leading to backlash and reputational damage – both socially and professionally.

The irony of this situation is not lost on me. The national conversation that sparked a dialogue addressing racial inequity has subsequently facilitated collective discomfort, shutting down those same conversations. This great silencing, if you will, is a function of harmful, modern cancel culture intertwined with excessive political correctness, warping and muting meaningful dialogue.[5] While there has been collective recognition of DEI's importance across the profession, this current atmosphere stifles open dialogue, the key to genuine understanding and progression. The net effect has been reductive, boiling down nuanced discussion to a simplistic Black/white binary, where whites are biased and Blacks are marginalized. This issue alone problematizes the deep, transformative conversations necessary to improve workplace culture. Cancel culture aside, the profession will not make meaningful progress until it can confront the elephant in the room: deep-rooted postracial beliefs and a reluctance to engage in conversations that challenge the status quo.

A Different Approach

For many employees, the UC and IB training they received in the wake of George Floyd's murder heavily focused on race. As a result, DEI training experienced a subtle but distinctly race centric shift, positioning dominant majority whites as wrongdoers, and people of color as communities to be placated. For many, the risk was too high, a single misstep, regardless of good intention, could lead to severe professional repercussions. Training then drifted away from critical conversations and attendance became perfunctory – comply but hold back.

Forward progress requires DEI learning environments that foster honest assessments of deeply held internalized beliefs about race. Focus must lean toward

[5]Cancel culture is a socially driven phenomenon where individuals, organizations, or groups face public rejection, ostracization, or professional consequences due to perceived offensive, controversial, or morally objectionable opinions or actions. Often fueled by social media, it can serve as a form of accountability but also devolve into a toxic or disproportionate response, leading to harm, fear of open discourse, and the suppression of nuanced conversations.

unpacking unconscious bias and its relationship to decision-making, leading to positive changes in behavior. Learning programs need to provide education about the specificities of race and society, enabling better understanding of the roles each person plays within it. This provides an opportunity to create healing solutions at the individual and organizational level and so drive systemic change. Programs that offer more than a simplistic view of race serve as the foundation for identifying barriers in the workplace. Raising individual awareness enables accountability as we learn to do better. However, this approach assumes awareness equates to agreement, and that a willingness to change exists. Put simply, change of this type requires buy in from top to bottom. Disrupting bias is the first step in addressing workplace inequities and fostering inclusive cultures.

Unconscious bias training, while well-intentioned, is doomed to fail until people discover how internalized beliefs subconsciously influence self-perception, self-esteem, and emotional well-being.

Learning environments have the potential to aid people in feeling supported, offering space to grow at a pace that is right for them. For some, the journey will be troubling, for others validating. For some, it will clarify. For others, it will raise questions. DEI programs must be safe spaces, allowing participants to feel:

- Safe expressing deeply held views, even if they are upsetting and unsavory.[6]
- Missteps and mistakes will be met with grace and empathy.
- Discussions will be respectful, holistic, and preserve the dignity of all.

Current approaches to DEI training skip a critical first step in managing reactivity – a person's involuntary emotional and psychological response to change and challenging situations. Even for those motivated to change, it is still difficult. Change involves the disruption of ingrained habits, resulting in feelings of insecurity and uncertainty – a kind of psychological resistance, an imperceptible barrier, resistant to new thoughts and behaviors. It activates a natural defense mechanism, making it difficult to think clearly and respond rationally in the moment. As a result, well-intentioned efforts to change may wane over time. The current approach to DEI training skips a critical first step – managing reactivity, our automatic, often unconscious, emotional and psychological responses to change and challenging situations. Instead, I argue for an alternative approach, one centered on self-awareness, intentionality, and ownership. Self-awareness requires an investigation of beliefs to better understand oneself and understand the perceptions of others. Intentionality requires identifying normative beliefs and behaviors in a diverse and equitable work environment.[7] Ownership requires taking individual responsibility for driving change. On their own, each requires deep introspection, personal commitment, and resilience.

[6]A safe space must be safe for all, meaning that hate speech is rejected, and the risks of such exploration are clearly outlined to participants.

[7]A normative belief is a person's observation of the degree to which others who are significant believe they ought or ought not to perform certain behaviors, often shaping an individual's action from that point forward.

Taken as a whole, they cross into the level of emotional work that is not often associated with workplace training.

The REM 360 Framework©

Understanding and managing reactivity is crucial in bridging the gap between unconscious resistance to change and conscious desire to work on change. By connecting the dots between internal (often unconscious) and external reactivity to experiences in the workplace, it provides people with the tools to regulate their emotions. While this model applies to all emotions and situations, it is particularly helpful in navigating difficult or negative experiences. This model acknowledges and reinforces the importance of emotional connection and psychological safety for building trust within teams and across organizations. This trust is the foundation, one that must be laid before the behavioral change work associated with DEI efforts can take place.

To this end, I have developed the REM 360 Framework© model (illustrated below in Fig. 10.1) to aid in the development of the emotional intelligence and resilience required to bridge the gap in workplace interactions, relationships, and communications.

This framework is particularly suited to difficult conversations around race, but it can be applied elsewhere. The process revolves around three interconnected abilities:

(1) Real-Time Awareness©
(2) Emotional Anchoring©
(3) Mindful Recovery©

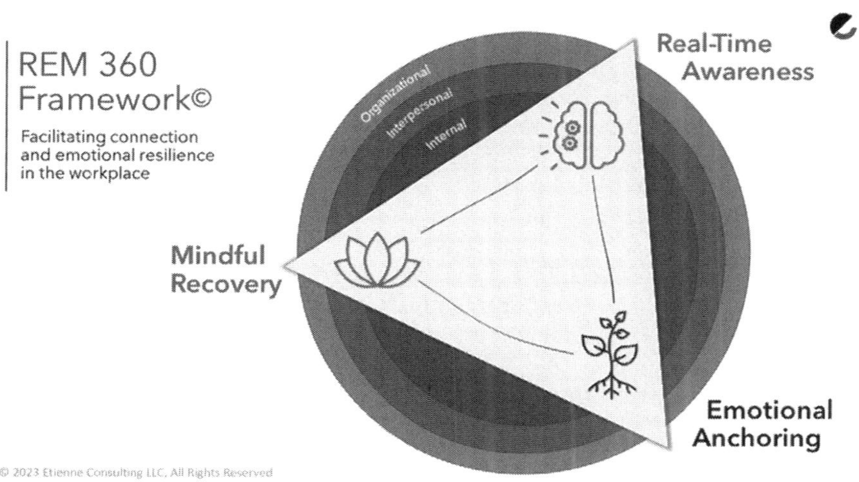

Fig. 10.1. REM 360 Framework© Model.

Real-Time Awareness©

I define Real-Time Awareness© as:

> The ability to immediately recognize and understand one's reactions, both internal and external, to various stimuli such as situations, people, or environments. This skill facilitates a shift from reactive to intentional responses, allowing for more deliberate and thoughtful engagement.

Our brain is constantly scanning our environment for danger. When a threat is detected, our brain prepares the body to react: fight or run away (think sweaty palms, racing heartbeat), or freeze (think "deer in the headlights"). Known as the "fight, flight, or freeze" response, it was important when survival depended upon the ability to evade dangerous predators or rival tribes. Fast forward to modern times – human brains have evolved to the point where people can do incredible calculations, solve complex problems, ideate, and more. Yet, the part of the brain responsible for this response remains largely unchanged. While people today rarely face life-threatening situations like humanity's cave-dwelling ancestors, their bodies still respond to stress with the same fight or flight response. People are often triggered into the fight or flight responses by social and emotional threats.[8] Emotionally charged or distressing experiences and situations, such as a triggering discussion (what feels like an attack on your racial identity, a challenge to your integrity and personal values, or a deeply hurtful or demoralizing remark) in a high-stakes environment (the source of your livelihood), can activate an instinctual, automatic physiological response to a perceived threat.

Unconscious bias training includes topics that can activate this response. What starts as an uncomfortable subject can quickly escalate internally and cause one to feel triggered. When triggered, an individual's senses, like sight, hearing, smell, and touch, send signals to their brain which starts a series of automatic responses to prepare their body to deal with the threat. When it comes to learning, reactivity is the enemy. Instinctive and involuntary reactions can immediately, and sometimes significantly, impact our thinking and decision-making in a negative manner, making it difficult to stay present and engaged, vulnerable and open, curious and respectful. While outwardly one may seem calm, internally, they may be experiencing a number of different reactions. For example:

- one's ability to make clear, rational decisions may be compromised;
- one may struggle to process or retain new information;
- one might become irritable and more prone to anger;

[8]The term "trigger" in psychology refers to a stimulus that activates a physical, emotional, or psychological reaction or worsens the symptoms of a mental health condition. More recently, it has been used as a nonclinical term to describe situations or experiences that elicit a strong, negative emotional response to a current situation. Feeling triggered is more than just being uncomfortable, feeling unsettled, or something rubbing you the wrong way.

- one may experience anxiety;
- one's heart may start racing to the point of feeling palpitations;
- one might experience a shortness of breath;
- one may feel nauseous, dizzy, or unsteady.

Real-Time Awareness© provides the tools for noticing an individual's reaction to a situation, person, or environment, muting reactivity. Instead, intentionality is accessed as the right response. Learning to recognize the impact of one's environment helps diminish reactivity, creating space to recognize one's feelings. The aim is to notice reactivity in the moment, identify potential triggers, and recognize how being in a triggered state impacts thoughts, actions, and decisions. This is how awareness is brought to the present moment, allowing intentionality to be accessed.

Emotional Anchoring©

I define Emotional Anchoring© as:

> The ability to maintain emotional stability and remain open, respectful, and engaged during conflict, facilitating calm and constructive collaboration in good faith.

Learning to regulate emotions in a triggered state is the second step. Once the emotional threat has passed, instinctual responses are reversed, and human bodies calm down. This can be initiated with the right tools and strategies. Otherwise, people resort to surface acting or assimilation tactics which can exacerbate psychological strain and impair well-being.[9] Being triggered undermines one's ability to align words, actions, and behaviors with intention. As a result, people may say the wrong thing, make rushed decisions, or exhibit behaviors that impact others in unintended ways.

Emotional Anchoring© practices foster the quieting of the mind and restore calm to people's bodies. This creates a connection with one's intention and thoughtful reflection about how one is showing up to others. Conscious communication requires that when people express themselves, they are:

- clear about the purpose of their communication;
- mindful of the impact they are having on others;
- listening and engaging with empathy and compassion for others;
- paying attention to nonverbal communication;
- acknowledge others, even if they don't agree.

---

[9]Surface acting refers to the action of simulating emotions that are not honestly experienced. It involves dishonestly replicating expected emotions. Zapf, D., Kern, M., Tschan, F., Holman, D., & Semmer, N. K. (2021). Emotion Work: A Work Psychology Perspective. https://doi.org/10.1146/annurev-orgpsych-012420-062451

Most importantly, it allows them to pay attention to how their internal communication is impacting their external communication. It allows them to own their contribution and separate context from content in order to stay present and engaged. The goal is to acknowledge the impact without losing control, so they can maintain a balanced state and remain emotionally intact despite being triggered.

Mindful Recovery©

I define Mindful Recovery© as:

> The ability to reflect and reassess with self-compassion after intense situations, to recalibrate emotionally, facilitating a return to a balanced sense of physical, mental, and emotional well-being.

Stressful situations, particularly triggering events, can leave people feeling emotionally drained, mentally scattered, and even physically exhausted. *Mindful Recovery©* is a reset button on one's emotional state. This is important for several reasons. It helps:

- prevent a negative spiral that could lead to heighted stress or anxiety;
- avoid escalation, resentment, and grudges;
- build resilience to strengthen one's ability to handle future triggering situations or experiences;
- develop healthy coping strategies;
- boost self-awareness;
- restore a sense of equilibrium and balance;
- provide a sense of control and personal agency.

Mindful Recovery© enables engagement in a reflective process through the lens of self-compassion rather than self-criticism. It does not ignore or suppress emotions but rather seeks to acknowledge and understand them. Disentangling from the immediacy and intensity of feelings, individuals can recalibrate, eventually drifting back to a state of equilibrium, where they can react rationally, and maintain a healthy perspective on experiences.

Mindful Recovery© holds a special significance for minorities, especially after triggering events. These events often stem from, or are heightened by, experiences of bias, marginalization, or discrimination, adding an extra layer of emotional complexity. For people of color, it is more than regaining emotional balance; it is about dealing with deeper issues related to identity, sense of belonging, and respect. It is more than a coping mechanism, rather it is a core process that helps Outsiders reaffirm self-worth and maintain dignity in demanding situations. Centrally, it is the ability to react in ways rooted in self-compassion and resilience, instead of internalizing negative biases. Practicing *Mindful Recovery©* empowers minorities to efficiently process hard experiences while upholding integrity and well-being in work environments that can sometimes be challenging to navigate.

Overall, the REM 360 Framework© provides guiding principles for a range of situations and scenarios, particularly those prone to triggering reactivity, emotional imbalance, or counterproductive behaviors. It allows DEI efforts to be introduced without breaking people down. When people possess the skills to engage in conversations outside their comfort zone, challenge existing norms, and disrupt the status quo, the process of safely and constructively re-examining views of diversity and equity can begin.

Meaningful DEI efforts do not seek to accommodate minorities so "they" feel comfortable. Meaningful efforts reimagine organizational culture or norms in a way that reflects diversity holistically. Where people feel safe expressing their views and making mistakes, where learning and growth are prioritized over punishment and fear, only then can a culture of genuine inclusivity and understanding be fostered, moving beyond superficial compliance to a meaningful change.

Conclusion

All too often, the profession ignores, downplays, or dismisses emotions at work. Public displays of positive emotions are accepted, while negative emotions are actively hidden, often subconsciously. Visible reactivity is limited to happy emotions (think: laughing at a joke or expressing interest in attending a company social event). Yet, visible reactivity to sadness, fear, disgust, and anger are managed. Navigating emotion at work is an active, complex, and dynamic process governed largely by a mix of norms (gender norms, workplace behavioral norms, etc.) and unspoken rules. Emotions can be organized in three buckets: expected (what people are assumed to be experiencing), displayed (what people are actively expressing publicly), and felt (what people are experiencing internally).

Traditionally, in the accounting profession, DEI work has failed to help individuals and organizations navigate treacherous emotional terrain. Often, DEI has been presented as a binary choice between valued hard technical skills, ones most likely to lead to partnership, and devalued soft people skills that will not. This false dichotomy only adds to the difficulties already inherent in such work. The salience of culture wars and the global activities of BLM pushed DEI front and center in accounting, where it was hijacked by cancel culture, which sought to obfuscate nuanced dialogue, reshaping equity and inclusion work into an unsafe space to speak one's true feelings. DEI became perilous work for dominant majority white workers, fearful that one wrong word will result in sanctions, or job loss.

As an alternative, I have argued for a different path, outlined in the REM 360 Framework©. Within this framework, the essence of discord is removed as reactivity to the perilous nature of DEI is detached, leaving a truly safe space to uncover and rediscover belongingness to one another across difference. This is the value of social connectedness that DEI, when implemented correctly, can bring, reducing feelings of Otherness and disconnection through a sense of shared humanity. This is the "new DEI" work to be done.

References

Ahmed, S. (2012). *On being included. Racism and diversity in institutional life*. Duke University Press.

AICPA. (2021). *Trends in the supply of accounting graduates and the demand for public accounting recruits*. Association of International Certified Public Accountants. https://www.thiswaytocpa.com/collectedmedia/files/trends-report-2021.pdf

Alston, C., Rukasuwan, L., & Lewis, A. (2023, September/October). What can the profession do? Looking closely at each piece of the puzzle. *The CPA Journal*, *36*. https://www.cpajournal.com/2023/12/04/what-can-the-profession-do/

Annisette, M., & Prasad, A. (2017). Critical accounting research in hyper-racial times. *Critical Perspectives on Accounting*, *43*, 5–19.

Asare, J. G. (2022, October 4). New study finds that Black employees are penalized for self-promotion. *Forbes*. https://www.forbes.com/sites/janicegassam/2022/10/04/new-study-finds-that-black-employees-are-penalized-for-self-promotion/

Bertrand, M., & Mullainathan, S. (2023). *Are Emily and Greg more employable than Lakisha and Jamal? A field experiment on labor market discrimination*. National Bureau of Economic Research. https://www.nber.org/papers/w9873

Coqual. (2019). *Being Black in corporate America: An intersectional exploration*. https://coqual.org/wp-content/uploads/2020/09/CoqualBeingBlackinCorporateAmerica090720-1.pdf

DiAngelo, R. (2018). *White fragility. Why it's so hard for white people to talk about racism*. Beacon Press.

Gino, F., & Coffman, K. (2021, September/October). Unconscious bias training that works. *Harvard Business Review Magazine*. https://hbr.org/2021/09/unconscious-bias-training-that-works

Hammond, T. A. (2002). *A white-collar profession: African American certified public accountants since 1921*. The University of North Carolina Press.

Kalev, A., Dobbin, F., & Kelly, E. (2006). Best practices or best guesses: Assessing the efficacy of corporate affirmative action and diversity policies. *Sociological Review*, *71*, 589–617.

Lewis, A. (2012). *A critical analysis of the Black accounting experience in the U.K. tales of success and failure in the British professional workplace*. Lambert Academic Publishing.

Lewis, A. (2015). Frankenstein is Black. A tale of Black accountancy. *International Journal of Linguistics, Literature and Culture*, *2*(1), 1–21.

McKinsey & Company. (2021, February 21). *Race in the workplace: The Black experience in the U.S. private sector report*. https://www.mckinsey.com/featured-insights/diversity-and-inclusion/Race-in-the-workplace-The-Black-experience-in-the-US-private-sector

Saatkamp, A. (2022). *Portrait of a "gentlemanly" profession: Whiteness and the persistent racial Imperviousness of accounting* (p. 1536) (Doctor of Philosophy Dissertation). Illinois State University. https://ir.library.illinoisstate.edu/etd/1536/

Twyford, E. J., Tanima, F. A., & George, S. (2022). Critical race theory, counter-accounting, and the emancipatory potential of counter-stories. *Accounting, Auditing & Accountability Journal*. (ahead-of-print). https://doi.org/10.1108/AAAJ-12-2020-5035

Chapter 11

Critical Perspectives on Accounting and Race: Shifting the Focus From Periphery to Centre Using a Critical Race Theory and Critical Dialogic Accounting and Accountability Approach

Erin Twyford[a], *Farzana Tanima*[a] *and Sendirella George*[b]

[a]University of Wollongong, Australia
[b]Victoria University of Wellington, New Zealand

Introduction

Accounting and race have received considerable scholarly attention over the last 30 years. However, much of this research presents race unproblematically, an accepted and taken-for-granted element that is a 'normal and ubiquitous part of our daily fabric' (López et al., 2018). This attention, while not limited, remains insufficient when viewed from the broader context in which race, racism and racialisation are so prevalent.[1] This leads to almost asserting Goldberg and Searls-Giroux's (2014) belief in a 'post-racial' world – instead of the hyper-racial reality we live in (Annisette & Prasad, 2017).

Predominantly, studies in accounting focus on historical instances of race-related issues. Again, these studies focus on race as 'objective, inherent or fixed' instead of viewing 'races [as] categories that society invents, manipulates, or retires when convenient' (Delgado & Stefancic, 2012, p. 8). Emphasising the social construction of race rather than normalising it challenges entrenched discriminatory practices. By acknowledging race as a product of societal forces rather than biological determinism, we can dismantle structures that perpetuate racial

[1]We adhere to Hochman's (2019, p. 1246) definition of racialisation as 'the process through which groups come to be understood as major biological entities and human lineages, formed due to reproductive isolation, in which membership is transmitted through biological descent'. People are then able to be racialised by being understood as members of a 'race' according to the context of the time.

Voices of Change, 145–157

doi:10.1108/978-1-83753-030-420251028

inequality and promote a more inclusive society. Historical studies focus on accounting for enslaved people, people as chattel, or ideological racialisation through programmes such as the Holocaust (see, for example, Fleischman & Tyson, 2000, 2004; Oldroyd et al., 2008; Twyford, 2018; Twyford & Funnell, 2023). Contemporary studies are more likely to call out the inconsistencies with accepting the pseudo-scientific categorisation of race and grapple with issues of racialisation more strongly. For example, Lehman et al. (2016) examine racialised accounts from within carceral systems, while Lehman et al. (2018) consider racialised accounts of immigration in Canada. These studies are the impetus for pushing race and accounting research boundaries, though much more is needed.

We argue that scholars who wish to engage with issues of race tend to avoid delving into the subject's complexities beyond merely acknowledging its influence within a given context for two reasons. The first is that race is a complex phenomenon, racism even more so, and applying a theoretical framework to better understand racialised accountings seems daunting, perhaps even impossible. Second, racism is such an insidious practice, seamlessly permeating and infiltrating everyday lives, that it can be difficult to call attention to, particularly as embedded within neoliberal constructs such as capitalism, white-CIS male heteronormativity and patriarchal colonial rule. These systems have so vastly shaped our society that their influence is hardly noticed.

In this chapter, we aim to bridge the gap between conducting research where race is simply a contextual factor and conducting research that explicitly examines and problematises race, racism and racialisation. We understand that new theoretical tools are required to grapple with these concepts. We offer an avenue for undertaking research on accounting and race that draws from Critical Race Theory (CRT) and Critical Dialogic Accounting and Accountability (CDAA) to reflect the need for focus on how race intersects with modern-day practices such as accounting.

CRT highlights race and racialisation as a central aspect of research rather than a peripheral consideration in a study's context. CDAA positions accounting as a practice that holds the potential to broaden spaces of understanding and reposition accounting as a tool for emancipation, drawing out social and moral elements rather than mere technical elements (Brown, 2009; Carnegie et al., 2021). Here, scholars advocate for extending 'pluralism by engaging with divergent ideological perspectives and associated power struggles, to critique and transform accounting' to address accountability for marginalised Others (Tanima et al., 2024, p. 2). CDAA theorists focus on analysing the interrelations between accounting and accountability by bringing ideological understandings to the forefront (Tanima et al., 2020). For instance, 'neoliberal discourse theorises "accountability" is a way that privileges financial capital and brings that meaning to "accountants" and "accounting" practices', whereas CDAA 'theorises "accountability" in terms of political struggles whereby citizens exercise democratic rights over powerholders' (Tanima et al., 2020, p. 3). Accordingly, 'by rearticulating accountability, CDAA resignifies the meaning of "accountants" and "accounting", and its critique of neoliberalism provides a conceptual base for developing alternative accounting practices' (Tanima et al., 2020, p. 3). This chapter shows how researchers can centralise racialisation by combining these two theories while ensuring that accounting and accountability remain predominant.

This chapter proceeds as follows. First, we uncover the critical literature that examines accounting and race as central and peripheral elements. We then give a historical overview of the CDAA project, arguing that the amalgamation with other theoretical frameworks is its current trajectory. A convergence between CRT and CDAA is then presented. We then briefly illustrate the potential utility of the proposed framework using the Australian immigration policy for asylum seekers as our case. We finish by commending scholars towards future research possibilities utilising the framework.

Accounting and Race

The literature informs us that race is ever-present yet remains largely unproblematised. However, where there have been attempts to re-centre race, this has been done primarily through theoretical means. Lewis (2015) (re)problematises Black accountants' career entry and progression and challenges what is a gendered and racialised profession in reality. He argues that race in accounting remains 'under-theorised and under-researched' (Lewis, 2015, p. 1) and was the first to offer CRT as a way to account for the role of race and racism in the accounting profession. Twyford et al. (2022) also use CRT to highlight the inherent racialisation of the continent called Australia's asylum seeker policy.[2] Ufodike et al. (2023) have contributed by organising the literature to collate other studies that explore 'anti-Black racism'. They call for further research that uses theorisations beyond CRT to examine contextual issues that influence anti-Black racism and extend 'racism' beyond the homogeneity with which it is currently treated to capture the nuances in distinct forms of discrimination.

These studies represent just the initial steps in an agenda aiming to shed light on race and racialisation in what we consider to be more significant ways. Some examples include calling out the problems with adopting race as a taken-for-granted categorisation or a fixed identity and examining the microaggressions and insidious nature of racialisation (Davis et al., 2021). It is not enough to explore a context and acknowledge there have been racialised practices – this will not achieve emancipation. Instead, there needs to be a re-centring on the violence inflicted through racialisation and *starting* at this point. There needs to be an underlying questioning of the inherent racism embedded in the structures and institutions that accountants inhabit and accounting serves. Instead of perpetuating the notion that race is fixed by not engaging or problematising this explicitly, research will need to be ontologically situated to acknowledge that 'racism remains a significant problem and a major cause of societal frustration'

[2]We note here that Australia is a colonised name given after invasion, and this continent comprises many distinct Aboriginal and Torres Strait Islander groups living on Country.

(Ufodike et al., 2023, p. 377). At the very least, research should 'problematise [the] dominant ideologies in which knowledge is constructed' (Tyson, 2003, p. 20).

We propose that part of the difficulty in problematising race lies in theoretical framing. Race and racism are dynamic and complex phenomena influenced by every discipline, class and system, so much so that explanations or understandings can only ever be deeply contextualised, nuanced and individualised. While CRT has been utilised in law (where it originated) and education disciplines, it has yet to receive similar uptake in accounting. We understand this theory requires investment and is not explicitly built for accounting. However, we also note that other theorists, for example, Foucault, were similarly not focused on accounting but have been used significantly to enrich our understanding of accounting and accounting practices. CRT will require more explanations and usage, illustrations and demonstrations before other work flows as Foucauldian studies have.

We contend that pairing CRT with the more well-known and used (in the accounting literature) CDAA framework can provide opportunities for research into accounting and race. We intend to ensure that both racialisation and accounting can be featured without either being reduced to a contextual feature as we work towards an emancipatory project that values, uplifts and prioritises the work and experiences of racialised people instead of relying on Anglo-centred views of what constitutes good research or sound data. In this way, we also intend to push the boundaries of what constitutes accounting, recognising that traditional (and again Western-centric) visions of accounting tend to be rigid, numerical and presented as ostensibly objective facts. We now outline the extant literature on CDAA, drawing out not gaps but the potential for expanding the CDAA project into racialisation.

The CDAA Project

CDAA has evolved from dialogic accounting, which in some ways has become co-opted by studies that are only tangentially associated with dialogics.[3] Tregidga (2022) has questioned whether a *reassessment* of dialogic accountability is necessary to return to the foundational premise of dialogics – the political intent. To this end, recent work has sought to establish that distinction between work that aligns with a dialogic form and reinstates the political and critical imperatives – CDAA. For example, George et al. (2023) theorise CDAA by assessing how counter-accounts can challenge neoliberalism by applying an agonistic lens to frame the struggles of social movements, while Tanima et al. (2023, p. 1) engage competing discourses and construct counter-narratives, 'based on poor women's lived experiences with neoliberal microfinance programs' to foster 'critical dialogic praxis' to 'support marginalised groups' struggles to hold powerholders accountable for their (in)actions'.

---

[3]Dialogic accounting involves ongoing communication and collaboration among stakeholders to understand and interpret an organisation's performance and impact. It emphasises transparency and trust-building for informed decision-making.

These studies place the original intent of dialogics, as established by the foundational work by Brown (2009, 2017), Brown and Dillard (2013) and Brown et al. (2015), back into accounting and accountability studies. These scholars have called for opening up monologic accounting to critical scrutiny by taking ideological conflicts seriously and developing approaches that assess accountability as a politically contested issue. They have also called for engaging with the voices of the marginalised to foster more democratic spaces.

In line with Tregidga (2022), we contend that for future enrichment of the dialogic project, beyond a reorientation through CDAA, alternative perspectives and theoretical approaches can be enmeshed within CDAA to offer a richer depiction, or better understanding, of phenomena. Other critical methods can be sought to continue the momentum of the dialogic project while returning to its initial premise.

CRT and Its Convergence With CDAA

As a possible avenue forward in pursuing research that centres racialisation while attending to accounting and accountability issues, CRT narrows its focus on the elements of race while CDAA broadens and opens up accounting to allow for social, moral and ethical considerations – including racialisation. We merge the two streams of theoretical frameworks to tackle racial elements while attending to the oft-repeated question of 'where is the accounting' – even in contexts where, arguably, accounting is peripheral or on the boundaries as race requires primacy. This framework is based on the core tenets of CRT.[4]

- Centrality of race and racism

Research applying a CRT lens centralises race and racism (Twyford et al., 2022). It examines how these constructs interact with other forms of marginalisation such as 'class, nationality, gender and sexual preference' (Twyford et al., 2022, p. 333). This stems from the ontological notion that race is a 'social construction' instead of a 'biological' truth and has marginalising impacts on the lives of predominantly non-white groups and individuals.

- Challenging the dominant perspective

This is based on the premise that white supremacy and the institutional systems designed to uphold it – such as patriarchy, neoliberalism, capitalism and heteronormativity – solidify and perpetuate racist practices. CRT directly acknowledges that our world, as we know it, is hyper-racial and turns attention to the need for countering dominant racialised hegemonies (Twyford et al., 2022).

[4]These tenets are based on the work of Crenshaw (1988), Crenshaw et al. (1995), Delgado and Stefancic (2012), Solórzano and Delgado Bernal (2001) and Howard and Navarro (2016). Further details on these tenets can be found in Twyford et al. (2022).

- Commitment to social justice

CRT encourages emancipatory outcomes through a focus on social justice. Emancipation is a broad term, but we articulate it as engendering tension with the prevailing norm by making visible 'the exploitative and repressive functioning of the status quo – and thus tends towards the latter's transformation' (Gallhofer & Haslam, 2019, p. 4) so that oppressive elements are no longer ignored but highlighted. The idea here is to tackle racialisation head-on through every available tool. For example, counter-storytelling mechanisms serve as a liberatory research methodology (Tyson, 2003) to challenge majoritarian narratives.

- Valuing experiential experience

In focusing on the emancipation of marginalised voices, CRT accepts lived experiences, testimonies and storytelling as valid and rigorous forms of data with a vast scope for methodology. Therefore, it embraces 'messiness' as an essential feature of learning, re-learning and unlearning – seeking to move beyond majoritarian narratives embedded in racialisation (Twyford et al., 2022). Counter-stories, for example, direct accounts of lived experiences of the marginalised, are accepted as mechanisms towards challenging and re-narrating existing taken-for-grant social practices grounded in racism.

- Being interdisciplinary

By acknowledging how complex the perpetuation of racialisation is, CRT calls for cooperation from all disciplines, including accounting. From a CRT perspective, while accounting is not 'the central cause' of racialisation, it illuminates that it does and can contribute to it (Twyford et al., 2022). Accordingly, practices such as accounting must be assessed through socio-politico-legal lenses requiring racism and racialisation to be analysed as a multidimensional social reality.

Taking these central themes, we interpose them over a CDAA framework to develop our four-tiered framework for CRT-based CDAA praxis. This framework includes the dominance of race in neoliberal governmental narratives, identifying counter-hegemonies and engaging divergent discourses, fostering platforms for multifaceted groups to share counter-stories and building alliances for transformative change.

This framework aims to illuminate the voices of racialised Others while fostering space for transformative change. It does so by centring counter-stories as a form of (counter) account to broaden the scope of what constitutes an account and thus accounting.

To illustrate the potential of a CRT CDAA convergence, the following section provides an example using the context of immigration.

CRT and CDAA: The Framework

This framework calls attention to agonistic understandings of pluralism – the need to take ideological and sometimes conflicting perspectives seriously (Brown, 2009). This includes the voices of racialised Others in accounting and accountability systems and fostering transformative social change through tools such as counter-accounts and counter-stories (see Twyford et al., 2022).

Accounting for Immigration

Immigration is a complex and wide-ranging phenomenon, ranging from bureaucratic programmes for skilled workers to asylum seekers who must move outside official channels to avoid persecution. To demonstrate the possible utility of a CRT-CDAA approach, we examine the latter, specifically the offshore detention centres run by the Australian government in Nauru.

The Dominance of Race in Neoliberal Governmental Narratives

Within Western democracies, the balance of power is usually predicated on several issues, including immigration. Immigration, whether through official channels or asylum-seeking, is politicised to invoke voter attention, passion and racism. Often, a narrative of 'us vs them' or a zero-sum argument reverts to the movement of earmarked resources for citizens moving to newcomers. Political rhetoric often couches this in terms of 'we should help our own before we help others'. This mode of thinking is inherently racist and Othering, not the least, because 'our own' who need help are also marginalised, vulnerable and never the recipient of additional funding. There is not one pool of funding to 'help' people, and addressing it as such pits citizens against immigrants rather than other powerful actors who can change funding requirements by increasing the funding pool – namely religious institutions, large corporations, extractive industries and super-wealthy individuals – in other words, tax-exempt, tax-evasive or tax-avoider individuals and entities.

Identifying Counter-Hegemonies and Engaging Divergent Discourses

Counter-hegemonies require identification to critically take up the mantle of challenging taken-for-granted narratives around Others. They manifest through counter-accounts, which oppose the dominant discourse propagated by governmental bodies. By facilitating the telling of stories by marginalised voices on their own terms, counter-accounts, specifically counter-stories, facilitate the convergence of CDAA and CRT. Through these divergent discourses, we interrogate hegemony and refute the notion that accounts must be quantifiable, objective and numerical to be valid. Instead, we acknowledge the value of lived experiences denoted through *storytelling* and recognise counter-stories as a rigorous and scientific method akin to the hegemonic accounts traditionally deemed as representing reality and truth (George et al., 2024).

True counter-hegemonies emerge within these counter-stories, wherein racialised voices, experiences and truths are forefronted without intermediaries. For the academy to legitimise counter-stories as a valid form of discourse, it must foster environments where counter-hegemonies and divergent discourses flourish. However, merely amplifying these counter-stories is insufficient. There must be substantial engagement from professionals, policymakers, academia and educators to take these discourses seriously and commit to challenging the status quo, embracing discomfort and striving towards a more egalitarian society.

Divergent discourses within offshore immigration prove challenging to engage with due to legal restrictions and anti-whistle-blower provisions (Twyford et al., 2022). Yet, instances such as the leaked Nauru files in 2016 and Behrouz Boochani's memoir 'No Friend but the Mountains' (2018) exemplify the power of counter-hegemonic perspectives. Boochani's first-hand account, gathered at significant personal risk, illustrates the emancipatory potential of divergent narratives in exposing the realities of Australia's mandatory offshore detention system (Twyford et al., 2022). These narratives illuminate the complexities of human experience and highlight the constraints of acceptable behaviour. This acceptability falls on a spectrum that, for Australian citizens, would be tolerated by the community but are instead written up as 'incidents' or delivered poetically through memoir to highlight the humanity and complexity of people. These discourses allow us to peer around the legislation, official accounts and other instruments of obfuscation to 'see' the realities of offshore detention through the harm recorded and accounted for as if such violence and suffering were diarised and normalised.

Fostering Platforms for Multifaceted Groups (Such as Racialised Others, Activists and Academics) to Share Counter-Stories

The rigid structures of hegemony and the institutions it upholds often impose boundaries around who can speak, when they can speak and where they can speak, resulting in 'social closure' (Hammond et al., 2009). This social closure excludes certain voices from platforms where their messages could be heard and potentially acted upon. While distinct from CRT, social closure shares the overarching aim of exposing marginalised perspectives to provide a more comprehensive understanding of society.

Numerous platforms exist for marginalised groups to share their counter-stories, including social media, news media, memoirs and participation in social movements (George et al., 2023). For academics, several avenues exist to provide or hold space for counter-stories. Methodological choices and research objectives can be centred on amplifying the voices and experiences of people of colour. Engaging in policy work, such as submissions to government inquiries, providing expert testimony and advocating for policy reform, can also amplify marginalised perspectives. Additionally, fostering collective action among like-minded researchers to prioritise issues of race and elevate alternative and Indigenous research methods can be impactful (George et al., 2023). Further, as educators, we can seek to highlight Other voices in our curriculum, critique traditional views of accounting as a mere technical practice and draw out the social and moral imperatives while highlighting race and racialisation as issues of our time.

It is necessary to broaden the interpretation of what constitutes an account to foster platforms for counter-stories. Scholars have argued for the inclusion of various forms of storytelling, such as memoirs, incident reports, oral histories and testimony, as valid forms of accounting (Brown, 2017; Brown & Dillard, 2014; George et al., 2023). This recognition acknowledges that accounting is not solely a technical practice but also a social and moral one (Carnegie et al., 2021). By embracing these diverse forms of storytelling, scholars challenge conventional notions of rigour and data, acknowledging traditional research paradigms' inherent biases and limitations. Therefore, in carrying out research where we centralise the (counter) stories of racialised people, we include any form of account in which they tell their stories in a manner that feels organic and authentic to them. We then, as scholars, spotlight these stories and defend their use to 'gatekeepers' who seek (consciously or not) to exclude that which falls outside the hegemonic, white and Western ideals of research.

However, it is essential to approach counter-stories with a degree of scepticism. Despite their potential to empower marginalised voices and drive social change, counter-accounts can inadvertently perpetuate harmful language and stereotypes (Martin & Fozdar, 2022). Ethical considerations arise regarding their impact on marginalised communities and potential unintended consequences. Evaluating counter-accounts' success in achieving their objectives remains a complex challenge (Laine & Vinnari, 2017). While instances like Behrouz Boochani's detention account have garnered international attention and contributed to shifting public discourse and policy, the long-term impact of counter-stories on driving comprehensive and lasting political change is still subject to ongoing examination (Laine & Vinnari, 2017; Twyford et al., 2022).

Building Alliances for Transformative Change

To blend CRT and CDAA effectively, our research must mobilise alliances and collective action to achieve transformative change, in line with Laclau and Mouffe's (1985) 'chains of equivalence'. These alliances foster strategic collaborations among individuals and groups with diverse struggles, leveraging their collective experiences to challenge hegemonic structures comprehensively.

In race studies within accounting, these chains of equivalence hold significant implications, enabling scholars, activists and marginalised communities to pool their efforts against racial inequalities (Twyford et al., 2022). By recognising a shared goal of dismantling racial biases, these alliances amplify the collective voice for change, fostering an environment where diversity of perspectives is respected and actively sought. Chains of equivalence encourage counter-stories that challenge dominant narratives, facilitating the deconstruction of oppressive systems and redefining notions of 'rigour' by centring on diverse lived experiences (Brown, 2017).

Building alliances in race studies within accounting requires more allies to engage with race-related issues and Others to privilege their stories. Differing groups working together and engaging in dialogue can connect various tools to tackle complex social factors – for example, activists' expertise in fostering 'collective action' and academics' knowledge and application of theoretical lenses to understand and analyse issues. The exhausting (mentally, physically, psychologically) and traumatic work of activists who advocate for racialised people is often performed by those who identify as marginalised and victims of racism. While many people may feel hesitant about engaging in race-related issues for fear of saying or doing the wrong thing, this fear should not prevent allies from taking up part of the mantle and doing some of the work.

While recognising the challenges and potential pitfalls, scholars can play a crucial role by promoting diversity, advocating for non-Western-centric methodologies and theories and fostering dialogue with marginalised communities (Brown & Dillard, 2014). We suggest scholars with more capital or gravitas actively include early career academics in their projects and groups to foster and mentor research that begins with race as a central question. Collaborations across disciplines and with civil society allies can provide a multifaceted approach to tackling complex social factors, as demonstrated by academic-activist alliances in prior research efforts (Twyford et al., 2022).

By 'building chains of equivalence', scholars can empower marginalised voices and challenge hegemonic knowledge paradigms, creating platforms for Others to share their racialised experiences authentically in ways where it otherwise may be difficult or near impossible to. These alliances not only foster transformative social change but also redefine research methodologies to privilege counter-stories and divergent discourses, particularly those of people of colour, thus advancing a more inclusive and equitable scholarly landscape.

Summary

While critical accounting literature has explored race and racialisation within accounting and accountability, there's a lack of substantial engagement with these issues. To bridge this gap, a new theoretical approach is needed. By integrating CRT and CDAA, scholars can better address racialisation within accounting. This approach offers a familiar framework for examining race in accounting research, encouraging scholars to tackle these issues with greater confidence and depth.

This chapter has provided a theoretical starting point, showcasing the value of a CRT-CDAA perspective through the example of Australia's offshore detention policy. We have underscored the importance of considering social and moral dimensions of accountability, particularly in relation to racialisation dynamics and the potential for emancipation through counter-stories and counter-accounts. This framework offers theoretical avenues for challenging dominant discourses, shedding light on marginalised perspectives and advocating for transformative change within accounting and accountability, especially in contexts marked by racialisation.

We hope that illuminating the possibilities fills the silences on accounting and race, encouraging studies that prioritise these issues rather than merely including them without critical examination. It is crucial to acknowledge racism as an ongoing societal problem and race as a socially constructed concept, challenging the notion of a post-racial narrative propagated by white hegemonic interests. Accounting scholars have ample opportunity to explore racialisation across various domains, including education, society, and the profession. By utilising frameworks like CRT-CDAA, we hope to inspire more research on accounting and race, contributing to a more emancipatory vision of society.

References

Annisette, M., & Prasad, A. (2017). Critical accounting research in hyper-racial times. *Critical Perspectives on Accounting*, *43*, 5–19.

Boochani, B. (2018). *No friend but the mountains*. Pan Macmillan.

Brown, J. (2009). Democracy, sustainability and dialogic accounting technologies: Taking pluralism seriously. *Critical Perspectives on Accounting*, *20*(3), 313–342.

Brown, J. (2017). On the need for broadening out and opening up in accounting. In J. Brown, P. Soderbaum, & M. Dereniowska (Eds.), *Positional analysis for sustainable development reconsidering policy, economics and accounting* (pp. 45–60). Routledge.

Brown, J., & Dillard, J. (2013). Agonizing over engagement: SEA and the "death of environmentalism" debates. *Critical Perspectives on Accounting*, *24*(1), 1–18.

Brown, J., & Dillard, J. (2014). Integrated reporting: On the need for broadening out and opening up. *Accounting, Auditing & Accountability Journal*, *27*(7), 1120–1156.

Brown, J., Dillard, J., & Hopper, T. (2015). Accounting, accountants and accountability regimes in pluralistic societies: Taking multiple perspectives seriously. *Accounting, Auditing & Accountability Journal*, *28*(5), 626–650.

Carnegie, G., Parker, L., & Tsahuridu, E. (2021). *Redefining accounting for tomorrow*. International Federation of Accountants (IFAC). https://www.ifac.org/knowledge-gateway/preparing-future-ready-professionals/discussion/redefining-accounting-tomorrow. Accessed December 19, 2021.

Crenshaw, K. (1988). Race, reform and retrenchment: Transformation and legitimation in antidiscrimination law. *Harvard Law Review*, *101*(7), 1331–1387.

Crenshaw, K., Gotanda, N., Peller, G., & Thomas, K. (1995). *Critical race theory: The key writings that formed the movement*. The New Press.

Davis, P., Dickins, D., Higgs, J., & Reid, J. (2021). Auditing while Black: Revealing microaggressions faced by Black professionals in public accounting. *Current Issues in Auditing*, *15*(2), 24–33.

Delgado, R., & Stefancic, J. (2012). *Critical race theory: An introduction*. New York University Press.

Fleischman, R., & Tyson, T. (2000). The interface of race and accounting: The case of Hawaiian sugar plantations, 1835-1920. *Accounting History*, *5*(1), 7–32.

Fleischman, R., & Tyson, T. (2004). Accounting in service to racism: Monetizing slave property in the Antebellum South. *Critical Perspectives on Accounting*, *15*(3), 376–399.

Gallhofer, S., & Haslam, J. (2019). Some reflections on the construct of emancipatory accounting: Shifting meaning and the possibilities of a new pragmatism. *Critical Perspectives on Accounting*, *63*, 1–18.

George, S., Brown, J., & Dillard, J. (2023). Social movement activists' conceptions of political action and counter-accounting through a critical dialogic accounting and accountability lens. *Critical Perspectives on Accounting*, *91*, 1–27.

George, S., Twyford, E., & Tanima, F. A. (2024). Authoritarian neoliberalism and asylum seekers: The silencing of accounting and accountability in offshore detention centres. *Journal of Business Ethics*, *194*, 861–885. https://doi.org/10.1007/s10551-024-05770-4

Goldberg, T., & Searls-Giroux, S. (2014). *Sites of race*. Polity Press.

Hammond, T., Clayton, B., & Arnold, P. (2009). South Africa's transition from apartheid: The role of professional closure in the experiences of black chartered accountants. *Accounting, Organizations and Society*, *34*, 705–721.

Hochman, A. (2019). Racialization: A defense of the concept. *Ethnic and Racial Studies*, *42*(8), 1245–1262.

Howard, T., & Navarro, O. (2016). Critical race theory 20 years later: Where do we go from here? *Urban Education*, *51*(3), 253–273.

Laclau, E., & Mouffe, C. (1985). *Hegemony and socialist strategy: Towards a radical democratic politics*. Verso.

Laine, M., & Vinnari, E. (2017). The transformative potential of counter accounts: A case study of animal rights activism. *Accounting, Auditing & Accountability Journal*, *30*(7), 1481–1510.

Lehman, C., Annisette, M., & Agyemang, G. (2016). Immigration and neoliberalism: Three cases and counter-accounts. *Accounting, Auditing & Accountability Journal*, *29*(1), 43–79.

Lehman, C., Hammond, T., & Agyemang, G. (2018). Accounting for crime in the US: Race, class and the spectacle of fear. *Critical Perspectives on Accounting*, *56*, 63–75.

Lewis, A. (2015). Counting black and white beans: Why we need a critical race theory of accounting. *European Journal of Contemporary Economics and Management*, *2*(2), 1–13.

López, N., Erwin, C., Binder, M., & Chavez, M. (2018). Making the invisible visible: Advancing quantitative methods in higher education using critical race theory and intersectionality. *Race, Ethnicity and Education*, *21*(2), 180–207. https://doi.org/10.1080/13613324.2017.1375185

Martin, C., & Fozdar, F. (2022). The master's tools: Media repurposing of exclusionary metaphors to challenge racist constructions of migrants. *Discourse & Society*, *33*(1), 56–73.

Oldroyd, D., Fleischman, R., & Tyson, T. (2008). The culpability of accounting practice in promoting slavery in the British Empire and antebellum United States. *Critical Perspectives on Accounting*, *19*, 764–784.

Solórzano, D., & Delgado Bernal, D. (2001). Examining transformational resistance through a critical race and LatCrit framework: Chicana and Chicano students in an urban context. *Urban Education*, *36*, 308–342.

Tanima, F. A., Brown, J., & Dillard, J. (2020). Surfacing the political: Women's empowerment, microfinance, critical dialogic accounting and accountability. *Accounting, Organizations and Society*, *85*, 101141.

Tanima, F. A., Brown, J., & Hopper, T. (2024). Doing critical dialogic accounting and accountability research: An analytical framework and case illustration. *Accounting, Auditing & Accountability Journal*, *37*(1), 1–30.

Tanima, F., Brown, J., Wright, J., & Mackie, V. (2023). Taking critical dialogic accountability into the field: Engaging contestation around microfinance and women's empowerment. *Critical Perspectives on Accounting*, *90*, 1–27.

Tregidga, H. (2022). Is it time to abandon "dialogic accounting"? In *Plenary session Australasian Centre for Social and Environmental Accounting Research Conference*, Wellington, New Zealand.

Twyford, E. (2018). *The state in pursuit of thanatopolitics: Accounting and the citizenry* (Doctor of Philosophy Thesis). School of Accounting, Economics and Finance, University of Wollongong. https://ro.uow.edu.au/theses1/569

Twyford, E., & Funnell, W. (2023). Accounting for the Nazi Aryanisation of German banks. *Accounting, Auditing & Accountability Journal*, *36*(1), 1–23.

Twyford, E., Tanima, F., & George, S. (2022). Critical race theory, counter-accounting, and the emancipatory potential of counter-stories. *Accounting, Auditing & Accountability Journal*, *35*(9), 330–358.

Tyson, C. (2003). Research, race and an epistemology of emancipation. *Counterpoints*, *195*, 19–28.

Ufodike, A., Egbe, I., Ogharanduku, B., & Akinyemi, T. (2023). A knowledge synthesis of anti-Black racism in accounting research. *Accounting Perspective*, *22*(3), 253–426.

Chapter 12

Exploring the Spaces in Between Professional Accounting Practice and Academia: What Could a Transdisciplinary Approach Offer Diversity in Accounting?

Orthodoxia Kyriacou

Middlesex University, UK

My Positionality and Searching for the Spaces in Between

My creative writing journey began in my childhood. I enjoyed writing stories and always wrote them following the traditional structured form, 'once upon a time…'. These stories were about princesses, fairies and witches, and they centred on the general idea of good winning over evil. I noticed very early on at school that the ability to write and express oneself through this form of communication was an advantage and the only way that I could achieve a competitive advantage over others in my class. I was one of a few ethnic background children out of a class of 30. I could see from a very early age that the 'white' children were favoured. I was something in between. Not totally white, not having the ability to converse in a fluent manner meant that I was at the back of the queue with regards to getting the teacher's attention. Although my writing abilities improved over time, my competitive advantage lay in my ability to handle numbers. Through school, I excelled in understanding 'numbers' and I observed that they could be manipulated. I sat my Maths exam three years early.

My interest in numbers began to grow. I noticed that numbers could act as 'translators' in their ability to explain and reflect elements of what was happening in nature. I noticed that the Fibonacci sequence – (the golden ratio) could be seen in nature such as in the snail's shell and even in Greek bobbin lace making and crochet that I would often practice with my mother as a young child. This 'awareness' and ability to notice meant that I could make connections between highly theoretical subjects such as Maths and their relationship to reoccurring patterns and sequences in both nature and craft making, such as crochet.

Voices of Change, 159–174

Published under exclusive licence by Emerald Publishing Limited
doi:10.1108/978-1-83753-030-420251030

I further noticed that certain people in society were being treated differently and in the most horrible ways because they were 'black'. I observed this when I was watching Alex Haley's 'Roots' (1976/1991). I was dumfounded when I saw Kunta Kinte being beaten up. I will never forget asking my mother 'why is this happening?'. I recall her reply; 'this is how it is'. This answer troubled me in my teenage years; I couldn't understand why this had been her reply. It was only years later as a postgraduate student studying communication that I understood why this was so. Her answer lay embedded in historical structural and social inequalities built on white privilege.

My abilities as a communicator in Maths and (English) language continued through school. I enjoyed the work of Doris Lessing (1955, 'Through the Tunnel'), Henry James and his Gothic novels ('Turn of the Screw', 1898) and the work of F. Scott Fitzgerald (1925), 'The Great Gatsby'. These works enabled me to look for deeper meanings contained within the pages of these works through the writer's clever use of language, metaphor and reoccurring imagery. These literary devices taught me that a point could be reinforced just through the use of words or through the creation of an idea. For example, the use of the reoccurring 'sea' imagery in 'The Great Gatsby' reinforced the notion that death and sadness lay ahead.

At University, I embarked on a degree in Accounting and Finance as I thought that this would be ideal as I was 'good' at numbers. After three years of learning that 'dead rabbits can't run', I decided that I didn't want to be a communicator of Financial Accounting reality anymore. I wanted to do something more exciting which was to try and understand the assumptions behind the accounting numbers. I quickly learnt that accounting was socially constructed (Hines, 1988) and could be manipulated and crafted according to the preparers' world view (Morgan, 1988). In essence, I noticed the missing elements or 'figures' in accounting. Where were the very people who were responsible for the construction of numbers, who were they? Women? Men? What was their ethnic background? I wanted to know who they were. I developed an interest in the constructors of accounting, the individuals behind the numbers and their stories and what had brought them into the accounting world. The discovery of this would only become apparent when I embarked on my PhD exploring gender and ethnicity in UK Accounting.

This notion of race and inequality which I had been exposed to as a child while watching 'Roots' allowed me to explore these issues in my thesis, through the utilisation of Oral History as methodology (which historically lies in the giving of voice to the silenced). I wanted to explore the lived experiences of Black women in UK Accounting. Their presence was invisible in the official statistics coupled with no record at all of their membership within the profession. They were truly invisible. Through my research, I brought visibility to women who had historically been rendered invisible through a white male version of accounting history. I now brought to the table a 'herstory' to replace the traditional white male history to accounting by documenting their lived experiences and acknowledging my positionality through utilising a semi-autobiographical approach as an ethnic researcher who has faced marginalisation within the UK education system. The author as knower and as agent who could make change happen through their creativity and agency was still missing from the discipline. My research continues to shed light on these issues, and through my creativity, my purpose has been to hold a metaphorical mirror up to the profession. Through writing as research, my journey continues...

My Wayfaring Journey Into Transdisciplinarity

From 1998 to 2020, I was a full-time accounting academic with many research interests ranging from accounting education, accounting stereotypes, to the exploration of diversity and inclusion in the profession of accounting. Perhaps a more relevant description of my role was that of a 'translator' of the language of accounting to student audiences (Harding, 2021). While teaching this numerical language, I continued to query the assumptions lying behind the seemingly 'rational' numbers and to further question what lay behind the numbers and the identity of those responsible for their construction (Hines, 1988).

My academic accounting journey and the development of my research interests were characterised by 'wayfaring' (Ingold, 2011). In other words, a path which is not undertaken in a planned way but one which evolves out of getting lost in the dense (knowledge) 'forest' and following other paths which may appear on the journey, not quite knowing where these will lead (Adams & Maguire, 2022). Some of these paths lead to dead ends, while others eventually lead to something insightful and full of promise. Such a path opened up for me in late 2020.

In late 2020, I began working with the transdisciplinarity (TD) professional doctorate team at Middlesex University because I wanted to experience something different from teaching the discipline of accounting to undergraduate students, and the professional doctorate team gave me the opportunity to work with professional doctoral candidates. More specifically, I was seeking to obtain an appreciation of different knowledge landscapes through the eyes of the practitioner (Wenger-Trayner & Wenger-Trayner, 2014).

I began to appreciate that multidisciplinary perspectives and interdisciplinary perspectives, although insightful for accounting, may have had their day as far as other professions were concerned. Through my interactions and conversations with other (international) professionals ranging from engineers, psychologists, coaches, organisation transformation experts and senior healthcare leaders, it was evident that these professions are trying to adapt to what has commonly been termed a VUCA world (Bennis & Nanus, 1985). A VUCA world is characterised by volatility, uncertainty, complexity and ambiguity. In other words, professionals have been required to remain agile in response to changing environments over which they themselves may have no direct control. It was becoming clear that accounting as a profession also must adapt to survive challenges from different external and internal environments. However, in order to achieve the level of adaptability the future will require, the profession must undergo a paradigm shift (Kuhn, 1962) with regard to the fundamental assumptions upon which accounting is built. Some of these strands I will attempt to unravel later in this chapter.

While trying to engage with and work towards an understanding of TD concepts and themes, I noticed that some aspects of what encompasses a TD approach were aspects that I have been utilising either consciously or unconsciously for some time without naming them. This is because I was not aware of their formal existence let alone that they have been 'named' into existence by significant authors.

As an accounting academic working within the critical school, I was used to working within the accounting discipline and highlighting core assumptions which appeared contradictory or needed theoretical unpacking in order that they make sense. One such example is the doctrine of 'True and Fair' which essentially crosses over into notions of social construction and ethics, which it has been claimed is the backbone of all accounting practice (Sikka et al., 2007). With these ideas, I began to connect with other spaces within accounting and across accounting, into other disciplines, enabling a deeper reflection upon the practice of accounting and my gradual movement towards 'becoming knowledgeable' (Ingold, 2011).

Currently, I am moving beyond the accounting discipline and into new spaces and territories as well as those in between (Montuori, 2010). The spaces in between these can act as vantage points allowing for new insights to develop, and this work emerges from such a position. These new territories for me now include the area of futures literacy and how we as individuals can 'anticipate' the multiplicity of futures which lie ahead and to work towards making adaptions to our practice and knowledge (Mangnus et al., 2021). My current work aims to contribute to, and further this debate as far as the profession of accounting is concerned. In the next section, I explore some of the fundamental shifts and turns within the diversity and inclusion literature in accounting, and by doing so, I hope to reveal the silences and gaps within the field before moving towards a discussion of what TD can offer the (future) diversity debate in accounting.

Exploring the 'Diversity Turn' in Accounting: From Complete Visible Silence to Invisible Presence

Since the 1990s, there has been an awareness and recognition within the accounting discipline that issues concerning diversity (in all its forms) and notions of inclusion are of importance. A handful of landmark studies have left a lasting legacy educating us about the past and the awful experiences which early African-American accountants faced (Hammond, 1990, 1997, 2002; Hammond & Streeter, 1994). These studies were groundbreaking in their attempts to document for the first time the lived experiences of those marginalised and struggling to enter and progress in the American profession. These pioneering studies are written with such authenticity, warmth and emotion in their attempts to convey and document the previous silence of those struggling to join accountancy. These studies are littered with visible and at times insurmountable barriers and obstacles by those simply seeking a career in accountancy but denied it based on their ethnic and cultural background.

Attempts to document the voice of those previously marginalised in accounting gathered pace in the late 1990s, when Hammond and Sikka (1996) called for the use of more qualitative interpretive methodologies. Hammond and Sikka (1996) argue that Oral History would have the potential to not only break the silence concerning those who have previously remained silenced but also offer an alternative history of accounting based on oral tradition. These powerful early studies awakened my sociological imagination (Wright Mills, 1959) and gave me permission to follow in their footsteps, yet carving out a different journey and path (Macfarlane, 2012), this time exploring the lived experiences of those from ethnic minority background in the UK Accounting profession, in the late 1990s (Kyriacou, 2000). Despite these modern times and the start of a new millennium approaching, the experiences of people from marginalised ethnic backgrounds remained undocumented.

A peppering of studies began to emerge on the issue of race from historical perspectives such as the work of Annisette (2000, 2003). Annisette's work (2000, 2003) shows how notions of race were mobilised as part of the professionalisation project in Trinidad and Tobago. For the first time, we were given rare insights into how race was interconnected with professional identity to exclude or limit participation of those 'socially defined as black' (Annisette, 2003, p. 639).

More recently, the importance of access to networks within the accounting profession has been highlighted as well as the careful negotiation of an individuals' identity in order to progress. The influential studies of Ashong-Lamptey (2015, 2016, 2018) provide both theoretical argument and empirical evidence to illustrate that non-white individuals must manage biculturalism in order to progress in accountancy. The findings from Ashong-Lamptey's body of work also echo the sentiments put forward in the work of Lewis (2011, 2015, 2020). Lewis argues that what is needed is a critical theory of race to help unpack the intersections of race, class and professional identity within the accounting space.

Managing one's identity appears to be key to progress within accounting as individuals are having to negotiate the structures or codes of accountancy in order to advance professionally. Some of my earlier work focused on these structural and institutional aspects of the accounting profession. It was evident that aspects pertaining to an individual's identity are mediated through notions of invisibility and visibility in the structured work and workplace of accountancy (Johnston & Kyriacou, 2011). The important work of Kirkham and Loft (1993) highlighted the historically white masculine structures of UK Accountancy, which treated those who were not white and male as Other. Growth in gender studies in accounting over the past 30 years has clearly illuminated the different journeys of women in accounting and the slow progress that has been made (Ciancanelli et al., 1990). We are now more knowledgeable about journeys into motherhood and accounting through the pioneering work of (Haynes, 2008). Furthermore, we are now beginning to hear the stories and experiences of non-Western women in accounting: through the work of Kamla (2012, 2019) on Syrian women, Chinese women (Li, 2022; Zhao & Lord, 2016). Women's voices are now being heard and the previous silence is slowly being broken.

Another important area which has gained some visibility is the previously unexplored area of disability (Duff & Ferguson, 2007a, 2007b, 2011, 2012; Duff, 2011). Representations of disability were bought to our attention for the first time, and it was clear to see the ways in which representations of disability are largely invisible within the structures of UK Accounting. Through the use of Oral History and qualitative methodologies, the lived experiences of a number of disabled accountants were explored, '*highlighting how organizational practices in accounting serve to marginalize disabled accountants*' (Duff & Ferguson, 2011, p. 351).

The diversity debate in accounting has been enriched as a direct result of our attention to diversity in all its forms. We now know so much more about gender, ethnicity, intersectionality and about disability issues in accounting, but there is still more to learn and do, not only from an academic stand point but also professionally.

In recent years, we have seen the accounting diversity debate make a welcome move into the LGBTIQ arena (Rumens, 2016). Although this part of the diversity debate is still in its infancy with regard to the development of methodological approaches and praxis frameworks, it is gaining momentum through the visibility of articles calling for the equality of all individuals in accounting, the acknowledgement of difference and the development of a 'queering manifesto' (Ghio et al., 2023).

These studies implicitly and in some places explicitly call for the development of appropriate methodologies in order to acknowledge difference and to allow individuals the space and safety to be their 'authentic' selves within the organisational accounting setting (Egan & de Lima Voss, 2022; Hammond, 2018; McGuigan & Ghio, 2018). I would like to echo this call, and in the next section, I explore some of these strands regarding the notion of authenticity within accounting research.

Progress has been made with respect to illuminating the diversity agenda in accounting from an academic perspective. However, it is clear that there appears to be a missing element in the debate concerning the position of the profession itself. From an academic perspective, we have come so very far in the past 30 years, but from a practitioner and organisational angle, little change has actually happened with regard to acknowledging this intersectionality and how it plays out within the (real) accounting organisational setting. In the next section, I highlight some aspects borrowed from a TD perspective which perhaps may aid in furthering the diversity debate.

TD and Its (Future) Offerings for Accounting Space(s)?

My engagement with and reflection upon the above literature has led me to notice that a number of spaces within the diversity in accounting literature require some attention. I attempt to draw out and discuss some of these areas and how they may benefit from a TD offering or reconceptualisation.

As I outlined earlier, my 'journey to become knowledgeable' with respect to TD can be likened to that of a 'wayfarer' (Ingold, 2011), never quite knowing where the journey would take me. I started out as an accounting academic questioning the obvious and then began to look more deeply behind the numbers and questioning the assumptions through developing a sense of noticing (Mason, 2002). My sense of noticing has developed further through my recent engagement with coaching at a professional level. I have recently undertaken a coaching qualification and become a newly qualified European Mentoring and Coaching Council (EMCC) coach. This event signalled my journey into professionalisation (Johnson, 1972). I acknowledge that my professional identity, through my attempts to develop into a reflective practitioner (Schon, 1983/2000), is shifting and being (re)shaped through my engagement with various bodies of literature which expresses itself through my practice. I believe I now occupy a unique position, moving from academic to practitioner allows me to view the spaces in between these boundaries. This has afforded me with further opportunities to deepen and enhance my 'professional sensitivities to notice' (Mason, 2002). Furthermore, coaching has also reinforced certain values and attributes relating to my 'being' (Griffin, 1996), awareness and agency that I believe are fundamentally relevant to enhancing the accounting debate on diversity.

Calling for a 'Being' Turn

It has been well documented that accounting operates in fast-paced, complex, interconnected financial sectors and markets and that its function is to mobilise capital (Sikka, 2001). The boundaries between the local, national and global markets are often blurred (Cooper et al., 2003). However, what is often not considered is the notion of what this fast-paced industry and work does to the individual in accounting and how the accounting organisational setting and its structures relate to the individual experience. We have little insight into the interplay between the macro, meso and micro levels of accounting and how each one of these levels filters through to the individual experience at the micro level. Further, the fast pace of accountancy and the 'rush', 'rush' 'rush' to mobilise capital leaves little or no time for reflection in action and reflection on action (Schon, 1983/2000). In this way, notions of '*eros*' and the love of the everyday (Griffin, 1996) are getting lost in the rush to complete time sheets and to manage one's accountability in terms of allocating time in the apportionment of costings. A focus on 'being' is absent from the accounting literature and even more so from the accounting diversity debate. In this piece, I argue that the diversity debate can be enriched through the process of acknowledging our 'being'. This can be achieved through acknowledging our awareness in terms of our consciousness and presence in the accounting social setting. Moustakas (1995) suggests that 'being' encompasses a number of facets – *'being-in', 'being-for' and 'being-with'*. Moustakas (1995) further suggests that 'being' is situational and also relational; it concerns the acknowledgement of relationships with others and also with one's self. Being with oneself can encourage creativity, freedom and authenticity to emerge. However, Moustakas (1995) argues that although being with oneself while alone can lead to creativity, there can also be a paradox at play in the sense that being alone inspires more intimate contact with others and the need for connection. Freedom for the individual can emerge from within these boundaries leading to an authenticity of self to emerge:

> The aim is to evoke a human presence, a freedom to enter into peaks and valleys of experience, courage to walk through darkness and traverse shadows of life itself. To achieve these aims, one must become internally alive, embrace one's own perceptions and senses, and face whatever appears in one's awareness and understanding – the imponderable and unknown regions of the self that inevitably occur in individual and communal living. (Moustakas, 1995, p. xix)

Moustakas's (1995) sentiments appear very relevant to our notion of accounting work and how this reality is experienced within the VUCA world. I argue that individuals who are aware of their 'being' and have insights into their selves and its relational aspects have the capacity and ability to enhance the accounting social setting, by encouraging a safe environment for all and therefore embracing diversity in all its different forms. With permission to be free and to be ourselves, we can bring our authentic self to the organisation. In other words, we can bring ourselves to '*accounting and everyday life*' (Hopwood, 1994).

One potential barrier or obstacle to achieving this is rooted in a fundamental assumption of accounting. Lying at the core of accounting practice is the assumption of classification, and classification systems are established ways of organising knowledge and offering explanations to reduce uncertainty (Gunnlaugsdottir, 2003; Padian, 1999). The unclassified is potentially problematic for accounting and by extension individuals too. Individuals cannot be classified according to accounting assumptions, and an individual's identity is a personal matter not up for classification in some fixed taxonomy. Rather, our identity is being shaped and being transformed through our 'being'. For accounting to move beyond the rigidity and structure of its taxonomic tendencies would entail a significant paradigm shift (Kuhn, 1962). In part, what is needed is 'freedom' (Moustakas, 1995) which will assist in the emergence of the authentic self which transcends classification systems.

The accounting profession has previously exercised such classification systems through its various attempts over the decades to systematically collect and monitor information regarding gender and ethnic background of professional accountants in the United Kingdom. I previously held the view that the engagement of such an activity would be highly beneficial for the profession to record membership details and to make some inroads into active monitoring of what are now considered protective characteristics (Equality Act, 2010). However, terms usually used on monitoring forms to 'classify' are highly problematic as an individual's identity cannot be pigeon-holed into these somewhat binary classifications (such as Black, white) and 'other-please explain' categories. My personal experience meant that I was always left hovering over the 'other' category and forced to explain as far as possible what my unique identity was.

Assumptions and definitions based on classification lie at the core of accounting and by extension have been applied to individuals and their classification. The fundamental issue here is whether classification serves a meaningful role in increasing diversity or whether it provides opportunity for discrimination. Future directions exploring diversity in accounting could possibly engage and seek collaboration from the workforce as their voices would be an important part of the process in designing these monitoring systems and questionnaires. Inclusion of voices in the system's design who have historically been forgotten would signal an important step towards inclusion.

The accounting profession appears to be lacking in agility where diversity is concerned. The profession's unique history where issues of diversity are of focus illustrates that it has been slow to act and to break down its codified, exclusionary institutional structures (Kyriacou, 2000). Hence, the profession's willingness to bring diversity issues to the table has often been slow or non-existent. This may be due to the complexity surrounding issues of diversity. My suggestion to bring about a 'being' turn in accounting can be considered in a number of ways.

Towards 'Being -in', 'Being-for' and 'Being-With'

I argue that an acknowledgement of 'being' (in) accounting is much called for. Individuals reflecting on their experiences of being in accounting and engaging in reflection-in action and reflection(s)-on action (Schon, 1983/2000) have the potential to illuminate our experiences of accounting. We have the potential to learn so much more about diversity in all its forms and how discriminatory practices can operate and effect individuals in negative ways. If we are able to heighten our awareness and develop our sense of noticing (Mason, 2002) and work towards becoming unconsciously competent (Burch, 1970), then this will be a significant breakthrough. If we are able to work on this skill of noticing, in time, it will become natural to us in the sense that we will be practising it at an unconscious level. Therefore, we will become competent at noticing how discriminatory practices work at subtle levels and then we can work in positive ways to eradicate them. One way to facilitate this awareness of 'being-in' is to encourage the development of autoethnographic studies in accounting which focus on the authentic voice, reflecting on experiences of accounting to develop learning through one's writing. Although we have seen the emergence of a handful of studies written in a semi-biographical manner by academics who have practised accounting (Haynes, 2006, 2008), this is an area within the accounting discipline which has largely remained unexplored. Insights into critical incidences and knowledge learning can be revealed through the process of reflecting (Kyriacou, 2000).

'Being-For' requires individuals to stand by their values, beliefs and convictions and not be swayed by others in any shape or form (Moustakas, 1995, p. xx). In other words, individuals need to be in congruence with themselves and to stand by their beliefs. However, this can be problematic for accounting as historically, when individuals have tried to stand by their beliefs and engage in resistance, they have been charged with an unwillingness to 'conform' to the institutional structures of the profession (Hammond, 2002; Kyriacou, 2000). The issue here appears to be one pertaining to structural issues whereby accounting structures need to be more flexible and agile and more humane with regards to being more accepting of individuals who may not necessarily conform to its structural requirements such as working to rigid timesheet patterns. If accounting continues to operate in this way, then working mothers, those experiencing pregnancy and menopause and those involved in caring responsibilities, are excluded from the working accounting world.

'Being with' is a way of 'facing the fears and doubts of existence as well as the enticements and attractions of life' (Moustakas, 1995, p. xx) through listening to the inner silences. For accounting, this suggests that individuals can seek a fulfilling existence within the work through its communal nature. Accounting as a social function is both practised alone and with others in organisational groups with the view of reaching a consensus across teams. The best teams are diverse teams which come together to reach decisions with different skill sets. A diverse workforce (in all its forms) is what is needed to keep accounting agile. This also means that accountants need to work with others beyond accounting to solve problems. This argument is partly echoed in the studies of Quattrone (2000); Whittington (2011) and Christ and Burritt (2018) calling for the use of TD approaches in accounting. Further, Bebbington et al. (2017) argue that moving forward, we need to look at ways in which we can make accounting sustainable. One way is to consider our 'being' through acknowledging the complexity of the spaces that we occupy within, across and beyond disciplines. However, the notion of practice and our situational relationship to it needs to be embraced.

Moving From Being, Doing to Knowing

The work of accountants as codified practice is well argued within the literature (Llewellyn & Milne, 2007). However, what still remains in its infancy is what can best be described as the 'practice' turn within the literature. Whittington (2011) calls for accounting researchers to explore 'practice' and its possibilities for accounting. However, at the same time, he provides a warning that there are difficulties with employing such an approach:

> When studying societal practices such as accounting..., we should always recall that they are the negotiated products of agency, with some aspects defined quite firmly by the wider apparatus of their respective professions, some highly adaptive to local contexts and others richly permissive of individual improvisation in the moment. Thus in a world of tight entanglements, practice research involves a constant parsing out of the individual, the local and the societal. For accounting,...and similar societal practices, practice-theoretic research can never be purely 'micro' or 'macro'; the other is always present, even if temporarily not centre-stage. (Whittington, 2011, p. 185)

Although Whittington (2011) provides some interesting cautionary insights into the practice turn for accounting and its offerings, I am of the belief that this is a worthwhile pursuit. A fresh approach could lie in moving the debate forward through change agents – both practitioners and academics working together in collaboration to bring about transformation. Utilising insights largely borrowed from a broad transdisciplinary perspective which acknowledges the presence and importance of 'being', 'doing' and 'knowing' (Adams & Maguire, 2022). I argue that it is possible to acknowledge our 'being' in the organisational space through our awareness of presence, the '*doing*' of accounting and academic work is more authentic, together with our '*knowing*' through our tacit knowledge (Polanyi, 1966/2009) we can push the notion of diversity further as new ways of knowing emerge. Through self-reflexivity, our 'knowing' can facilitate our agency and act as a key to transformation. Inviting diversity experts from other fields and those working in practice can enrich our understanding of the complexities concerning the diversity agenda. Those involved in policymaking and regulation can have input into the diversity agenda to re(imagine) accounting as a profession which treats everyone equally and respects diversity. Therefore, collaboration with significant others who are diversity experts, stakeholders, academics and indeed accountants can contribute to advancing the diversity debate. A fundamental question here for contemplation concerns the nature of such collaborations. Individuals with particular expertise need to come together to share ideas about best practice and how they can create a future for accounting which acknowledges and respects difference along diversity lines. With this comes an understanding of people and their histories. I argue that history is key to understanding the present and indeed the future of accounting. If the profession is able to embrace diversity and individual experience, only then can the profession claim that it will be sustainable. The profession needs an agile and diverse workforce to keep it relevant and able to face the challenges that an uncertain future brings.

Concluding Remarks

My 'wayfaring' journey into TD through my positionality as a critical accounting researcher has been the background for this piece. I have explored how some of the new ideas that I have encountered have caused me both to reflect and consider shifting my perspectives where accounting as a disciplined is concerned. Recently, I have been moving into new territories and those spaces in between (Montuori, 2010) to argue that the diversity debate in accounting has much to benefit from the utilisation of a broad TD approach.

It is evident that the diversity literature in accounting has come a long way in 30 years, and we know so much more about some of the intersections of gender, race and ethnicity. Our knowledge with respect to the multiple aspects of diversity is increasing, but more needs to be achieved. Emergent studies in the field of disability and the LGBTIQ+ arena highlight the need for equality within the accounting profession (Duff & Ferguson, 2011; Ghio et al., 2023). The diversity field in accounting has the potential to further our knowledge through the development of appropriate methodologies and praxis frameworks, acknowledging difference which allows individuals the space and safety to be their 'authentic' self both within the organisational accounting setting and the academic domain (Egan & de Lima Voss, 2022; Hammond, 2018; McGuigan & Ghio, 2018). I argued earlier that autobiographical and autoethnographic studies have the potential to enlighten our understanding of how diversity is experienced by an individual as these studies often reveal what is hidden from sight; the critical incidences faced by the researcher and making visible their influences and choices in exploring a particular theme, hence encouraging authenticity. I am of the belief that authenticity is key to the future development of the diversity agenda in accounting as individuals need to feel safe and free to be their 'authentic' selves (Hammond, 2018; McGuigan & Ghio, 2018). I noted, at times, this may be stifled and thwarted by accounting's rush for capital accumulation and mobilisation, and as such, the love of everyday accounting life and life itself can be lost (Griffin, 1996). Acknowledgement of our 'being' within the accounting context can further the authentic self to emerge. I argued that one barrier to achieving this lies at the very heart of accounting and its practice, which is the assumption of classification. Classification systems are used in accounting to reduce uncertainty and risk and thus place monetary values on items. Anything which is unclassified in accounting is potentially problematic. Our literature in accounting exploring diversity appears to illustrate this position, whereby those who have historically not conformed to the image of the construction of the professional person have remained unclassified or treated as the Other (Kirkham & Loft, 1993).

My call to utilise a TD approach to the diversity in accounting debate could be beneficial with regard to facilitating the professions' efforts to implement monitoring systems with regard to protective characteristics as defined by the Equality Act, 2010. My suggestion to involve the accounting workforce in collaborative discussions with outside experts such as lawyers and diversity experts could lead to a much more useful monitoring system and ethnicity questionnaires. However, for this to be successful, the voices of those who have historically remained invisible need to be included in the process. For the whole process to be useful and rewarding, it needs to be transparent, inclusive and equitable and sustainable.

Reflection and awareness of our 'being', doing and knowing (Adams & Maguire, 2022) can lead to new ways of knowing and new knowledge landscapes through our agency. We need to move beyond a belief in knowledge islands and that accounting as a profession exists in isolation. To enable equity to prevail, members of the accounting profession need to build connections and alliances with other experts, professionals and policymakers.

Accounting as a profession needs to be ready for the future and indeed the multiplicity of futures that may lie ahead. This, therefore, means both respecting the diversity in our workforce and developing our current workforce to be agile enough to deal with the complexities of the future. Through encouraging creativity, curiosity and feeding our sociological imagination (Wright Mills, 1959), we can envisage an inclusive accounting profession for the future.

References

Adams, D., & Maguire, K. (2022). Transdisciplinary practice: Being, doing, knowing. In R. J. Lawrence (Ed.), *Handbook on transdisciplinarity: Global perspectives*. Edward Elgar Publishing. (forthcoming).

Annisette, M. (2000). Imperialism and the professions: The education and certification of accountants in Trinidad and Tobago. *Accounting, Organizations and Society*, *25*(1), 631–659.

Annisette, M. (2003). The colour of accountancy: Examining the salience of race in a professionalisation project. *Accounting, Organizations and Society*, *28*(7–8), 639–674.

Ashong-Lamptey, J. (2015). Bicultural experience in the legal profession: A developmental network approach. *Fordham Law Review*, *83*(5), 2369–2385.

Ashong-Lamptey, J. (2016). *Crafting an identity: An examination of the lived experience of minority racial and ethnic individuals in the workplace*. Unpublished doctoral thesis. London School of Economics and Political Science.

Ashong-Lamptey, J. (2018). An exploration of minority ethnic culture as a professional resource. *Journal of Business Diversity*, *18*(2), 113–132.

Bebbington, J., Russell, S., & Thomson, I. (2017). Accounting and sustainable development: Reflections and propositions. *Critical Perspectives on Accounting*, *48*, 21–34.

Bennis, W., & Nanus, B. (1985). *Leaders: The strategies for taking charge*. Harper and Row.

Burch, N. (1970). *The four stages for learning any new skills*. Gordon Training International.

Christ, K. L., & Burritt, R. L. (2018). The role of transdisciplinarity in water accounting by business: Reflections and opportunities. *Australasian Journal of Environmental Management*, *25*(3), 302–320.

Ciancanelli, P., Gallhofer, S., Humphrey, C., & Kirkham, L. (1990). Gender and accountancy: Some evidence from the UK. *Critical Perspectives on Accounting*, *1*(2), 117–144.

Cooper, C., Neu, D., & Lehman, G. (2003). Globalisation and its discontents: A concern about growth and globalization. *Accounting Forum*, *27*(4), 359–364.

Duff, A. (2011). Big four accounting firms' annual reviews: A photo analysis of gender and race portrayals'. *Critical Perspectives on Accounting*, *22*(1), 20–38.

Duff, A., & Ferguson, J. (2007a). Disability and accounting firms: Evidence from the UK. *Critical Perspectives on Accounting*, *18*(2), 139–157.

Duff, A., & Ferguson, J. (2007b). Issues concerning the employment and employability of disabled people in UK accounting firms: An analysis of the views of human resource managers as employment gatekeepers. *The British Accounting Review*, *39*(1), 15–38.

Duff, A., & Ferguson, J. (2011). Disability and the socialization of accounting professionals. *Critical Perspectives on Accounting*, *22*(4), 351–364.

Duff, A., & Ferguson, J. (2012). Disability and the professional accountant: Insights from oral histories. *Accounting, Auditing & Accountability Journal*, *25*(1), 71–101.

Egan, M., & de Lima Voss, B. (2022). Redressing the Big 4's male, pale and stale image, through LGBTIQ+ Ethical Praxis. *Critical Perspectives on Accounting*. Available online September 11, 2022, (in press).

Equality Act. (2010). https://www.legislation.gov.uk/ukpga/2010/15/contents

Fitzgerald, F. S. (1925). *The great Gatsby*. Charles Scribner's Sons.

Ghio, A., McGuigan, N., & Powell, L. (2023). The queering accounting manifesto. *Critical Perspectives on Accounting*, *90*.

Griffin, S. (1996). *The Eros of everyday life: Essays on ecology, gender and society*. Anchor

Gunnlaugsdottir, J. (2003). Seek and you will find, share and you will benefit: Organising knowledge using groupware systems. *International Journal of Information Management*, *23*, 363–380.

Haley, A. (1976/1991). *Roots: The saga of an American family*. Vintage Books.

Hammond, T. (1990). *The minority recruitment efforts of the major public accounting firms in New York: A sociological analysis*. Unpublished Doctoral Dissertation. University of Wisconsin-Madison.

Hammond, T. (1997). From complete exclusion to minimal inclusion: African Americans and the public accounting industry 1965–1988. *Accounting, Organizations and Society*, *9*(3), 79–97.

Hammond, T. (2002). *A white-collar profession: African American certified public accountants since 1921*. University of North Carolina Press.

Hammond, T. (2018). LGBTQ+ accountants: A call for oral history research. *Sustainability Accounting, Management and Policy Journal*, *9*(5), 615–624.

Hammond, T., & Sikka, P. (1996). Radicalizing accounting history: The potentialities of oral history. *Accounting, Auditing & Accountability Journal*, *9*(3), 79–97.

Hammond, T., & Streeter, D. W. (1994). Overcoming barriers: Early african-American certified public accountants. *Accounting, Organizations and Society*, *19*(3), 271–288.

Harding, S. (2021). 'Becoming Knowledgeable': Ingold's 'wayfaring' and the 'art of translation' as a politics of difference. *The Translator*, *27*(4), 351–367.

Haynes, K. (2006). Linking narrative and identity construction: Using autobiography in accounting research. *Critical Perspectives on Accounting*, *17*(4), 399–418.

Haynes, K. (2008). Transforming identities: Accounting professionals and the transition to motherhood. *Critical Perspectives on Accounting*, *19*(5), 620–642.

Hines, R. (1988). Financial accounting: In communicating reality, we construct reality. *Accounting, Organizations and Society*, *13*(3), 251–261.

Hopwood, A. (1994). Accounting and everyday life: An introduction. *Accounting, Organizations and Society*, *19*(3), 299–301.

Ingold, T. (2011). *Being alive: Essays on movement, knowledge and description*. Routledge.

James, H. (1898). *The turn of the screw*. Penguin Classics.

Johnson, T. J. (1972). *Professions and power*. Macmillan Press Ltd.

Johnston, R., & Kyriacou, O. (2011). Exploring inclusion, exclusion and ethnicities in the institutional structures of UK accountancy. *Equality, Diversity and Inclusion*, *30*(6), 482–497.

Kamla, R. (2012). Syrian women accountants' attitudes and experiences at work in the context of globalization. *Accounting, Organizations and Society*, *37*(3), 188–205.

Kamla, R. (2019). Religion-based resistance strategies, politics of authenticity and professional women accountants. *Accounting, Organizations and Society*, *59*, 52–69.

Kirkham, L., & Loft, A. (1993). Gender and the construction of the professional accountant. *Accounting, Organizations and Society*, *18*(6), 507–558.

Kuhn, T. (1962). *The structure of scientific revolutions*. University of Chicago Press.

Kyriacou, O. (2000). *Gender, ethnicity and professional membership: The case of the UK accounting profession*. Unpublished PhD Thesis. University of East.

Lessing, D. (1955). *Through the Tunnel*. Creative Education.

Lewis, A. (2011). *A study of the black accounting experience in the UK* Unpublished Doctoral Dissertation. Leeds Metropolitan University.

Lewis, A. (2015). Counting black and white beans: Why we need a critical race theory of accounting. *European Journal of Contemporary Economics and Management*, *2*(2), 1–13.

Lewis, A. (2020). *Counting black and white beans: Critical race theory in accounting*. Emerald Publishing Limited.

Li, Q. (2022). *Accountants in China: An alternative feminist discourse on the changing professional and gender identities*. Unpublished Doctoral Thesis. Herriott Watt University.

Llewellyn, S., & Milne, M. J. (2007). Accounting as codified discourse. *Accounting, Auditing & Accountability Journal*, *20*(6), 805–824.

Macfarlane, R. (2012). *The old ways: A journey on foot*. Penguin.

Mangnus, A. C., Oomen, J., Vervoort, J. M., & Hajer, M. A. (2021). Futures literacy and the diversity of the future. *Futures*, *132*, 102793.

Mason, J. (2002). *Researching your own practice: The discipline of noticing*. RoutledgeFalmer.

McGuigan, N., & Ghio, A. (2018). Queering accountants: Opening up and connecting professional services firms. *Sustainability Accounting, Management and Policy Journal*, *9*(5), 625–635.

Montuori, A. (2010). Transdisciplinarity and creative inquiry in transformative education: Researching the research degree. In M., Maldonato & R., Pietroban (Eds.), *Research on scientific research: A transdiciplinary study*. Blackwells.

Morgan, G. (1988). Accounting as reality construction: Towards a new epistemology for accounting practice. *Accounting, Organizations and Society*, *13*(5), 477–485.

Moustakas, C. E. (1995). *Being-in, being-for, being-with*. Rowman & Littlefield Publishers Inc.

Padian, K. (1999). Charles Darwin's views on classification in theory and practice. *Systematic Biology*, *48*(2), 352–364.

Polanyi, M. (1966/2009). *The tacit dimension*. University of Chicago Press.

Quattrone, P. (2000). Constructivism and accounting research: Towards a trans-disciplinary perspective. *Accounting, Auditing & Accountability Journal*, *13*(2), 130–155.

Rumens, N. (2016). Sexualities and accounting: A queer theory perspective. *Critical Perspectives on Accounting*, *35*, 111–120.

Schon, D. A. (1983/2000). *The reflective practitioner: How professionals think in action*. Arena Ashgate Publishing.

Sikka, P. (2001). Regulation of accountancy and the power of capital: Some observations. *Critical Perspectives on Accounting*, *12*(2), 199–211.

Sikka, P., Haslam, C., Kyriacou, O., & Agrizzi, D. (2007). Professionalizing claims and the state of UK professional accounting education: Some evidence. *Accounting Education*, *16*(1), 3–21.

Wenger-Trayner, E., & Wenger-Trayner, B. (2014). Learning in a landscape of practice: A framework. In E. Wenger-Trayner, M. Fenton-O'Creevey, S. Hutchinson, C. Kubiak, & B. Wenger-Trayner (Eds.), *Learning in landscapes of practice: Boundaries, identity, and knowledgeability in practice-based learning*. Routledge.

Whittington, R. (2011). The practice turn in organization research: Towards a disciplined transdisciplinarity. *Accounting, Organizations and Society*, *36*(3), 183–186.

Wright Mills, C. (1959). *The sociological imagination*. Oxford University Press.

Zhao, Y., & Lord, B. R. (2016). Chinese women in the accounting profession. *Meditari Accountancy Research*, *24*(2), 226–245.

Chapter 13

Operationalising Oral History for Social Justice in Accounting

Sedzani Musundwa[a] *and Theresa Hammond*[b]

[a]University of South Africa, South Africa
[b]San Francisco State University, USA

> ...this was first time since I'd left school that I was looked at as a full human being rather than a subhuman. The release of oppression it left in my body and soul is hard to describe. The opportunity to compete with other aspirant accountants on an equal basis, regardless of race, gender or religion, was inspiring and exhilarating. My destiny was now in my own hands. (Jeff van Rooyen, 2022)

Every personal story is born from a much wider social context. This chapter is inspired by contemporary global movements, such as #BlackLivesMatter, that seek to draw attention to the injustice faced by Black people in everyday society. Beyond spotlighting these injustices, the movements reward the victims of violence with a platform for communicating, in their own intimate expression, the personal impact of the wrongs inflicted upon them. Similarly, in the study of the sociology of accounting, methods such as Oral History provide a catalyst for justice by allowing for the experiences of those marginalised in the accounting profession to share their lived experiences. The opening quote above is shared from the recently published autobiography of one of the first Black CAs to qualify in South Africa. In this short excerpt, the author shares his personal testimony of what achieving an accounting qualification means to him. Bursting with emotion, the author's account reflects, simultaneously, the effusive exhilaration and hope engendered by his achievement and the divided state of South Africa at the time.

The authors of this chapter use their experiences and engagements with Oral History on separate projects within scientific work to reflect on how this

Voices of Change, 175–188

Published under exclusive licence by Emerald Publishing Limited
doi:10.1108/978-1-83753-030-420251032

methodological approach can be used to generate new knowledge in the profession.[1] They use racial injustice in South Africa as a backdrop for making meaningful suggestions. The chapter provides some context on how Oral History has been previously used, along with a discussion of the theories that have supported the method in previous studies. The operationalisation of the method then follows with specific attention given to strategies for recruitment, conducting interviews and data analysis. The authors then highlight possible complexities that researchers may encounter when using this method and how they can be overcome. This chapter, therefore, serves as a suitable guide for researchers interested in taking up the method, especially within social justice–related studies.

Why Oral History?

Accounting has long been purported to be factual and neutral in nature (Ghio et al., 2023; Hammond & Sikka, 1996). The dynamic nature of accounting professionals and the various roles they fill in the profession and society at large dictate that accounting is, in fact, socially constructed. The dominant voices in accounting literature lay direct blame on marginalised groups for lowered performance in the profession and thus focus on strategies to essentially correct the perceived deficiency of persons from these groups. These voices also tend to be supported by statistics that reinforce the notion that persons from marginalised groups are poor performers (Musundwa, 2024). The authors of this chapter use Oral History to counter this narrative by demonstrating that the challenges faced by marginalised groups can be attributed to legal, structural and systemic challenges. The authors therefore propose that the focus with Oral History should thus be shifted to understand the nature of the barriers faced by Black aspirants for the purpose of identifying and implementing effective mechanisms to dismantle them.

Oral History essentially reveals the deeper fissures in society and thus provides an alternative method to the dominant positivist perspectives for preserving the lived experiences of those affected by the profession. Commonly used methods in qualitative accounting studies such as unstructured interviews run the risk of being too narrowly focused and miss delving deep into the contextual history of why becoming an accountant can be such a big achievement. Oral History can fill this methodological gap and has for years been celebrated for its ability to prioritise individuals' experiences (Yow, 2005). These testimonies, derived from respondents who have been allowed to reflect on their broad personal histories, provide a perspective which is critical to understanding how people are affected by the construction of society and community. By inviting victims of marginalisation in the profession to narrate their

[1]The combined experience of both authors spans across decades. Hammond has studied the experiences of Black South African accountants since the early 2000s. She later served as study advisor to Musundwa who completed her PhD in 2022 and has continued to specialise in the same arena. Data from both Hammond and Musundwa's research are referenced in this chapter.

own stories using their own words (Kyriacou, 2009), the method allows for empathetic engagement with those interviewed, while liberating the researcher to explore without any of the limitations of a scripted dialogue (Hammond, 2017). Within the context of social justice in accounting, this method facilitates an approach that allows researchers to therefore better understand the lived realities of marginalised accountants as a means for advocating for their dignity and freedom within the profession (Gordon, 2020).

Contextualising Oral History

Oral History is not a novel endeavour in accounting. It was adopted as early as 1980s as a means to provide ongoing visibility of various societies affected by accounting (Hammond & Sikka, 1996). While it has not been fully exploited, it has been applied (albeit to a limited extent) to expose the lived experiences of those who are marginalised based on ethnicity, gender, race and disability. Acting as a data retrieval instrument in environments where data are seldom gathered, Oral History offers a way to highlight the mostly unheard narratives that remain outside the mainstream domain (Kyriacou, 2009). It also proves invaluable in situations where obtaining conventional quantitative data is unfeasible due to its non-existence or where distributing survey instruments would pose challenges (Moses & Hopper, 2022).

James and Otsuka (2009) used Oral History to explore the difficulties faced by Chinese accountants in finding employment in mainstream corporates in Australia. In Kim's (2004a, 2004b) research, the Oral History method was used to consider the role of race, ethnicity and gender in the accounting profession in New Zealand. Through a feminist lens, Haynes (2010) used this method to investigate the experiences of women as a minority in the profession in the United Kingdom complementing Kyriacou (2009) who used the feminist research lens to explore the experiences of ethnic women. Duff and Ferguson (2012) used Oral History to gain insight into the difficulties experienced by accountants with disabilities. The authors of this chapter used Oral History to explore the lived experiences of Black South Africans in their pursuit of the Chartered Accountancy (hereafter CA) certification in separate studies conducted in the early 2000s and later in 2022. Both explorations were informed by the marginalised status that Black accountants held in a country where the Black demographic is in fact the majority. The early and more contemporary adoption of the method in the South African context forms the base for the suggestions made in this chapter.

Theories That Support This Method

Weber's theory on social closure has provided a reliable platform for the authors of this chapter to effectively apply Oral History and understand the role of race in accounting. The theory promotes shifting blame from the marginalised persons to the social systems and apparatus that oppress them. A similar theory that can be applied to racial studies in accounting is Critical Race Theory (CRT). CRT allows the researcher to illuminate race while silencing all other forms of oppression that tend to be used to justify racism (Lewis, 2016) thereby dedicating full focus on the root cause of injustice. Because the accounting profession is under consideration, professional closure theory can also be adopted which focuses on how credentialling is used as a catalyst for exclusion (Annisette, 2017). In addition, feminist theories similarly shift focus from the dominant, in this case male, perspective on issues and invest in understanding the experiences of women (Lehman, 2019). The African philosophy of Ubuntu promotes the recognition of community and the value of collective effort in society if social justice is to be achieved (Ngubane & Makua, 2021). Ultimately, the choice of theory should be informed by its ability to allow the researcher an opportunity to critically examine how systems of power and oppression interact to the detriment of selective population groups in society and thus promote social justice.

The Mechanics of the Method

The operationalisation of Oral History must consider all aspects of data gathering methodology, but in this chapter, the authors only focus on the recruitment of suitable participants, conducting the interview and data analysis as this requires much discretion.

Fig. 13.1 represents the components of Oral History arranged in no particular order. This is done deliberately to emphasise that they do not follow a linear path nor have a particular start point or end point that the researcher can follow. The theoretical lens facilitates a coherent flow throughout. To achieve success with the method, the researcher must remain agile. The depiction of interlocked gears, essentially depicting constant motion, illustrates the iterative nature of the process. Each component is discussed below.

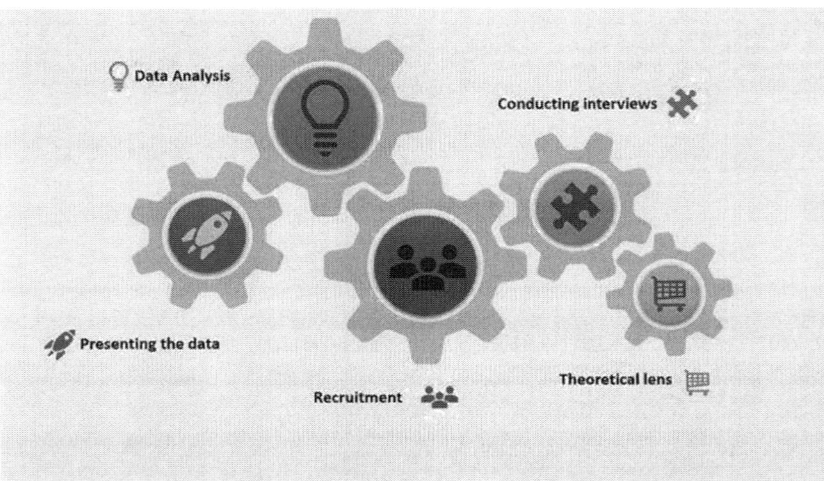

Fig. 13.1. The Mechanics of Oral History. Reference: Authors' own.

The Recruitment of Suitable Participants

The researchers must recognise that a multiplicity of realities can co-exist, but they target participants who can answer the specified research question. Meeting the project objectives is therefore critical since quality social justice research rests on recruiting the most suitable respondents. Obtaining their perspective contributes to new knowledge as they capture voices not commonly represented in accounting research.

Ideally, the researcher should target respondents from the said marginalised groups. Maintenance of this perspective throughout the process is critical and is thus discussed further in the data collection and analysis sections below. In our past research projects, we recruited based on questioning how Black CAs in South Africa are consistently under-represented in a country where they form the majority demographic.

More contemporary considerations can be expanded to include sub-classifications of the traditional constructs. Within race studies, for example, recruitment can be based on space, family structure and household income, among other classifications which are discussed below.[2]

Space

In considering space, the researcher relies on the complexity of geography as a marker for recruitment. For instance, Blacks under apartheid in South Africa were relegated to townships and rural areas which were significantly far from the economic hubs of the country and were disadvantaged with substandard services including education (Gallo, 2020). To further entrench the distance and inaccessibility of education and work, pass laws were imposed to restrict movements of Blacks. Access to employers and universities that offer accredited accounting degrees and relevant foundational education were all located away from Black communities. Distance as a barrier is demonstrated in the following two quotes shared by one of the early qualifying accountants in South Africa:

> I mean there was a school in that little village, but it was for whites only. So, we used to walk to the nearest school for Blacks which was 8 kilometres away. (TN, 2002)

Going to a purely Black school also meant substandard education as demonstrated in the following quote in which the same respondent shared the

---

[2]An opportunity continues to exist to explore the experiences of professional accountants based on their gender, race, class and religious compasses. For example, during recruitment, the researcher may encounter respondents that meet more than one of the inclusion criteria set for recruitment. In such cases, the researcher should remain open to the opportunities presented by intersecting criteria. This demonstrates a race and gender intersection which can yield results that differ from those evident when race and gender are studied independently. The intersection in itself may also birth a new sub study.

difficulties in attaining a postgraduate qualification. He had obtained the undergraduate in his rural town; however, the institution was not accredited for postgraduate qualifications:

> And then the following year [after attaining the degree] I then registered for the rest of the subjects to qualify for CTA,[3] so I did the conversion courses for two years before I qualified for the Honours, just to patch up on the subjects that I didn't do in the Transkei. (TN, 2002)

If the researcher had accepted that the respondent achieved the postgraduate qualification without further exploration, they would have overlooked the context which showcases the inequality in the system that contributed to the respondent having to "catch up" and thus delay his eventual certification. Thus, recruiting respondents based on their residence (i.e. in a township, rural area or even metropolis in the South African context) will yield deep insights regarding the barriers of access for Blacks into the profession and how these barriers manifest depending on one's proximity to a metropolis.

Interviewers must be well trained in Oral History in order to mitigate risks around potential omissions or neglecting critical data for the study. It may also be advisable to have a minimum of two interviewers facilitating a single interview at a time so that the second interviewer can catch what is missed by the first. In both cases, a broad interview protocol should guide the questions to be asked. Probing questions emanate from the responses of the participants.

Family Structure

Research shows that many Black families in South Africa are either single-parent or even child-headed households. Much of this is reported to be attributable to the migrant labour system entrenched into society under apartheid where males literally left their homes in pursuit of jobs in the metropolis. It is similar in the United States where, instead of leaving for work, Black men are the targets of gun violence and incarceration, leaving many homes without the male head. The impact of family structure on the pursuance of professional certification and the barriers it poses to Black individuals and their family's success is rarely considered within accounting. To aid in understanding this context, the following excerpt from Musundwa's (2022) dissertation is shared:[4]

---

[3]The Certificate in the Theory of Accounting is completed concurrently with the postgraduate accounting qualification. To qualify to sit for the South African Institute of Chartered Accountants (SAICA's) first professional assessment, graduates must possess this certificate.

[4]Musundwa collected data on the lived experiences of 22 Black aspirant CAs in South Africa. The aspirants' experiences were captured from commencement of their undergraduate qualifications to the attainment of the CA designation.

> I want to say, I've known that my dad's never going to do anything to change our financial situation at home. And I'm sort of the next person after my mom, I've got two younger brothers who are five and seven years younger than me. And in CTA [post graduate year] specifically that was probably my biggest source of anxiety to know that yes all of us are struggling, and yes all of us are sort of accepting that failure looks like the only option. But I actually can't do that. Because we will literally starve at home if I do it [fail]. My mom worked a government job and gets a fairly good income I guess compared to the rest of South Africa. But our financial situation for various reasons just was not very favourable. And I knew that if I don't focus on the fact that I have to pass and it's not an option to fail. We were going to be in trouble the next year. (CA4, 2022)

The respondent essentially highlights that she is lined up as the next breadwinner at home, and the expectation is that she will contribute to alleviating the financial pressure on the household. The conditions under which certification was achieved serve to broaden the researcher's understanding of prevalent systemic challenges.

Household Income

The impact of finances on private households when one family member decides to pursue an accounting qualification can never be overestimated. Families invest heavily in their family member not only financially but also in time and resources in the hope that it will eventually yield financially for the household. It is not a solo pursuit. The following quote provides an example of the opportunity costs when one family member pursues an accounting qualification:

> within the culture here most families amongst the Blacks, they will give, they will do everything possible to get their kids up to the degree level. But to persuade the parents that they [Black students] must stay in the educational system for another year, they don't understand that because now it's payback time, they're expected to go and work and start paying back. (ND, 2002)

The students themselves are also conscious of the pressure the family is under. It weighs so heavily that it contends with the focus they should rather be directing to their studies, resulting in these students earning the status of "poor performers." A respondent shares:

> And then halfway through [the qualification] it was bad. It was really bad. They trying to chase me out of the residence [university accommodation] because I needed to pay 20% or 50% back then.

> And now they're telling me I must go to fees office and sign an acknowledgement of debt. The security guard is refusing me access to my room. And then this other guy comes the next day is like, what's going on? I'm like, No, I'm supposed to sign an acknowledgement of debt. So, the guy takes me to his desk. And then he gives me an acknowledgement of debt [form]. And he says, Look, your mother has to pay R3500 a month. Do you think she's able to do that? At the time? I think she was earning R2000 a month? And then I was like, Yeah, she's going to pay. But the reality is how is my mother going to payR3500 when she's earning R2000. And she has to share that R2000 with my sisters and myself. (CA13, 2022)

What is essentially understood from the respondent's experience is that his fight to remain on campus and pursue his qualification emanates from a far larger systemic issue that renders the majority of Black South Africans poor. Without the context of his mother's income and the strain on the family, the student may have been perceived as a financial delinquent and expelled from the institution for something for which he was not responsible. The recruitment of respondents based on household income can therefore enhance the understanding of how barriers to access in the profession manifest in relation to disposal income and varying households.

The three subclassifications considered thus far do not by any means constitute a comprehensive list. Other constructs that can be considered include higher education institutions attended (Historically Disadvantaged Institutions vs historically white universities) as sociology research shows that this impacts employment post-qualification (Haltia et al., 2023), firms where accounting articles (also known as training) are completed and first-generation graduates.[5] The researcher should dedicate time to carefully explore communities that operate on the periphery of the accounting profession to identify a relevant set of constructs that can be used to demarcate their areas of interest.

Conducting the Interview

How the interviews are conducted matters for purposes of extracting "thick, rich data" from participants from marginalised groups. The researcher should commence the interview by establishing credibility and trust with the respondent by being transparent about the purpose of the study and the researcher's background and motivation. Examples that may be included are that the researchers themselves come from the marginalised group that is the subject of the study, that they are part of a group advocating for a cause with which the marginalised group is associated or even that they teach in a school or university where the academic performance of

[5]Historically Disadvantaged Institutions (HDIs) in South Africa are akin to Historically Black Colleges and Universities (HBCUs) in the United States.

marginalised groups is constantly questioned. Establishing a common motivation and trust with the recruited respondent is founded on whatever is communicated through both the recruitment and credibility stages of the research.

The researcher, now interviewer, should ideally follow an open-ended questioning strategy. Research shows that unstructured interviews can lead into unexpected areas of interest based on the participants' responses (Adams, 2015) as this organically enhances the richness of the data collected. The knowledge of what is essential to discuss lies with the respondent, and the platform for them to transfer this knowledge should therefore be provided. The interviewer may probe; however, this should be done without interjecting, judgement or even badgering the respondent. Active listening techniques should be engaged to ensure the interviewer is relaying empathy to the participants. Field notes comprising important points raised by the respondent and even their emotions which are visibly obvious during the interview should be documented.

Pre-COVID interviews were conducted in person, but lockdowns necessitated remote interviews. There are practical considerations that the researcher will need to bear in mind to create an environment supportive of a successful interview. Good quality connectivity may be taken for granted in first-world countries, but developing countries lack the structural infrastructure that makes connectivity possible. In addition, unaffordable costs associated with acquiring devices and data can make a good interview impossible. These critical factors pose significant threats to gaining access to respondents from the marginalised groups to be interviewed and thus limit access to new knowledge. If South Africa is considered as a case study, the hundred-year-old electrical infrastructure of the country is currently failing and resulting in timed rolling blackouts. The researcher and respondents may therefore struggle to find a common time when they would both have electricity and can be online simultaneously, assuming they are both in the country. While some may be of the opinion that researchers must revert to "being physically in the field" to conduct interviews, this automatically narrows the research that can be conducted as access poses a threat. We therefore suggest that online interviews be pursued as a means to gain access to marginalised groups and thus increase knowledge in the field.

Data Analysis

The principles generally applied to qualitative data analysis would apply to data collected using Oral History. The emphasis in this chapter is to ensure that the interviewer retains the multifaceted perspectives of the respondents interviewed rather than to attempt to reduce them to a single narrowed one. When 25 participants are interviewed, the perspectives should be treated as uniquely different. There should be no desire to be reductionist in their interpretations. To neutralise conflict within perspectives, researchers must report them as conflicting and analyse them further to understand the context from which the narratives are drawn. The value of the data collected lies in "why" the two participants are experiencing the same phenomenon differently. This can be achieved by directly quoting the participants verbatim when presenting the data. Modern tools like NVivo™ coding have made the process of analysing codes more efficient. In doing so, the authentic lived experiences of the marginalised respondents are preserved. The voices are also strong enough to then counter the dominant narratives directed at them that infiltrate the literature to date.

Every step in actioning the method up to this point (i.e. recruitment, establishment of credibility and trust, spending time with the respondent through an engaged interview) will contribute to an effective analysis process. With social justice at the core, it is the respondent's views and perspectives that must prevail. The researcher may begin with a process of elucidating statements made by respondents that provide insight to the research objectives of the project at hand. Themes can be identified and verified through the use of multiple authors or through Artificial Intelligence such ATLAS.ti™. While electronic data analysis tools have presented a level of efficacy, authors should take care to critically assess their outputs. Where significant thematic areas have been omitted, manual intervention remains a possibility.

The researcher must make note of instances where the respondent communicates what they were feeling. Emotions provide added context by allowing the researcher to understand the participant's full experience at the time that they encountered an event. For instance, a participant communicating their frustrations about a particular event means little if only words are considered; however, the underlying emotional frustration helps one understand its severity and how it contributed to the experience. At times, the emotions are communicated overtly; in other cases, the emotions are demonstrated physically during the interview. The researcher would have made notes of these in their field notes, as discussed under conducting the interview, and they can now be incorporated into the data analysis.

Complexities of Researcher Positionality and How to Mitigate Against Possible Bias

The study of people's lived experiences, namely phenomenology, places emphasis on giving prominence to the multivariant nature of lived realities rather than striving for a neutral perspective. Power dynamics between the researcher and their subjects, however, influence how the experiences are captured and ultimately reported. In earlier research, Kim (2008) identified three nodes of power play that call on the researcher's sensitivity when engaging in research of this nature. These three concerns are discussed below premised on race in South African accounting.

(1) The authenticity of the research if cultural identity is used as a base for assuming academic authority

    The accounting profession has been criticised for its domination by whiteness and white privilege which contributes to marginalisation of anyone who does not fall under this umbrella (Ghio et al., 2023). Research trends show that even though contemporary research claims that matters of diversity, equity, inclusion and belonging are significant, the core focus remains on white accountants, and consequently, research is operationalised through a white lens (Ufodike et al., 2022).

Suggestions for overcoming threats of academic authority assumed through cultural domination can include the overt disclosure by the researcher of their privileged position. The researchers can also share the intent of the research and the recruitment strategy based on marginalisation factors. They can also ensure protection of respondents' identities to mitigate this potential bias. The overriding objective should be elevating the narratives that counter the existing perception that persons from marginalised groups are inferior.

(2) The asymmetrical relationship between the researcher and their participants

Research dictates that there will be an asymmetrical relationship between a researcher and their subjects regardless of whether the researcher is a PhD student or an experienced researcher collecting data for a larger project. The issue with collecting data in studies that relate to injustice is that the subject will come from a "disenfranchised" perspective while the researcher presents from a position of "privilege" (Annisette & Prasad, 2017).

The subjects' positionality in society makes their recruitment to such studies difficult from the outset as they face threats of further marginalisation, discrimination and even oppression within their academic or even professional environments. Considering these threats, most subjects choose not to participate, which leaves the researcher with a marginal few to work with, resulting in findings that fail to broaden existing limited insights. Researchers can mitigate such risks in recruitment through adopting strategies such as purposive, instead of random, sampling where respondents are specifically targeted. A great advantage of this strategy is that only the initial participants need to be recruited. Thereafter, the researcher can fully rely on the identified subjects' networks, which provides a safety net for further potentially interested subjects. A disadvantage is that the pool of participants would contribute to limited inherent insight. Since the subjects come from the same networks, those of differing circumstances would be excluded from the study.[6]

Protection of the marginalised must remain a priority. The standard manner of achieving this is the requirement for ethical clearances by Institutional Ethics Boards including protection in the form of anonymity, confidentiality, the option of pulling of out of the process if they feel violated and, in some cases, psychological support. Interviewers must follow these protocols and empathetically engage their subjects in order to gain trust (Wertz, 2005).

(3) The inadvertent absolving of the researcher from acting against identified injustices encountered by participants

This dimension of research authenticity speaks to an element of ethics applicable to the researcher. Beyond the formalised ethics clearances, the

[6]In Musundwa's PhD, for example, the closed network of referrals resulted in a concentration of female participants. In future studies therefore, the researcher may consider deliberately recruiting males for a comparative perspective.

research has practical implications that can be used within everyday teaching and learning practices, recruitment practices by employers and funding vehicles, among others. There is a moral responsibility to honour the histories shared by the participants by taking action based off of that acquired knowledge.

Within teaching and learning for example, movements towards inclusive teaching and learning practices can be implemented. Accounting standards, for example, are set from the perspective of first-world countries with formal economies and trade exchange platforms; however, their adoption is enforced worldwide even where such economies do not exist. Researchers can therefore promote critical class discussions on how unrecognised economies prevalent in Africa can and should account for their transactions. Democratic citizenship education can be used to promote experiential learning where students from different backgrounds are grouped together to relay their experiences of accounting for finances in their households. Black tax which affects many marginalised communities can be incorporated into curriculum as a means of (i) acknowledging the overbearing presence of persons affected by this tax in society and (ii) teaching students to advocate for equitable tax reforms in their respective jurisdictions.[7] Bearing in mind the process undertaken to acquire knowledge, it is essentially inhumane for researchers to sit on the knowledge acquired through social justice without acting on it. Part of the process is thus to invite participants to submit suggestions on how the injustices can be countered.[8]

Conclusion

The aim of the chapter was to provide guidance to researchers employing Oral History as a method within social justice studies in accounting. Theories not widely used such as Ubuntu have been demonstrated as suitable alternatives to disrupting the conventional dominant narratives that seek to problematise marginalised professionals. With previous studies as a backdrop, the authors have suggested avenues for further exploration simply through dissecting what is already known of oppression using the major social constructs of class, race, gender and religion. A myriad of suggestions for recruitment strategies, conducting interviews and analysing data specifically within these complex contexts have been provided. Critical research by nature is complex, and as such, careful consideration and sensitivity will have to be applied in across all the ethical

[7]Black tax in South Africa can be described as a sense of obligation to support members of an extended family or kinship circle financially, alongside the endeavour to establish financial stability (Mangoma & Wilson-Prangley, 2019), whereas in the United States, it is understood to be the extra weight imposed on African Americans, requiring them to exert double the effort to demonstrate their value (Strand & Mirkay, 2019).

[8]The suggestions made within this section incorporate those rendered by participants. The invitation was put forward in all research conducted.

matters engaged. We trust that this chapter has also served as an invitation to those researchers who have not yet considered employing the method.

References

Adams, W. C. (2015). Conducting semi-structured interviews. In K. N. J. Wholey & H. Hatry (Eds.), *Handbook of practical program evaluation* (4th ed., pp. 492–505). John Wiley and Sons Incorporated.

Annisette, M. (2017). Discourse of the professions: The making, normalizing and taming of Ontario's "foreign-trained accountant". *Accounting, Organizations and Society*, *60*, 37–61. https://doi.org/10.1016/j.aos.2017.06.006

Annisette, M., & Prasad, A. (2017). Critical accounting research in hyper-racial times. *Critical Perspectives on Accounting*, *43*, 5–19. https://doi.org/10.1016/j.cpa.2016.06.002

Duff, A., & Ferguson, J. (2012). Disability and the professional accountant: Insights from oral histories. *Accounting, Auditing & Accountability Journal*, *25*(1), 71–101. https://doi.org/10.1108/09513571211191752

Gallo, M. A. (2020). *Bantu education, and its living educational and socioeconomic legacy in apartheid and post-apartheid South Africa*. https://fordham.bepress.com/international_senior

Ghio, A., McGuigan, N., Stewart, O. J., Tharapos, M., & Wood, L. I. (2023). Diversity, equity, and social justice in accounting education. *Issues in Accounting Education*, *38*(1), 1–5. https://doi.org/10.2308/ISSUES-2022-089

Gordon, L. (2020). *Freedom, justice, and decolonization*. Routledge.

Haltia, N., Isopahkala-bouret, U., & Mutanen, H. (2023). Getting a head start: Capital inheritance and the labour market entry of finnish business graduates. *British Journal of Sociology of Education*, *44*(4), 669–686.

Hammond, T. A. (2017). Oral history. In K. H. Zahirul Hoque, L. D. Parker, & M. A. Covaleski (Eds.), *The routledge companion to qualitative accounting research methods* (1st ed., pp. 200–214). Taylor & Francis.

Hammond, T., & Sikka, P. (1996). Radicalizing accounting history: The potential of oral history. *Accounting, Auditing & Accountability Journal*, *9*(3), 79–97.

Haynes, K. (2010). Other lives in accounting: Critical reflections on oral history methodology in action. *Critical Perspectives on Accounting*, *21*(3), 221–231. https://doi.org/10.1016/j.cpa.2009.11.002

James, K., & Otsuka, S. (2009). Racial biases in recruitment by accounting firms: The case of international Chinese applicants in Australia. *Critical Perspectives on Accounting*, *20*(4), 469–491. https://doi.org/10.1016/j.cpa.2008.02.005

Kim, S. N. (2004a). Imperialism without empire: Silence in contemporary accounting research on race/ethnicity. *Critical Perspectives on Accounting*, *15*(1), 95–133. https://doi.org/10.1016/S1045-2354(03)00004-2

Kim, S. N. (2004b). Racialized gendering of the accountancy profession: Toward an understanding of Chinese women's experiences in accountancy in New Zealand. *Critical Perspectives on Accounting*, *15*(3), 400–427. https://doi.org/10.1016/S1045-2354(02)00208-3

Kim, S. N. (2008). Whose voice is it anyway? Rethinking the oral history method in accounting research on race, ethnicity and gender. *Critical Perspectives on Accounting*, *19*(8), 1346–1369. https://doi.org/10.1016/j.cpa.2007.03.009

Kyriacou, O. (2009). On trying to do Oral History in accounting research. *Accountancy Business and Public Interest.*, *8*(2), 44–64.

Lehman, C. R. (2019). Reflecting on now more than ever: Feminism in accounting. *Critical Perspectives on Accounting*, *65*, 102080. https://doi.org/10.1016/j.cpa.2019.04.001

Lewis, A. (2016). A critical race theory discussion of neutrality and colorblindness in accounting. *Advances in Public Interest Accounting*, *19*, 113–134. https://doi.org/10.1108/S1041-706020160000019005

Mangoma, A., & Wilson-Prangley, A. (2019). Black tax: Understanding the financial transfers of the emerging black middle class. *Development Southern Africa*, *36*(4), 443–460.

Moses, O., & Hopper, T. (2022). Accounting articles on developing countries in ranked english language journals: A meta-review. *Accounting, Auditing & Accountability Journal*, *35*(4), 1035–1060.

Musundwa, S. (2022). *Developing a framework to address the underrepresentation of Black citizens in the chartered accountancy profession: Case of South Africa*. University of South Africa.

Musundwa, S. (2024). Towards inclusive teaching and learning practices: A guideline for commerce academics. In E. Loots & J. Oberholster (Eds.), *Rethinking commerce education in South Africa: The case for change to develop future-fit business leaders* (pp. 95–110). AOSIS Books. https://doi.org/10.4102/aosis.2024.bk454.07

Ngubane, N. I., & Makua, M. (2021). Intersection of ubuntu pedagogy and social justice: Transforming south african higher education. *Transformation in Higher Education*, *6*, 1–8. https://doi.org/10.4102/the.v6i0.113

Strand, P. J., & Mirkay, N. A. (2019). Racialized tax inequity: Wealth, racism, and the US system of taxation. *Northwestern Journal of Law and Social Policy*, *15*, 265.

Ufodike, A., Igbe, I., Ogharanduku, B. E., & Akinyemi, T. E. (2022). The sociology of exclusion: A knowledge synthesis of anti-black racism in accounting research. *SSRN Electronic Journal*, 1–47. https://doi.org/10.2139/ssrn.4006758

van Rooyen, J. (2022). *Unshackled*. Bookstorm PTY Limited.

Wertz, F. J. (2005). Phenomenological research methods for counseling psychology. *Journal of Counseling Psychology*, *52*(2), 167–177. https://doi.org/10.1037/0022-0167.52.2.167

Yow, V. R. (2005). *Recording oral history: A guide for the humanities and social sciences*. AltaMira Press.

Chapter 14

Decolonizing the Accounting Curriculum

Sedzani Musundwa[a], *Joanne Sopt*[b], *Nadra Pencle*[c] *and Jean Wells*[d]

[a]University of South Africa, South Africa
[b]San Francisco State University, USA
[c]Ball State University, USA
[d]Howard University, USA

Introduction

Decolonization is being discussed within certain business schools. There have been various webinars held over recent years seeking to explore the nature of decolonization and its intersection with the curriculum.[1] Additionally, an article was recently published by the Association to Advance Collegiate Schools of Business (AACSB) to acknowledge and advocate for decolonization within business schools (Everett, 2023). While this position is not a formal statement from the AACSB, it does indicate an appetite to engage with this issue. These conversations are being carried out concurrently with calls by various journals for submissions interrogating diversity, equity, inclusion, and belonging issues centering the topic of race (Ghio et al., 2023). The common driver within the space of education appears to be the desire to uncenter white, Western knowledge and thus decolonize. The difficulty however has been in identifying appropriate alternative paths forward that will be inclusive of all currently marginalized perspectives.

We begin with a reflection on definitions of colonization and decolonization within the context of universities. The heart of this chapter then centers on decolonization within the accounting curriculum as an instrument for change. This chapter concludes by offering some practical examples to close this gap as a springboard for the further explorations by accounting academics.

[1]Hosted through the Alternative Accounting Research Network (https://www.alternativeaccounting.org/), the EAA, ETHOS: The Centre for Responsible Enterprise, among others.

Voices of Change, 189–201

doi:10.1108/978-1-83753-030-420251033

Foundational Questions

What Is Colonization and Decolonization? And What Is the Role of Universities?

In the wake of social protests following the death of George Floyd in 2020, a renewed interest around race and decolonization of the curriculum in business schools has been noted. However, there has been a certain level of discomfort with the term decolonization among faculty including accounting academics. Some fail to see the impact colonization continues to have on modern society and question the relevance of decolonization today. Others may be uncomfortable to discuss its intersection with race. Similar trends are noted in Annisette and Prasad's work which reflected on the lack of articles on race in accounting journals due to the belief that we live in a postrace world. This ideology of postraciality is partly a function of the neoliberal ideology which casts blame on the individual for shortcomings rather than the institutions that contribute to them (Annisette & Prasad, 2017). While it has been suggested that the project might have a broader reach if another term was used, this chapter recognizes the importance of engaging with colonialism and race. We see a risk labeling an initiative as "decolonization" when it does not substantially deliver on that promise.

According to Kessi et al. (2020), "colonialism and coloniality can be defined teleologically: the subjugation and subjection of people, societies, and experiences for the purposes of accumulating knowledge, wealth, and power that serve, directly or indirectly, white Western hegemony" (pp. 271–272). The production of knowledge has a role to play with the languages that are chosen and deployed in modern science and our educational systems (Clapham, 2020). A choice exists regarding what knowledge is placed on a pedestal; systems are subsequently created to ensure that it remains so. Within the context of colonization, that choice has resulted in the domination of knowledge from the "white, the Western and Eurocentric, and the male" (Everett, 2023). If how we understand the world and its problems is framed according to that viewpoint, there will be little room for critical thought. The power structures will remain to benefit those who have created those understandings. It is also supported by a continual process that encompasses many overlapping attempts that are meant to support the overall system in place (Roberts, 1990). For example, this can be seen with the sources of knowledge that are allowed and their accompanying research methodologies (Banerjee, 2022). Accounting, which is predominately viewed as a neutral science, contributes by offering "hard evidence" to support a neoliberal project which views the marketplace as an equal-playing field and a determinant of success while avoiding conversations about systemic racism.

Colonialism has been at play for centuries, yet we have recently seen a movement toward political and intellectual decolonization beginning around the 1950s and 1960s (Clapham, 2020). A variety of understandings exist around the term decolonization, but it can traditionally be recognized as the fall of colonized nations as "vassals" of Empire and their subsequent rise as independent nation-states, which has occurred in phases from the mid-1940s to the late 1970s

(Kennedy, 2016). While there are specific historical moments when a transfer of power did take place between the colonizer and the colonized, Jansen and Osterhammel (2017) highlight that decolonization is a process which is ongoing into the present day in the form of delegitimizing subjugation by the powerful elite that are viewed "by a broad majority of the population as alien occupants" (p. 13). One way to support this process is to create legitimate cracks in dominant Western knowledge paradigms to allow for additional voices.

Universities have a role to play due to their part in producing and disseminating knowledge. Several articles have highlighted key moments in the process of decolonization of universities such as the #RhodesMustFall movement in South Africa and Georgetown University in the United States (Chigudu, 2020; Kessi et al., 2020). However, the main thrust is happening within research communities and classrooms to decolonize thinking, involving "unlearning and dismantling unjust practices, assumptions, and institutions – as well as persistent positive action to create and build alternative spaces and ways of knowing" (Kessi et al., 2020, p. 271). In other words, the goal of epistemic decolonization is to situate learning beyond Euro-American theory and challenge what is considered to be scientific knowledge. In order to begin that process, questions such as who is generating the knowledge, from where, and for what purpose are needed (Okech, 2020). This struggle has already begun in the fields of business and organizational studies particularly among critical and qualitative researchers (Banerjee, 2022; Sauerbronn et al., 2021).

It is important to recognize that decolonization is context specific with each site engaging with colonization differently. From the perspective of those engaging in African studies in Africa, part of the struggle is to "decolonize the mind" by situating African scholarship at the center of the dialogue and recognizing the legitimacy of African humanity apart from the West (Creary, 2012; Wa Thiong'o, 1992). It is important to recognize that the elites that took over power once the colonizers left was not in and of itself decolonization as noted by Fanon (1961) since the structures of colonialism continued with them. Neocolonialism is evident with the practices of the West via organizations like the United Nations using soft power to influence former colonies (Sauerbronn et al., 2021; Watts, 2009). Tuck and Yang (2021) also warn about the risk of decolonization becoming a metaphor if the repatriation of disposed Indigenous land does not get addressed.

Engaging with decolonization from the West is also complicated due to the extent to which it can even be called such. Sauerbronn et al. (2021) highlight the debate, for example, between postcolonial critical theory which largely resulted from authors from the Global South residing in the United States and the United Kingdom and decolonial epistemology movement from those residing in Latin America. To put it bluntly, "according to Walsh (2007, p. 235), we need to understand Latin America (or any other context) without reading Foucault, Bourdieu, Deleuze, or Lacan, for instance" (Sauerbronn et al., 2021, p. 9). What this would mean is once again re-centering where knowledge originates, honoring what it might look like, and using caution in labeling an action as decolonization. The authors argue that "the decolonial shift is a project of de-linking while post-colonial criticism and theory is a project of scholarly transformation within the academy" (Mignolo, 2007, p. 452 as cited in Sauerbronn et al., 2021, p. 9).

While several studies exist on decolonization from the perspective of African studies (Auma et al., 2020; Kessi et al., 2020; Okech, 2020), specific movements such as #RhodesMustFall (Chigudu, 2020), humanitarian and development work (Marchais et al., 2020), and forestry (Sungusia et al., 2020), there has been less of an emphasis on business schools. However, this is needed due to the power that business schools possess in attracting students to the Western model and management techniques taught in schools that have been spreading epistemic coloniality throughout the world to maintain Western dominance (Banerjee, 2022; Jammulamadaka et al., 2021).

What Is the Curriculum?

We specifically locate the discussion within the decolonization of the curriculum since that is the instrument adopted to transfer knowledge within a formal educational environment. Young (2014) describes curriculum more aptly as specialized apparatus used to achieve precise learning outcomes. This apparatus is operationalized through an assortment of learning tools such as "study plans, syllabi, and modules." Although designed within higher education institutions and their frameworks, students form the core of the curriculum as they are the ultimate beneficiaries and custodians of the learning process.

Where the institution consciously situates itself as an extension of all its students' everyday lived realities, the curriculum can be positioned to provide an opportunity to expand students' knowledge beyond the limitations of their social boundaries (Reiss & White, 2014). It can be adopted as a platform for the universalization of essential skills and knowledge (Tedesco et al., 2014) through equalizing and expanding on the knowledge that students bring into the environment from their varying backgrounds. In doing so, the curriculum has the potential to facilitate equality and social justice beyond the classroom as the students become an extension of the societies from which they come and therefore form the vessels for iterative transfer of knowledge between society (communities) and higher education institutions. Tedesco et al. (2014) and Young (2014) in their independent writings posit that the common contemporary objective of a quality education should be in this direction of social justice:

> Instead of being viewed simply as a collection of study plans, syllabi, and teaching subjects, the curriculum becomes the outcome of a process reflecting a political and societal agreement about the what, why, and how of education for the desired society of the future. (Tedesco et al., 2014, p. 528)

The connection to society as outlined in this quote suggests that curriculum development is underpinned by a social morality, and it becomes difficult to develop without the consciousness of its effects. Carnegie et al. (2021) argue that accounting is more than just a technical practice and in fact has a role to play in building a moral society. A moral education is one where knowledge acquired promotes behaviors that lead to peace and social justice, whereas the absence of it suggests the promotion of the opposite contributing to the degeneration of society (Obiagu, 2023). It is within this frame that Obiagu argues that a moral education can make a significant contribution in alleviating many of Africa's and the world's social ills. This emphasis on the deliberate shift in education toward social justice speaks directly to the notion of Ubuntu which recognizes the connectedness of all people and their interdependence on each other in building a coherent society (Ngubane & Makua, 2021). Such theories on collectiveness have however been underutilized in accounting education as Western ideologies encouraging individualism have been elevated, justified through narratives factuality and neutrality. A shift toward social consciousness thus provides an opportunity for curriculum to be adapted to promote "moving accounting's capabilities and inherent influence to create a better world consistent with a more balanced perspective on planet, people and profit" (Carnegie et al., 2021).

The complexity of delivering a curriculum that meets these ideals rests with the influence of the curriculum designer. We suggest that academics approach curriculum development subjectively and thus project their consciousness about themselves into the process. This chimes well with Wimpenny et al.'s (2022) position that curriculum practices are in fact centered at the intersection of the academics' self-consciousness, their subjective approach to curriculum, and their positionality as providers of global education and thus have a significant influence on the lens through which students receive knowledge. Conversely, we proffer the consciousness of accounting academics is instead submerged beneath the whitened and Western curriculum demands of the profession enabled through accreditation processes imposed on business schools by professional accountancy bodies (PAOs) (Venter & de Villiers, 2013). By accrediting programs, knowledge content is standardized, and racialized to white normativity, therefore what is deemed appropriate and authentic accounting knowledge is consequently estranged from the lived realities of students of color expected to embrace said knowledge. Additionally, the reality for many accounting academics is that they are not trained in pedagogical practices, including curriculum development, and thus rely on the guidance of PAOs to know what to teach (Lubbe, 2020). The problem in this approach of academics funneling information from the PAOs is it removes students from the center of learning, particularly students of color where there is an opportunity for a plurality of perspectives to coexist. It also reduces the environment to one of pure knowledge transfer. As Paulo Freire reflects:

> It is not our role to speak to the people about our own view of the world, nor to attempt to impose that view on them, but rather to dialogue with the people about their view and ours. We must realize that their view of the world, manifested variously in their action, reflects their situation in the world. (Freire, 1970, p. 96)

In environments where students are not engaged on their perspectives, rote learning together with simple mastery and narrowed application are then prioritized (Wong et al., 2021). Such environments also make it conducive for promoting narrower perspectives which does not bode well for building moral and integrated societies. A danger Mahabeer (2020) clearly sees as a tunneled educational approach that is nothing more than a means of conditioning apathy and ignorance toward global matters in learners. The authors of this chapter therefore argue that academics have a moral obligation to self-reflect on their own racialized positionalities (among many others), personal values, outlooks, and apprehensions as they relate to those adopted by their curriculum practices.

In summary, this chapter recognizes that there is a place for different universities and those implementing curriculums, including those situated in the West, to work in this space by first centering colonialism as an object of study and understanding how it has shaped our contemporary world and secondly allowing the space for alternative ways of thinking about the world. In addition, it is important to engage with the effects of neocolonialism and its intersection with financialization to understand accounting's role which is discussed next.

Decolonization and the Accounting Curriculum

It should now be understood from earlier excerpts in the chapter that decolonization essentially seeks to uncenter the Western filter dominant in the world by promoting the peaceful coexistence of a multiplicity of perspectives (Mahabeer, 2020). It has also thus far been established in this chapter that education and curriculum should serve to expand on the lived reality of students and so if we are to embrace diversity in society, it would be logical to do the same within curriculum practice. To not do so runs the risk of harming Black and Brown students of color who do not believe that their lived experiences belong in accounting because they do not see themselves reflected in programs of study. Decolonizing curriculum has thus been accepted as the means by which universities will redress past inequity and injustice, challenge Western-orientated hegemonies in academia, and interrogate coloniality prevalent in curriculum practices (Wimpenny et al., 2022). The complexity involved in the process is acknowledged, and it is therefore also accepted that decolonizing would happen in increments for many years to come.

However, a problematic consequence of funneling knowledge through PAOs and other first world apparatuses is that it fails to recognize and embed Indigenous knowledge. Accounting, as with other disciplines, risks viewing Indigenous knowledge as "weak and untrustworthy" (Smith, 1999), thus justifying its exclusion from mainstream curriculum and international qualifications. Decolonizing the curriculum will therefore entail disrupting what has been naturalized as the best means of knowledge generation to make room for a new way of knowledge building (Wimpenny et al., 2022), while restoring Indigenous knowledge and dignity to the Indigenous people (Mahabeer, 2020).

We would like to acknowledge that steps have been taken toward problematizing Western dominance of accounting education via oppressive ideologies by using the work of Paulo Freire, a renowned Brazilian educator and philosopher (Chabrak & Craig, 2013; Thomson & Bebbington, 2004). Much of this work focuses on sustainability courses in accounting and the work involved to infuse more critical thinking in the classroom by applying the liberating pedagogies from Freire by partnering with students (Bebbington et al., 2007; Wong et al., 2021). While problems of colonization are not the main focus of these classroom interviews, Thomson and Bebbington (2005) note that:

> one cannot expect 'positive' results from an educational or political action programme which fails to respect the particular view of the world held by the people with whom one wishes to interact. Such a programme constitutes a similar process of cultural invasion or colonization. (p. 528)

Boyce (2002) also recognizes the need to bring race into the classroom if one is committed to taking a social justice perspective. It is also important to focus on the lived experiences of students (Boyce & Greer, 2013), which could be a good starting point if teaching an ethnically and racially diverse set of students.

Non-Western viewpoints, using Freire as inspiration, have been explored in a few studies. For example, Gallhofer et al. (1999) questioned the retention of Maori accounting students in New Zealand and posed interesting questions around how an accounting curriculum could reflect Maori values rather than only those imposed by a Western context. Ocampo-Gómez and Ortega-Guerrero (2013) also began to explore how alternative learning approaches similar to Freire in the accounting curriculum could be applied in Mexican universities. Contraffo et al. (2015) analyzed an activist project in a rural town in Peru with the goal of translating sustainability into actionable results. However, the work should not end with Freire. There are other theorists who have been more central to the decolonial epistemology movement in Latin America such as Anibal Quijano, Enrique Dussel, and Walter Mignolo (Sauerbronn et al., 2021).

While accounting educators have been engaging with the oppressive forces in the accounting curriculum, these studies highlight that more work can be done in this area specifically around problematizing colonization and race. In the section that follows, we provide some focused examples that can provide inspiration for those who would like to begin or continue with this work.

Practical Examples

For us, at least, it is vital to view decolonization in the accounting realm as an ongoing process rather than an outcome of that process. Colonization is the product of centuries of colonial dominance, and it is unreasonable, even unrealistic, to anticipate unraveling such deeply rooted systems in a short to intermediate term. Rather, within the curriculum, steps can be taken toward progressive milestones that aid on the journey toward decolonization. Hence, for decolonization to become a reality in accounting, accounting administrators, faculty, and staff will need to identify colonial systems, structures, and relationships and collectively work to challenge those systems (Keele University, 2018). We cannot simply make token, sporadic, marginal, inconsistent, half-hearted attempts. Rather, decolonization of the accounting curriculum requires a paradigm shift. A shift away from racial and cultural denial, Eurocentric primacy, and exclusionary practices to more cultural openness and acceptance and inclusionary systems, policies, and systems. To this end, critical accounting scholars have provided some insights into how we can take steps toward decolonization. We will give a brief synopsis of some of these below.

Recently, Pelzer et al. (2023) proposed the use of case studies as a tool for decolonizing the accounting curriculum. The author team ground their work in Banks' (2014) 4-level, curriculum transformation framework. This hierarchical framework outlines some steps that can be taken toward transforming a curriculum. The authors provide examples at each level in the hierarchy of how accounting can use cases to help in the decolonization process. Such examples range from developing and using cases that only highlight the contribution of various marginalized "heroes" to developing and using cases that address grand social concepts from varied perspectives. The paper challenges faculty and other stakeholders to intentionally develop cases that challenge the existing paradigm while simultaneously providing a more holistic education for students. The suggestions from this paper can be applied to all accounting disciplines as the authors note the lack of diverse representation in cases currently in use within the business school and accounting, more specifically.

Experiential learning is another tool that can be used to facilitate progress toward decolonizing the accounting curriculum. A practical example is how Dr Diane-Laure Arjaliès, PhD, opted to teach her impact assessment class when there was no textbook. Dr Arjaliès shared this experience at a British Accounting and Finance Association 2021 virtual session on decolonization. She recounted efforts to decolonize and indigenize by requiring that her students spend time over the course of the semester with Indigenous conservationists. She subsequently challenged the students to develop a "system of accounting," not based on existing standards, that would value the unique and diverse aspects of the Indigenous conservationists. Students created stories, pictures, narratives, and other accountings. The class presentations were held outside, without PowerPoints and other forms of technology, and attended by members of the Indigenous community.[2] This kind of experiential learning can challenge the dominant valuation systems that privilege financial accounting systems.

The tax curriculum should also be reviewed to start addressing the question that Jerome Culp, law professor, posed "To what extent have our tax laws been

---

[2]Arjaliès, Diane-Laure "Panel Discussion on Decolonising the Accounting and Finance Curriculum, (Annual Conference 2021)" British Accounting and Finance Association, April 2021, video, 26:01, https://www.youtube.com/watch?v=BQ1JeMtXIDs

distorted now and historically by the question of slavery and continuing racism?" (Culp, 1991): Law professor, Dorothy A. Brown, in her book, *The Whiteness of Wealth*, attempts to answer this question by challenging the theory of horizontal equity, which posits that taxpayers in similar circumstances, i.e., income earned, should be taxed the same. Brown debunks the theory by postulating that income and circumstances are not the same by using her two working Black parents, a nurse, and a plumber, each earning $50,000 as an example and comparing them to another married white couple with one working spouse – the husband, an investment banker, making $100,000. Brown points out that while the incomes are the same, the circumstances are not. Both her parents worked and had to find childcare for their children and spend time away from them while the investment banker's wife enjoyed all the luxuries of being a stay-at-home mom including being home to care for their children (Brown, 2022).

Academics can use real-world examples to engage students in a critical dissection of tax law and its administration. The curriculum can include additional context around how laws imposed taxes on the enslaved, who were treated as property, and then how those tax laws became a significant source of revenues for some state governments. Poll taxes were also used to deter Blacks from voting. As a final example, the 10 most audited counties in the United States were inhabited by mostly lower income Blacks in the Deep South in the 21st century. In contrast, the least audited counties were inhabited by a majority of higher income whites (Kiel & Eisinger, 2018).

A common thread throughout this chapter is to also center and involve students in the process of decolonization. Paulo Freire sees this as a matter of creating a "critical education" as outlined in his seminal work *Pedagogy of the Oppressed* in which he charts how this might look from his experiences in education working among the poor in South America. It provides a general framework on how to intervene in oppressed conditions for the purpose of revolutionary action. It is a powerful launching pad of how to frame one's intentions so that the oppressor does not co-opt them. For example, it is not enough to include diverse voices and knowledge in the curriculum; rather, the focus of pedagogy needs to be on structural imbalances caused by the racialization process which colonization produces. This is accomplished through partnership with students using a libertarian educational approach as opposed to an oppressive one.[3] By posing the problems of colonization, decolonization, and race to students, a dynamic process can occur with surprising moments of consciousness.

[3]He advocated for a combination of praxis and reflection which is needed so that truthful words can be communicated. Dialogue is crucial, but it is not simply idle chatter or individuals trying to impose their ideas on each other. Instead, its focus is on naming the world and transforming it with both the teacher-students and student-teachers. It requires acts of creativity with love, humility, faith, trust, hope, critical thinking, and communion to be present. Each of these elements requires its own discussion in future studies, but this brief summary provides an idea what this work can look like and how it can be conducted (Freire, 2005).

While previous studies and definitions of decolonization are a starting point, localized interventions are needed to make the concepts resonate with the lived experiences of those it is trying to impact. For example, the racial composition of the classroom and its location will have an impact on the type of curricular redesign one can develop. The authors of this chapter encourage context-specific actions by collaborating with similarly-minded individuals and using as inspiration the previously cited works. Collaborating in a cross-disciplinary manner can also prove important for those who have been trained in pedagogical practices. Accounting academics can draw insights from fellow academics in education but also from ethnic studies, political science, and other social sciences for exciting and dynamic paths forwards.

Conclusion

Decolonization is a definite possibility within the accounting profession. Through solidifying the definitions of colonization and decolonization and contextualizing them within accounting, the authors were able to identify opportunities for disrupting the existing narratives around Western domination. The influence of jurisdiction and its unique relationship with colonial histories revealed that the concept of decolonizing would require agility from all actors in the process. The existing hierarchical relationship between lecturer and student would need to be dismantled to accommodate a more dialogical approach that promotes the coexistence of multiple perspectives, in this way decolonizing. The practical examples of decolonizing demonstrated across different subjects not only reveal what can be done but place a spotlight on what has been and can be expanded and continued.

References

Annisette, M., & Prasad, A. (2017). Critical accounting research in hyper-racial times. *Critical Perspectives on Accounting*, *43*, 5–19.

Auma, M. M., Otieno, E., & Piesche, P. (2020). 'Reclaiming our time' in African studies: Conversations from the perspective of the Black Studies Movement in Germany. *Critical African Studies*, *12*(3), 330–353.

Banerjee, S. B. (2022). Decolonizing management theory: A critical perspective. *Journal of Management Studies*, *59*(4), 1074–1087.

Banks, J. A. (2014). *An introduction to multicultural education* (5th ed.). Pearson/Allyn and Bacon.

Bebbington, J., Brown, J., Frame, B., & Thomson, I. (2007). Theorizing engagement: The potential of a critical dialogic approach. *Accounting, Auditing & Accountability Journal*, *20*(3), 356–381.

Boyce, G. (2002). Now and then: Revolutions in higher learning. *Critical Perspectives on Accounting*, *13*(5–6), 575–601.

Boyce, G., & Greer, S. (2013). More than imagination: Making social and critical accounting real. *Critical Perspectives on Accounting*, *24*(2), 105–112.

Brown, D. A. (2022). *The whiteness of wealth*. Crown.

Carnegie, G., Parker, L., & Tsahuridu, E. (2021). It's 2020: What is accounting today? *Australian Accounting Review*, *31*(1), 65–73. https://doi.org/10.1111/auar.12325

Chabrak, N., & Craig, R. (2013). Student imaginings, cognitive dissonance and critical thinking. *Critical Perspectives on Accounting*, *24*(2), 91–104.

Chigudu, S. (2020). Rhodes must fall in Oxford: A critical testimony. *Critical African Studies*, *12*(3), 302–312.

Clapham, C. (2020). Decolonising African studies? *The Journal of Modern African Studies*, *58*(1), 137–153.

Contrafatto, M., Thomson, I., & Monk, E. A. (2015). Peru, mountains and los niños: Dialogic action, accounting and sustainable transformation. *Critical Perspectives on Accounting*, *33*, 117–136.

Creary, N. M. (Ed.). (2012). *African intellectuals and decolonization* (Vol. 90). Ohio University Press.

Culp, J. (1991). Toward a Black Legal Scholarship: Race and original understandings. *Duke Law Journal*, *40*(1), 39–67.

Everett, S. (2023, October 19). Decolonizing the business school curriculum. *AACSB*. https://www.aacsb.edu/insights/articles/2023/02/decolonizing-the-business-school-curriculum

Fanon, F. (1961). *The wretched of the earth*. Penguin.

Freire, P. (1970, 2005). *Pedagogy of the oppressed*. The Continuum International Publishing Group.

Gallhofer, S., Haslam, J., Kim, S. N., & Mariu, S. (1999). Attracting and retaining Maori students in accounting: Issues, experiences and ways forward. *Critical Perspectives on Accounting*, *10*(6), 773–807.

Ghio, A., McGuigan, N., Stewart, O. J., Tharapos, M., & Wood, L. I. (2023). Diversity, equity, and social justice in accounting education. *Issues in Accounting Education*, *38*(1), 1–5. https://doi.org/10.2308/ISSUES-2022-089

Jammulamadaka, N., Faria, A., Jack, G., & Ruggunan, S. (2021). Decolonising management and organisational knowledge (MOK): Praxistical theorising for potential worlds. *Organization*, *28*(5), 717–740.

Jansen, J. C., & Osterhammel, J. (2017). *Decolonization: A short history*. Princeton University Press. https://doi.org/10.1515/9781400884889

Keele University. (2018). *Keele manifesto for decolonising the curriculum*. https://www.keele.ac.uk/raceequalitycharter/raceequalitycharter/keeledecolonisingthecurriculumnetwork/keelemanifestofordecolonisingthecurriculum/. Accessed on May 13, 2022 and March 28, 2023.

Kennedy, D. K. (2016). *Decolonization: A very short introduction* (Vol. 472). Oxford University Press.

Kessi, S., Marks, Z., & Ramugondo, E. (2020). Decolonizing African studies. *Critical African Studies*, *12*(3), 271–282.

Kiel, P., & Eisinger, J. (2018). Who's more likely to be audited: A person making $20,000 — or $400,000? *ProPublica*. https://www.propublica.org/article/earned-income-tax-credit-irs-audit-working-poor

Lubbe, I. (2020). Towards a global model of accounting education – A South African case study. *Journal of Accounting in Emerging Economies*, *10*(4), 601–620. https://doi.org/10.1108/JAEE-01-2020-0017

Mahabeer, P. (2020). Decolonising the school curriculum in South Africa: Black women teachers' perspectives. *Third World Thematics: A TWQ Journal.*, *5*(1–2), 97–119. https://doi.org/10.1080/23802014.2020.1762510

Marchais, G., Bazuzi, P., & Amani Lameke, A. (2020). 'The data is gold, and we are the gold-diggers': Whiteness, race and contemporary academic research in eastern DRC. *Critical African Studies*, *12*(3), 372–394.

Mignolo, W. D. (2007). Delinking – The rhetoric of modernity, the logic of coloniality and the grammar of de-coloniality. *Cultural Studies*, *21*(2–3), 449–514.

Ngubane, N. I., & Makua, M. (2021). Intersection of Ubuntu pedagogy and social justice: Transforming South African higher education. *Transformation in Higher Education*, *6*, 1–8. https://doi.org/10.4102/the.v6i0.113

Obiagu, A. N. (2023). Toward a decolonized moral education for social justice in Africa. *Journal of Black Studies*, 1–28. https://doi.org/10.1177/00219347231157739

Ocampo-Gómez, E., & Ortega-Guerrero, J. C. (2013). Expanding the perspective and knowledge of the accounting curriculum and pedagogy in other locations: The case of Mexico. *Critical Perspectives on Accounting*, *24*(2), 145–153.

Okech, A. (2020). African feminist epistemic communities and decoloniality. *Critical African Studies*, *12*(3), 313–329.

Pelzer, J., Booker, D., Pencle, N., & Brown, V. (2023). Making the case for diversity: Exploring the use of case studies for URMs in the accounting curriculum. *Issues in Accounting Education*, *38*(3), 39–63.

Reiss, M. J., & White, J. (2014). In M. J. Reiss & J. White (Eds.), *An aims-based curriculum: The significance of human flourishing for schools* (1st ed.). Institute of Education Press. https://doi.org/10.1080/09585176.2013.875323

Roberts, A. D. (Ed.). (1990). *The colonial moment in Africa: Essays on the movement of minds and materials, 1900-1940*. Cambridge University Press.

Sauerbronn, F. F., Ayres, R. M., da Silva, C. M., & Lourenço, R. L. (2021). Decolonial studies in accounting? Emerging contributions from Latin America. *Critical Perspectives on Accounting*, 102281.

Smith, L. T. (1999). *Decolonizing methodologies: Research and indigenous peoples*. Zed Books.

Sungusia, E., Lund, J. F., & Ngaga, Y. (2020). Decolonizing forestry: Overcoming the symbolic violence of forestry education in Tanzania. *Critical African Studies*, *12*(3), 354–371.

Tedesco, J. C., Opertti, R., & Amadio, M. (2014). The curriculum debate: Why it is important today. *Prospects*, *44*(4), 527–546. https://doi.org/10.1007/s11125-014-9326-x

Thomson, I., & Bebbington, J. (2004). It doesn't matter what you teach? *Critical Perspectives on Accounting*, *15*(4–5), 609–628.

Thomson, I., & Bebbington, J. (2005). Social and environmental reporting in the UK: A pedagogic evaluation. *Critical Perspectives on Accounting*, *16*(5), 507–533.

Tuck, E., & Yang, K. W. (2021). Decolonization is not a metaphor. *Tabula Rasa*, (38), 61–111.

Venter, E. R., & de Villiers, C. (2013). The accounting profession's influence on academe: South African evidence. *Accounting, Auditing & Accountability Journal*, *26*(8), 1246–1278. https://doi.org/10.1108/AAAJ-06-2012-01027

Wa Thiong'o, N. (1992). *Decolonising the mind: The politics of language in African literature*. East African Publishers.

Walsh, C. (2007). Shifting the geopolitics of critical knowledge: Decolonial thought and cultural studies 'others' in the Andes. *Cultural Studies*, *21*(2–3), 224–239. https://doi.org/10.1080/09502380601162530

Watts, M. (2009). Neocolonialism. In R. Kitchin & N. Thrift (Eds.), *International encyclopedia of human geography* (pp. 360–364). Elsevier.

Wimpenny, K., Beelen, J., Hindrix, K., King, V., & Sjoer, E. (2022). Curriculum internationalization and the 'decolonizing academic'. *Higher Education Research and Development*, *41*(7), 2490–2505. https://doi.org/10.1080/07294360.2021.2014406

Wong, A., George, S., & Tanima, F. A. (2021). Operationalising dialogic accounting education through praxis and social and environmental accounting: Exploring student perspectives. *Accounting Education*, *30*(5), 525–550. https://doi.org/10.1080/09639284.2021.1919531

Young, M. (2014). What is a curriculum and what can it do? *Curriculum Journal*, *25*(1), 7–13. https://doi.org/10.1080/09585176.2014.902526

Chapter 15

Going Beyond Business-as-usual

Lauren Rukasuwan

Butler University, USA

> The classroom remains the most radical space of possibility in the academy. (hooks, 2014, p. 12)

Introduction

Throughout my accounting education, from a Bachelor's to a Doctorate, nowhere was I pushed to look beyond business-as-usual. I was never pushed to interrogate the practices or structures I had come to accept as normal in our "white supremacist, capitalist patriarchy."[1] Therefore, I wasn't able to see the systemic issues arising from the way our economic relations are structured and "the way information in the classroom is slanted to protect the interests of ruling class groups" (hooks, 2012, p. 42). Going into college, I passively accepted the "business isn't personal" perspective that was portrayed in TV and movies and that was being reinforced in my classrooms. A small part of that passivity was me wanting to fit into my new surroundings, but most of it came from my socialization within a western and US-centric paradigm. For the most part, the structuring of our economic system was a given, not to be challenged, questioned, or even named outright. No one talked about how "slavery as an institution pav[ed] the way for advanced capitalist society" (hooks, 2012, p. 40), let alone how continued colonial-imperialism and neoliberal economic policy maintains it. Instead of making these realities clear and discussing the ways that accounting practice has aided in the dehumanization and oppression of entire groups of people for centuries, my accounting education focused on technical application and passing exams.[2]

[1]A term used by bell hooks to describe our current system as these systems of domination are so intertwined that interrogating one without the others would lead to little, if any, change (hooks, 1996).

[2]This is true for slavery and colonization, where enslaved and Indigenous people were reduced to their economic value on balance sheets and annual reports, as well as the holocaust to obscure the human element associated with an attempt to annihilate an entire group of people (Funnel, 1998; Power & Brennan, 2022; Rosenthal, 2018).

Voices of Change, 203–219

doi:10.1108/978-1-83753-030-420251035

On top of this, the white-washed version of US history that was presented to me from the time I can remember led me to believe that racism was characterized by overt acts of bigotry that were a thing of the past.[3] I was taught that the Civil Rights movement rectified past injustices and the goal was to not see color. Legal equality had been won, and therefore, any evidence of inequity was representative of an individuals' failure to work hard enough. Growing up in the south, however, I quickly learned that this was the official party line, but behind closed doors, racist attitudes and behaviors remained strong. I knew something didn't add up, but even then, it was a long time before I was able to fully comprehend how racism is foundational to our current society and plays out in subversive, covert, and systemic ways (Delgado & Stefancic, 2023). In 2020, however, the inequitable economic impacts of a global pandemic and global racial protests made clear to me that business is personal, the personal is political, and an accounting education is not neutral. I was able to see how a few people making ethical decisions in an oppressive system didn't add up to much because the indifference of the majority drowned it out. Therefore, to address inequality and social injustices, we have to take radical approaches at the individual and system level.[4]

In preparing our students for their futures, providing them with the insights that will help them succeed under the current rules of the game is a pragmatic and valid pursuit. However, in teaching them how to play by the rules of the game, we are choosing to be a key agent in the maintenance of a system that is unsustainable and rigged to benefit a small group of, largely, white males. During my Doctorate, I had to stop and ask myself, as a future professor, does this serve my students or society in the long term? In my attempt to answer this question, I began to see the ways accounting curriculum could be transformed in substance and form, to address our gross socioeconomic inequalities and environmental crises. Instead of offering students the perspective that our economic reality exists independently of the work we do as accountants, we can teach them that, "in communicating reality, [we] construct reality" (Hines, 1988, p. 257). Then we can begin working with them to create more humane systems of accountability that position us in what economist Kate Raworth (2017) defines as "a safe and just space for us all." A space bounded by goals of human prosperity and ecological protection, rather than profit growth.

To be clear, the points I make in this chapter are not mine and mine alone. A number of critical accounting scholars have been pushing for this kind of professional reckoning for decades, including a robust critique of neoliberalism, capital, and the critical role accounting plays in social construction (Chiapello, 2017; Dillard & Vinnari, 2019; Hines, 1989a, 1989b; Manetti et al., 2021; Potter, 2005). However, much of this discussion occurs outside of the United States and

[3]Whitewashing is the act of simultaneously denying race while super-imposing white culture. It ignores the role that race plays in structuring the world while positioning whiteness as the default (Howell & Richter-Montpetit, 2019). For example, throughout US history books, European colonizers are presented as "settlers" and civilizing agents, while the Indigenous peoples of America are depicted as villains in need of saving and assimilation (Padgett, 2015).

[4]I define radical in the same vein as Angela Davis. In her book *Women, Culture, and Politics*, she explains that "radical simply means 'grasping things at the root'" (Davis, 1990, p. 14).

within scholarly journals that make the discussion largely inaccessible to the majority of the profession. Additionally, the isolation of this research in just a few journals sends a clear signal of how such endeavors are valued in the broader academy. Thus, the majority of US accounting scholars aren't introduced to this scholarship and conduct research within the traditional economic and finance–based accounting paradigm.[5] To combat this, I hope to introduce these ideas in a more accessible way, allowing a broader group of accounting scholars and practicing professionals to recognize the importance of thinking in systems and shifting from a profit-centered paradigm to a human-centered paradigm, integrating what we know with what we do on a daily basis.

Before I get into this discussion though, I first want to explain what I mean by business-as-usual and how this mindset keeps us stagnant. To offer a way forward, I will introduce education as the practice of freedom and how this pedagogical stance requires us to examine the current structure of the accounting curriculum and how it is delivered. Lastly, I will attempt to offer a few starting places for further discussion about how we can go beyond business-as-usual to transform our current oppressive realities while engaging our students in the process.

Business-as-usual

Business-as-usual, to me, is a process of maintenance informed by the values of late-stage capitalism and neoliberalism where ideas of the market, individual "freedoms," and capital accumulation are prioritized above all else.[6,7] It is the maintenance of an economic system where wealth is accumulated from the exploited labor of the global majority, who is forced to participate in their exploitation by

---

[5]This paradigm also takes the form of a positive science where the goal is simply to describe what is, not what should be. In doing so, accounting research could be understood as impartial and value free. In reality, however, the values of accounting research are merely obscured by economic assumptions about the market and profit growth that are embedded in our theories and models.

[6]neoliberalism is typically defined as "a theory of political economic practices that proposes that human well-being can best be advanced by liberating individual entrepreneurial freedoms and skills within an institutional framework characterized by strong private property rights, free markets, and free trade" (Harvey, 2007, p. 2). The emergence of neoliberal theory and policy made the capitalist system even more cut-throat, where any vulnerable population is exploited for profit. Knowing this led many of the racial justice revolutionaries of the Civil Rights movement to broaden their critique of racial oppression to include a critique of economic oppression.

[7]I place "freedom" in quotations to highlight the ways in which our collective ideas of freedom have been redefined as individual consumer choice and buying power rather than social equity and equal representation. In the United States at least, we largely view freedom as the ability to go into a market and choose what we buy and who we buy it from, even though we have little say in what is produced and how resources are allocated.

threat of poverty or death, and environmental degradation is viewed as a negative externality.[8] The inherent contradiction between the interests of the capitalist class and the working class is the subject of centuries of theory development, debate, and human conflict at the intersection of multiple systems of oppression.[9] This system of labor exploitation isn't in the forefront of most people's minds though. We talk all the time about how much we hate working in overly bureaucratic organizations, living paycheck to paycheck, and having little say in what we do with our time but, this is rarely framed in terms of class relations, or systems. Instead, the average person is too consumed with surviving under the current rules of the game, while also being depoliticized from decades of propaganda (Chomsky, 2002). As one of the world's leading capitalists Charlie Munger, Vice Chair of Berkshire Hathaway, explained it however:

> If you stop to think about it, what makes capitalism work is the fact that if you're an able-bodied young person, if you refuse to work, you suffer a fair amount of agony. And it's because of that agony that this whole economic system works. (Yahoo, 2022)

Even if we make a million-dollar salary, one bad investment, one recession driven lay-off, or one medical incident can lead us to economic ruin. Then, in our culture of hyper-individualism, pulling ourselves out of poverty is placed squarely on our shoulders in a system of cut-throat competition where basic human needs such as water, food, shelter, and healthcare are not a right. The stress of living under this system can then be linked to drug addiction (Bjerg, 2008) as well as severe anxiety and depression that is affecting people at significantly younger ages than ever before (James, 2008). Each of which are then criminalized and pathologized in the Black, Indigenous, and immigrant communities at a disproportionate rate (Purnell, 2022).

A thorough reading of history highlights how intricately social systems of oppression (i.e., racism, sexism, ableism, etc.) are tied to our oppressive economic system. If exploitation of a large working class is needed for infinite profit growth, then social hierarchies like race, gender, or ability define and rationalize who is exploitable and who is expendable through processes of dehumanization. As Fred Hampton, one of the greatest revolutionary minds of the Civil Rights movement,

---

[8]A negative externality from an environmental perspective could be when a corporation is responsible for pollution due to their own actions, but they will not bear that cost on the environment and society and hence not record it in their accounting.

[9]This dynamic and the inherent power imbalance between classes is why every gain made by the labor movement (i.e., the 40-hour work week, child labor laws, and workplace safety regulations) had to be fought for in militant ways and must remain consistently defended. Recently, there has been an increase in states easing child labor laws, including hour limitations and hazardous work environments (Marr & Rainey, 2023). Additionally, while the 40-hour work week has, for the most part, remained unchallenged (even though plenty of jobs require overtime), real wages have declined for decades and the minimum wage hasn't increased since 2009, effectively institutionalizing a poverty wage.

put it, "racism is an excuse used for capitalism, and we know that racism is a byproduct of capitalism" (Hampton, 1969).[10] Understanding this makes it clear why these oppressive social hierarchies have been near impossible to eradicate. Even if racism and misogyny were to miraculously disappear from society tomorrow, millions would still live under inhumane conditions because capital requires it. Exploitation and economic oppression would not disappear; who is exploitable would just be redefined.

Examining the material conditions of capital accumulation over the past century, including our turn to neoliberalism, Piketty (2014) provides empirical evidence, including comparative data across eight countries, regarding what he calls the "inequality regime." Most telling from his findings is that current wealth and income inequalities are as high now as they were leading up to the great depression (Piketty, 2014; Saez & Zucman, 2016). The neoliberal "restoration in class power" served to enrich the top 0.1%, increasing their share of wealth from 12% in 1980 to 20% in 2014, while the bottom 50% has declined by the same percentage with their average pretax income remaining around $16,000 (George, 1999; Piketty et al., 2018; Saez & Zucman, 2016). Quite literally, the gains of the past 40 years were siphoned from the working class to further enrich the capitalist class. Just in the years following the 2020 pandemic, the top 1% captured 63% of the $26 trillion of wealth created (Christensen et al., 2023), while billions have faced the difficult task of choosing between one life sustaining resource or another, water or electricity, food or housing, on a daily basis.

At the intersection of capitalism and race, even more telling is the U-shaped evolution of capital that Saez and Zucman (2016) evidence, depicting a similar pattern of progress and backlash that Critical Race Theory (CRT) scholars highlight in their work tracing the evolution of racism throughout US history.[11] Following every instance of progress toward racial equity, there was an equal, if not greater, backlash (Delgado & Stefancic, 2023).[12] For example, following the Civil Rights movement, the war on drugs and system of mass incarceration was introduced (Alexander, 2011). Within this framing, the rise in neoliberalism can be viewed as economic backlash from the ruling elite as they felt their financial standing being threatened by the economic policies, kicked off by Roosevelt's

---

[10]This fact has led many scholars to describe our current economic system more specifically as "racial capitalism." A way of acknowledging the inherent racialization of historic capitalist development (Melamed, 2015; Ralph & Singhal, 2019; Robinson, 2020).

[11]According to Lewis (2015, p. 2) CRT was "originally conceived in the field of Law and now used in multiple disciplines to examine how race and oppression impact professions, particularly racial ethnic minorities. Essentially a CRT standpoint centralizes race and racism in society."

[12]Alexander (2011) traced these cycles of backlash in her indictment of our current system of mass incarceration. As she outlines, following slavery, Black codes were put in place to restrict Black people from owning property, starting businesses, owning land, and freely moving throughout the country; after the passage of the 14th amendment, the violent system of Jim Crow was established and following the Civil Rights Movement the system of mass incarceration, each serving to reaffirm social control over the Black community.

New Deal after World War II (Harvey, 2007), policies that attempted to build a social safety net and level the playing field for socially marginalized and economically disadvantaged groups. Since the 1970s, this backlash has pushed the neoliberalization of states across the globe, freeing capital from regulation and increasing the threat of poverty by privatizing public services and infrastructure (Harvey, 2007). This ultimately serves to concentrate wealth in fewer and fewer hands, reinscribe power, and create unsustainable social inequalities and ecological degradation.

It's important to keep in mind though that while economic exploitation is a threat to all of us, intersectionality tells us the most structural violence from our current system will always be felt by those that sit at the intersection of multiple compounding oppressions. For example, the environmental effects of capitalist industry are disproportionately felt by the Black and Indigenous communities due to institutional racism such as redlining that has led to 71% of Black Americans living in counties that are in violation of air pollution standards (Thomas, 2022).[13] Systemic racism and various other systems of oppression in hiring, lending, housing, and policing practices all compound on the already cut-throat competition of our economic system to reduce opportunities for survival. This is why our examination of race and accounting must be deeply intersectional with an understanding that poor, Black, queer, trans, disabled, femmes are at risk of the most violence and harm. If our efforts are not aimed at lifting them, then our efforts are not truly liberatory.

Without this kind of critique, inevitably, the most marginalized groups will get left behind. The case of white feminism is a perfect example of how an effort to empower a historically marginalized group, without challenging the dominant economic system and deep-rooted culture of whiteness, can transform the most privileged of the group into the oppressor of those more marginalized (Schuller, 2021).[14] Girl boss culture assumes that white male power (i.e., becoming the oppressor) is the goal, but decolonization and liberation efforts aren't about sitting at the table with cis-hetero white men. The goal is to tear the table apart and build something new.[15]

---

[13]Redlining is a historical practice where financial and real estate agents "conducted widespread neighborhood appraisals of investment risk in the form of color-coded 'residential security' maps" (Swope et al., 2022, p. 960). Red neighborhoods were labeled as hazardous and unworthy of credit with comments mentioning race, ethnicity, and immigration status. The effects of this practice are still felt today as neighborhoods largely remain segregated with historically redlined neighborhoods experiencing higher poverty, subprime lending, lower home values, and adverse health outcomes (Swope et al., 2022).

[14]This brings into question the practice of including white women in diversity metrics going forward. Within public accounting, over the same time period, white female representation has increased more than any other marginalized group (American Institute of Certified Public Accountants, 2019).

[15]Cis-hetero refers to a heterosexual individual that identifies with the gender assigned to them at birth.

To move beyond business-as-usual, it is imperative for us to acknowledge the ways in which accounting practice serves as a tool of maintenance. Making sound decisions, whether personal or business related, requires that we crunch the numbers. What we decide to include, how we measure it, what we prioritize, and who validates it is the power of accounting. But business-as-usual values influence the way accountants construct and interpret financial statements, making accounting practitioners key agents in the development and legitimization of neoliberalism (Bakre et al., 2022; Chiapello, 2017). This link is acknowledged by critical accounting scholars, leading them to question "the training of accountants [as well as] the regulations governing them and what [standards] they must apply" (Chiapello, 2017, p. 59). As I see it then, radical change depends on whether or not we approach the classroom as a process of maintenance or a process of transformation to move beyond business-as-usual. As abolitionist writer and activist Derecka Purnell highlights, "[we] need to do more than break barriers to get into the system; we need [to] break the system itself" (Purnell, 2022, p. 69). This requires a twofold approach where we work to increase representation while also committing to the development of our and our student's critical consciousness. The embodiment of which is "education as the practice of freedom" (hooks, 2014).

Education as the Practice of Freedom

Deconstructing my preconceived notions about business and accounting practice changed everything for me in terms of pursuing my Doctorate and joining the academy. I began reflecting on the ways neoliberal capitalist thought was normalized and reinforced in my university classrooms without mentioning the gross inequalities created, and human suffering sustained by it. With the works of Paulo Freire and bell hooks, however, I began to see the accounting classroom as a possible site of transformation. Freire's *Pedagogy of the Oppressed* and bell hook's *Teaching to Transgress: Education as the Practice of Freedom* gave me the language to interrogate the questions I had and set me on a path to figure out how to "teach without reinforcing existing systems of domination" (hooks, 2014, p. 18). This is something I will spend my life in constant, imperfect, pursuit of.

The pedagogical philosophy outlined in their works is succinctly summarized by Robert Shaull in the introduction to the 30th anniversary edition of Pedagogy of the Oppressed. As he puts it:

> Education either functions as an instrument that is used to facilitate the integration of the younger generation into the logic of the present system and bring about conformity to it, or it becomes the 'practice of freedom', the means by which men and women deal critically and creatively with reality and discover how to participate in the transformation of their world. (Freire, 2006, p. 34)

This concept of liberatory pedagogy, at first, seemed impossible to me within the confines of a business college, arguably the largest site of capitalist cultural reproduction I could think of. As Lorenzi (2012) puts it, "the very foundation" of a business college is capitalism. As I reflected on it though, I realized that this is exactly where disruption is most necessary because it allows us to get at the root of the problem and I'm not sure I believe "the primary purpose of business schools [has to be] to teach wealth creation" (Lorenzi, 2012, p. 234). Additionally, the fact that accounting is a continuously evolving social project lends itself to this kind of transformation. We are constantly working to implement new standards, new processes, new policies, and new ways of measuring success, all of which aid in the construction of reality and can be used to maintain the oppressive status quo or transform it (Hines, 1989b). In our construction of this social project then, if our goal is human prosperity and ecological protection, the task at hand is determining what systems of accountability will get us there. The learning and unlearning required to get us there is education as the practice of freedom.

More than transforming the material we present, though, we also have to transform the ways in which we engage students with the material. Dialogue and critical reflection are key components to liberatory pedagogy. It wouldn't be enough to transform the accounting curriculum, without also working to facilitate a process of critical reflection and community building. That way, our students can locate themselves in the broader social, political, and cultural contexts to question dominant narratives and form their own conclusions. By engaging them in critical dialogue, "the student [becomes] fully involved in the educational process" (Armitage, 2011, p. 109). Ideas can be presented, challenged, and developed in community, in real time in what Freire denotes as the process of *conscientization*. A process grounded in the idea that we learn best in community rather than isolation, and the development of empathy and compassion for individuals that are different from us is key to collective struggle (Freire, 2006).

This is a hefty endeavor given that our students currently have to be prepared for licensing exams and obtain the technical knowledge necessary to practice accounting. After all, employment is required in our current system and CPA licensure is a somewhat clear path to class mobility.[16] The breadth of topics covered on the CPA exam, however, can make it seem like there is no space for covering anything else, effectively pushing critical dialogue to the fringes of the accounting academy and classroom. This is especially true if our students haven't been properly introduced to these concepts before entering their college classrooms as was the case for me. Therefore, if the goal is to go beyond business-as-usual, two questions arise. One, what role does the accounting classroom play in preparing students for the CPA exam? And two, how does our focus on teaching to the exam, intentionally or unintentionally, bar our students from the process of conscientization that Freire outlines?

---

[16]This mobility is not equally offered, however, as Black CPAs have historically faced barriers to entry and promotion as socialization to the professional standards of public accounting has been shown to enforce standards, norms, and values of whiteness leading to higher turnover rates for racialized individuals (Kim, 2004; Rukasuwan, 2022).

Going Beyond Business-as-usual

I remember being hopeful in my classes when we learned about B-corps, corporate social responsibility (CSR), and more recently Environment, Social, and Governance (ESG) reporting. However, in a well-evidenced interrogation of these practices over the past two decades, Anand Giridharadas brings to light how they have allowed the elite, who have a vested interest in the status quo, to dictate the way that social issues are solved. In his book *Winners Take All*, he notes:

> when elites assume leadership of social change, they are able to reshape what social change is. . .[in] ways that do not change the underlying economic system that has allowed winners to win and fostered many of the problems they seek to solve. (Giridharadas, 2019, p. 7)

This harkens back to the famous Audre Lorde (2012) quote, "for the master's tools will never dismantle the master's house" (p. 112), and highlights where we have fallen short in our efforts for change within the accounting academy and profession. In short, we cannot solve capitalist violence and exploitation with the tools of an oppressive capitalist system. We have to look for solutions beyond business-as usual.

In earning an undergrad accounting degree in the United States, it is commonplace that at least six classes are spent going over the technical ins and outs of Generally Accepted Accounting Principles (GAAP), journal entries, tax compliance, and auditing standards and practices. Almost no time is spent introducing students to the role accounting plays in constructing our social realities and thus how we can aid in transforming our current oppressive systems. It is claimed that this is all in an effort to better prepare students for the CPA exam and their future careers. This process of teaching to an exam, rather than teaching for critical consciousness, is what Freire refers to as the banking model of education. It is a model where students memorize the material presented to them, regurgitate it on an exam, and then never think about it again. Like deposits in the bank that are stored until they are needed, then withdrawn, used, and never seen again.

From my own experience, at mostly mid to large-size public universities, I retained very little of what was taught to me in undergrad or grad school, and my former classmates, I'm sure, would broadly agree. Most of the material was kept in mind long enough to take class exams and then it was all "relearned" while studying for the CPA exam, most of which was never used again in practice. It wasn't until I got halfway through my Master's, before I started enjoying the process of learning and really not until halfway through my doctorate that I began to do it critically. For this exact reason, the banking model brings into question the very use of exams that are largely based on technical knowledge with little real-world application, as benchmarks for learning. Within the accounting academy, however, we apply this model to a whole degree program and pat ourselves on the back for a job well done. Given the role that programs like Becker and Wiley CPA play in exam preparation, however, I argue that we could take this class time back to go beyond business-as-usual and increase the possibility of conscientization.

To do this, we first have to personally choose to not "act in complicity with greed and exploitation" (hooks, 2012, p. 46) and break free of the chains of capitalist realism. Our personal business-as-usual mentality that stems from our socialization in western, colonial-imperialist traditions, leading us to believe that our current structures are the pinnacle of human evolution. It is "a pervasive atmosphere, conditioning not only the production of culture but also the regulation of work and education, and acting as an invisible barrier constraining thought and action" (Fisher, 2009, p. 16). It is the mentality stemming from "a business ontology in which it is *simply obvious* that everything in society. . .should be run as a business" (p. 17). Therefore, to go beyond business-as-usual, we have to allow ourselves to envision our social and economic relations being structured in different, more humane, more sustainable ways. It's easier to do this once we realize where our current systems fall in the 6 million years of human history. Hadas Thier, in her book *A People's Guide to Capitalism*, provides a clear frame of reference. As she puts it, if all of human history were summarized in a 24 hour window, "capitalism only unfolded three minutes before midnight" (Thier, 2018, p. 11). Within this framing, it's clear to see that humans evolved for millennia outside of the constraints of our current system. Now, we have to reclaim our capacity to evolve beyond it.

Once we commit to this level of personal unlearning and deconstructing, our success is dependent "not only on debunking the old ideas but, more importantly, on bringing forth new ideas" (Raworth, 2017, p. 3). Ideally, this would be done in dialogue with all affected parties (i.e., faculty, students, and practitioners), but I will attempt to offer at least a few possible avenues to begin the discussion. One possibility is providing a true introduction to accounting. Currently, the typical introductory accounting class presents students with the nuts and bolts of debits and credits which usually scares or bores the majority of students from majoring in accounting (an issue that is extremely prevalent at the moment as programs across the country are experiencing a decline in enrollments). A true introduction to accounting could provide context for the role accountants play in constructing society and the systems of accountability that can be produced in practice. The social and historical background of the profession could also be introduced for students to grasp why accounting remains one of the whitest professions, even after decades of diversity initiatives (Lewis, 2015).

Accounting curriculum also has a critical role to play in the reframing of growth. For years now, environmental activists and sustainability scholars have been discussing a paradigm shift from growth to degrowth (Sekulova et al., 2013). Or, "a collective and deliberate process aimed at the equitable downscaling of the overall capacity to produce and consume and of the role of the markets and commercial exchanges as a central organizing principle of human lives" (Sekulova et al., 2013, p. 1). If this seems too extreme for those of us that were brought up and trained within a paradigm of endless economic growth, economist Kate Raworth offers an easier starting place. As she explains, "[w]hat we need are economies that make us thrive, whether or not they grow" (Raworth, 2017, p. 26).[17] Therefore, we should strive to "become agnostic about growth." To make this shift, accountants have a role to play in developing systems of accountability that have these goals at the outset.[18] This is a prime area for dialogue and critical reflection in the accounting classroom.

Critical dialogue can also focus on the ways that accounting practice serves to expand the reach of capitalist oppression. Throughout her work, Harvard Business School professor Shoshana Zuboff illuminates the lengths to which companies will go to predict and influence our actions to increase profits. Business practices that are reliant on large scale surveillance of our online presence to producing big data and ultimately a culture that challenges the democratic norms we hold dear (Zuboff, 2015, 2019b). As she states:

> [s]urveillance capitalism's 'means of behavioral modification' at scale erodes democracy from within because, without autonomy in action and in thought, we have little capacity for the moral judgment and critical thinking necessary for a democratic society. Democracy is also eroded from without, as surveillance capitalism represents an unprecedented concentration of knowledge and the power that accrues to such knowledge. (Zuboff, 2019a, online interview)

The collection and use of these big data sets to influence business strategy is a frontier that accounting programs are largely cosigning by developing entire data analytics programs with little reflection on the invasive and exploitative nature of

[17]In her revolutionary reframing of economics, Raworth (2017) makes it clear that this reframing of growth has to happen at the micro and macro level. At the individual level, there would be an interrogation of our consumerist tendencies leading us to always want more. As Tim Jackson put it, we're "persuaded to spend money we don't have on things we don't need to make impressions that won't last on people we don't care about" (Jackson, 2010). At the global level is the move away from "a metric so fickle, partial, and superficial as Gross Domestic Product" (p. 51) as the primary proxy for human welfare and prosperity. The framework guiding this pursuit is what she has termed "Doughnut economics" where the goal is a regenerative and distributive economy with "the social foundation of human rights and the ecological ceiling of planetary boundaries" (p. 42), effectively restoring the soul of economic policy.

[18]Dillard and Vinnari (2019) have introduced how this kind of accountability might be obtained. In their discussion, they compare two systems, accounting-based accountability and accountability-based accounting. The first system is limited by what is taken into account during the process of creating financial statements and what is disclosed. Our current system of ESG reporting, that has had marginal impact, would be an example. The latter system is where accounting processes, conventions, and disclosures are designed with specific interests of accountability in mind.

the field that disproportionately targets and harms vulnerable communities. Including this perspective into our classroom could allow our students to engage with the movement toward democratizing online spaces.

The tax classroom is also an exceptional opportunity for engaging students in critical reflection as the subject naturally falls at the intersection of the broader social, political, and cultural context. Framing taxes according to the neoliberal consensus and narrowly focusing on the technical application of our current system is all well and good if our goal isn't to acknowledge these linkages and embody a process of transformation.[19] If we want to take part in this process of transformation, however, we have to interrogate the dominant narrative and highlight the social implications of extreme income inequality and the prospect of tax policy as a redistributive mechanism.[20] We could also take the time to acknowledge the variety of ways in which seemingly neutral tax policy, because of its focus on equality of prescription rather than equity of outcomes, can intersect with other oppressive systems to produce social inequalities (Brown, 2021).

If we can acknowledge that the status quo is oppressive and the traditional approach to the accounting classroom, when unchecked, is a process of maintenance, then we as accounting academics have a choice to make. The choice to be part of the problem or part of the solution. Maintenance or transformation? Because make no mistake, overlooking or disregarding the politics and values inherent in the accounting classroom is a choice, and a loaded one at that.

Conclusion

Business-as-usual leads us to surface-level solutions and research questions where we think small. Our focus on statistical significance and the logic of cold hard numbers neutralizes our complex and messy reality that raises big questions. Like, why are we here? Is the point of life to sell our labor for what someone else thinks it's worth and barely earn enough to play the game? Capitalist realism would have

---

[19]Within dominant neoliberal ideology, taxes are seen as a drain on free enterprise. Thus, neoliberal tax policy has worked to reduce corporate and capital gains taxes, paying for them with cuts to social programs, while maintaining taxes on earned income (Harvey, 2007).

[20]This will be a challenge given the emotional reactions that arise around ideas of redistribution and the fact that most of our students come into the classroom already having absorbed the dominant narrative, that taxes are a burden and unnecessary annoyance. Collecting individual taxes for the benefit of broader society is antithetical to the hyper-individual culture we have been socialized to and the benefit of tax revenue hasn't been felt by the majority of us in quite sometime. We drive on roads that are falling apart, send our kids to schools that are consistently de-funded, and have to personally cover the ever-increasing cost of living and healthcare while banks get bailed out for billions and billionaires pay less tax than the average worker (Leiserson & Yaga, 2021). Challenging these preconceived notions is the point though, and from there, we can work with our students to imagine what tax policy could be if our system was designed to be redistributive from the outset.

us believe that this way of organizing socioeconomic relations is the best we can do. We just have to accept our fate to work until we retire, wasting resources that are finite and making profits for people that aren't us. Rather than focusing on solving problems, we focus on climbing higher and having more so the problems don't apply to us. This individual pursuit effectively blocks us from raising our class consciousness, building community, and crossing group lines (hooks, 2012). It also keeps us from realizing that in our pursuit of liberation, we have more commonalities than we have differences.

Personally, I don't believe we should have to spend most of our time away from our family and friends, earning what little we do while producing excess for a group of people who have more than they will ever be able to spend in 10 lifetimes. I believe we should be able to experience freedom without having to earn it. Freedom of time, authenticity, of our ability to live in the current moment instead of worried about tomorrow. Freedom to live a simple life focused on the work that would mutually benefit our direct community and society at large without any of us sacrificing our mental or physical health.[21] As much as I want to stop playing the game though, I can't. Playing the game is literally life and death. The game doesn't stop until we take our collective power back and choose to move us toward a new era, leaving the last 3 minutes behind.

This won't be easy. The effort required to approach the classroom with human emancipation at the core, standing 10 toes down when pushback comes, and living with integrity is a lot. But those of us who have the privilege of sitting at the edge of cultural reproduction, who are tasked with the education of young minds, have a responsibility to do this work. Not only within the world of accounting but also within the broader business college. A recent article published by the Association to Advance Collegiate Schools of Business (AACSB) titled *Decolonizing the Business School Curriculum* made it clear that, "[i]t is up to all of us in our fields to challenge our familiar mental habits, no matter how uncomfortable that is. We must all be involved, and we must all be responsible for achieving change" (Everett, 2023).

It is time to go beyond intellectualizing the issues and develop an anti-oppressive praxis, integrating what we know with what we do. The attempt to level the playing field during the mid-20th century brought about the racial and economic backlash that we have experienced for the past 40 years. If we are able to learn from history, then we can see how important this moment is. The fact that business and accounting scholars have researched and written about these issues for decades while little has changed in everyday practice makes it clear that we must be intentional, persistent, and committed to disrupting the oppression that is reproduced in our classrooms. If not, our reality and what's left of our

[21]As bell hooks puts it, "living a simple life [does] not mean a life without luxury; it [means] a life without excess" (hooks, 2012, p. 59).

democracy may not survive the cycle of backlash that is currently being wielded against our efforts to address systemic injustices.[22]

Fortunately, social media, as toxic as it might be, has provided us with an opportunity like no other. For the first time, we are able to hear about and learn from the experiences of others and stand witness to the suffering that has for so long been hidden from our collective imaginations. It directly challenges our hyper-individual culture and opens the door to critical reflection. This is an issue that affects all of us, Black, white, Latin-x, Indigenous, Asian, and all intersecting identities. We are never going to get anywhere in terms of racial or social justice if we can't first see the humanity in others and begin to operate in a way that doesn't reproduce hierarchies. We all have a lot at stake. Hope exists if we could only collectively recognize the stakes and go beyond business-as-usual personally, within our classrooms, and throughout our communities.

References

Alexander, M. (2011). The new Jim Crow. *Ohio State Journal of Criminal Law*, *9*, 7.

American Institute of Certified Public Accountants. (2019). *The supply of accounting graduates and the demand for public accounting recruits*. AICPA.

Armitage, A. (2011). Critical pedagogy and learning to dialogue: Towards reflexive practice for financial management and accounting education. *Journal for Critical Education Policy Studies*, *9*(2).

Bakre, O. M., McCartney, S., & Fayemi, S. O. (2022). Accounting as a technology of neoliberalism: The accountability role of IPSAS in Nigeria. *Critical Perspectives on Accounting*, *87*, 102282.

Bjerg, O. (2008). Drug addiction and capitalism: Too close to the body. *Body & Society*, *14*(2), 1–22.

Brown. (2021). *The whiteness of wealth: How the tax system impoverishes Black Americans–And how we can fix it*. Crown Publishing Group.

Chiapello, E. (2017). Critical accounting research and neoliberalism. *Critical Perspectives on Accounting*, *43*, 47–64.

Chomsky, N. (2002). *Understanding power: The indispensable Chomsky*. The New Press.

Christensen, M.-B., Hallum, C., Maitland, A., Parrinello, Q., & Putaturo, C. (2023). *Survival of the richest: How we must tax the super-rich now to fight inequality*. Oxfam International.

Davis, A. Y. (1990). *Women, culture & politics*. Vintage.

Delgado, R., & Stefancic, J. (2023). *Critical race theory: An introduction* (Vol. 87). NYU Press.

[22]Our democracy is also threatened by the logic of business-as-usual. In the *Dominion Voting System v Fox News defamation* case, phone and email transcript evidence shows that the show hosts knowingly broadcast lies about the "fraudulent 2020 election" to protect their ratings and profit (Peters & Robertson, 2023), a narrative that directly influenced the insurrection that was attempted on January 6th, 2021 at the US capital. Evidence that the business-as-usual logic will put profit above our democracy to the point where it is actively threatened.

Dillard, J., & Vinnari, E. (2019). Critical dialogical accountability: From accounting-based accountability to accountability-based accounting. *Critical Perspectives on Accounting*, *62*, 16–38.

Everett, S. (2023). *Decolonizing the business school curriculum*. Association to Advance Collegiate Schools of Business.

Fisher, M. (2009). *Capitalist realism: Is there no alternative?* John Hunt Publishing.

Freire, P. (2006). *Pedagogy of the oppressed: 30th anniversary edition*. The Continuum International Publishing Group Inc.

Funnel, W. (1998). Accounting in the service of the Holocaust. *Critical Perspectives on Accounting*, *9*(4), 435–464.

George, S. (1999). A short history of neoliberalism. In *Paper presented at the conference on economic sovereignty in a globalising world*, Bangkok, 24–26 March 1999.

Giridharadas, A. (2019). *Winners take all: The elite charade of changing the world*. Vintage.

Hampton, F. (1969). *Fred Hampton on revolution and racism*. https://www.liberationschool.org/fred-hampton-on-revolution-and-racism/

Harvey, D. (2007). *A brief history of neoliberalism*. Oxford University Press.

Hines, R. D. (1988). Financial accounting: In communicating reality, we construct reality. *Accounting, Organizations and Society*, *13*(3), 251–261.

Hines, R. D. (1989a). Financial accounting knowledge, conceptual framework projects and the social construction of the accounting profession. *Accounting, Auditing & Accountability Journal*, *2*(2).

Hines, R. D. (1989b). The sociopolitical paradigm in financial accounting research. *Accounting, Auditing & Accountability Journal*, *2*(1).

hooks, b. (1996). Killing rage: Ending racism. *Journal of Leisure Research*, *28*(4), 316.

hooks, b. (2012). *Where we stand: Class matters*. Routledge.

hooks, b. (2014). *Teaching to transgress*. Routledge.

Howell, A., & Richter-Montpetit, M. (2019). Racism in Foucauldian security studies: Biopolitics, liberal war, and the whitewashing of colonial and racial violence. *International Political Sociology*, *13*(1), 2–19.

Jackson, T. (2010). An economic reality check. In *Presented at TEDGlobal 2010*, London, 12–16 July 2010.

James, O. (2008). *The selfish capitalist: Origins of affluenza*. Random House.

Kim, S. N. (2004). Racialized gendering of the accountancy profession: Toward an understanding of Chinese women's experiences in accountancy in New Zealand. *Critical Perspectives on Accounting*, *15*(3), 400–427.

Leiserson, G., & Yaga, D. (2021). *What is the average Federal individual income tax rate on the wealthiest Americans?* The White House. https://www.whitehouse.gov/cea/written-materials/2021/09/23/what-is-the-average-federal-individual-income-tax-rate-on-the-wealthiest-americans/

Lewis, A. (2015). Counting black and white beans: Why we need a critical race theory of accounting. *European Journal of Contemporary Economics and Management*, *2*(2), 1–13.

Lorde, A. (2012). *Sister outsider: Essays and speeches*. Crossing Press.

Lorenzi, P. (2012). Business schools: Capitalism's last stand. *Society*, *49*(3), 230–239.

Manetti, G., Bellucci, M., & Oliva, S. (2021). Unpacking dialogic accounting: A systematic literature review and research agenda. *Accounting, Auditing & Accountability Journal*, *34*(9), 250–283.

Marr, C., & Rainey, R. (2023). *States look to ease child labor laws as federal scrutiny grows*. https://news.bloomberglaw.com/daily-labor-report/states-look-to-ease-child-labor-laws-as-federal-scrutiny-grows

Melamed, J. (2015). Racial capitalism. *Critical Ethnic Studies*, *1*(1), 76–85.

Padgett, G. (2015). A critical case study of selected US history textbooks from a tribal critical race theory perspective. *Qualitative Report*, *20*(3).

Peters, J. W., & Robertson, K. (2023, February 27). Murdoch acknowledges Fox News hosts endorsed election falsehoods. *The New York Times*. https://www.nytimes.com/2023/02/27/business/media/fox-news-dominion-rupert-murdoch.html

Piketty, T. (2014). *Capital in the twenty-first century*. Harvard University Press.

Piketty, T., Saez, E., & Zucman, G. (2018). Distributional national accounts: Methods and estimates for the United States. *Quarterly Journal of Economics*, *133*(2), 553–609.

Potter, B. N. (2005). Accounting as a social and institutional practice: Perspectives to enrich our understanding of accounting change. *Abacus*, *41*(3), 265–289.

Power, B. S., & Brennan, N. M. (2022). Accounting as a dehumanizing force in colonial rhetoric: Quantifying native peoples in annual reports. *Critical Perspectives on Accounting*, *87*, 102278. https://doi.org/10.1016/j.cpa.2020.102278

Purnell, D. (2022). *Becoming abolitionists: Police, protests, and the pursuit of freedom*. Astra Publishing House.

Ralph, M., & Singhal, M. (2019). Racial capitalism. *Theory and Society*, *48*(6), 851–881.

Raworth, K. (2017). *Doughnut economics: Seven ways to think like a 21st-century economist*. Chelsea Green Publishing.

Robinson, C. (2020). *Black Marxism, revised and updated third edition: The making of the black radical tradition*. UNC Press Books.

Rosenthal, C. (2018). *Accounting for slavery*. Harvard University Press.

Rukasuwan, L. (2022). *Examining the career progression of Black public accountants: A social identity approach and redesigned system of exclusion in the US*. Doctoral Dissertation, Texas Tech University. https://hdl.handle.net/2346/89298

Saez, E., & Zucman, G. (2016). Wealth inequality in the United States since 1913: Evidence from capitalized income tax data. *Quarterly Journal of Economics*, *131*(2), 519–578.

Schuller, K. (2021). *The trouble with white women: A counterhistory of feminism*. Bold Type Books.

Sekulova, F., Kallis, G., Rodríguez-Labajos, B., & Schneider, F. (2013). Degrowth: From theory to practice. *Journal of Cleaner Production*, *38*, 1–6.

Swope, C. B., Hernández, D., & Cushing, L. J. (2022). The relationship of historical redlining with present-day neighborhood environmental and health outcomes: A scoping review and conceptual model. *Journal of Urban Health*, *99*(6), 959–983.

Thier, H. (2018). *A people's guide to capitalism: An introduction to Marxist economics*. Haymarket Books.

Thomas, L. (2022). *The intersectional environmentalist: How to dismantle systems of oppression to protect people and planet*. Voracious, Little, Brown and Company.

Yahoo. (2022, February 16). *Charlie Munger: Nobody is going back to the office 5 days a week* [Video file]. https://finance.yahoo.com/video/workplace-changes-forever-charlie-munger-195526935.html?

Zuboff, S. (2015). Big other: Surveillance capitalism and the prospects of an information civilization. *Journal of Information Technology*, *30*(1), 75–89.

Zuboff, S. (2019a). High tech is watching you. *The Harvard Gazette*. https://news.harvard.edu/gazette/story/2019/03/harvard-professor-says-surveillance-capitalism-is-undermining-democracy/

Zuboff, S. (2019b). Surveillance capitalism and the challenge of collective action. *New Labor Forum*, *28*(1), 10–29. SAGE Publications.

Chapter 16

The Racially Conscious Accountant

Anton Lewis[a] *and Richard Hurt*[b]

[a]Governors State University, USA
[b]University of San Diego, USA

When thinking of a racial accountant, it seems to be a contradiction in terms. Time and again, the accounting profession presents itself as value free, devoid of feeling, removed from bias – a trusted if not dull arbiter of business information (Lewis, 2015). The message is that race and racism have no place in the hallowed halls of accounting. Unfortunately, this tale does not fit the facts as presented by Critical Race Theory (CRT) academics, Race Critical accounting scholars, and the AICPA's own difficult figures relating to low Black and Brown participation (AICPA, 2019).[1] But can more be done? The answer is yes. Accountants can alleviate the situation by developing a critical racial awareness, one that leads to action. This chapter is a call for a Racially Conscious Accountant, an individual the profession sorely needs. This chapter investigates what can be done to encourage active anti-racism in this number-crunching field.

Schooling the Racially Conscious Accountant

Improving racial awareness in the profession requires an overhaul of what currently typifies accounting education. From its inception in colleges and universities, accounting pedagogy evolved to formalize knowledge in its particular sphere, similar to that of other professions seeking Weberian market shelter and abnormal profits.[2] The difference, as noted by Macdonald (1995), is that accounting's esoteric domain actually encompasses several different areas of knowledge, some relating to other professions, and its authority derives from the claim that only it can perform the wide array of services demanded. The point

[1]Hylton marks a separation between scholars who research race using a variety of paradigms as race critical scholars and those who specifically apply CRT tenets to analysis as Critical Race Theorists (Hylton, 2009).
[2]Accounting as a subject is seen to incorporate many areas of knowledge such as Law, Bookkeeping, Economics, and Finance to just mention a few.

Voices of Change, 221–226

doi:10.1108/978-1-83753-030-420251037

here is that accounting as a profession has always incorporated diverse knowledge and skills, seen recently in the adoption of data analysis and Artificial Intelligence, among an array of IT skills not often associated with the traditional accounting function. We argue that a fundamental understanding of racial processes, as it pertains to practice, be included as an addition to formalized accounting knowledge, paving the way to modify the profession's racial landscape over time.

Central to this argument is the belief that changing the individual changes the profession. To mitigate institutional racism, companies and firms must strive to help "company men" (and women) become less racist, even anti-racist. Professions are capable of producing homogeneity among professionals, so this is feasible. Reproduction therefore is a process of creation/recreation of the new professional through dissemination of formalized esoteric knowledge, practical training from seniors in the field, and induction into professional mores characteristic of the authentic accounting professional. This should include standardized racial awareness education. When taught the essentials of race and racism, individuals are offered a chance to absorb a degree of empathy and understanding that may shape the essence of their future life and actions in the profession. If such an understanding and critical perspective is spread widely – throughout an entire generation of accountants – it can permeate the profession over time.

Moreover, historically, America's educational philosophy has centered on an understanding of democracy, the creation of knowledge, and the development of good citizens (Chan, 2016). One of the more notable analyses on the purpose of education classifies educational goals as political in nature. It categorizes these goals under the pillars of democratic equality as a public good, social efficiency as a private good, and social mobility as individualistic realizations for market (Labaree, 1997). This encourages accounting education to produce well-rounded professionals concerned with the virtues of good citizenry which is an objective accounting education has yet to achieve particularly in the arena of race (Alston et al., 2023). To counter this, the creation of a Racially Conscious Accountant is a social good beneficial to society.

In other fields, professionalism is characterized by moral action, by doing the right thing. In medical and law school, moral action imbues prospective professionals with an unparalleled sense of purpose. The Hippocratic Oath governs medical professionals who are the first to hold a baby as it takes its first breath of air. Medical professionals treat illnesses and are often the last to attend to dying patients, bearing witness to the final moments of a life. Legal professionals, driven by the 6th Amendment to the US Constitution, seek to guarantee everyone's right to a fair and speedy trial. The right to a defense is a cornerstone of democracy, as all are innocent until proven guilty. The importance of the law, its ethical justifications and reasoning, is imbued into the essence of the legal professional. What oath motivates our work in accounting? Where is the Hippocratic Oath for accountants – a call to do no harm, and in the context of what we propose here, a call to do no racial harm?

The act of producing the producers of accounting knowledge by widening the scope of what counts as valuable knowledge could lead to a greater appreciation of the importance of racial Others. To see a racialized perspective is, as Sopt et al. mention in this volume, a process of decolonizing the accounting curriculum. It is to extend a risky but required pedagogical invitation to the stigmatized, beckoning them to enter a realm that is desperately unsafe, one where few allies will be found in the pipeline. We argue such a stance is pivotal as it pertains to accounting education, specifically when attempting to attract African Americans. The old-style curriculum of esoteric knowledge acquisition stands in the way. The omission of Black, Brown, or Native viewpoints – an environmental microaggression – tacitly states that the profession is not interested in the racialized Other. As Derald Wing Sue (2010) specifies, "the term 'environmental microaggression' refers to the numerous demeaning and threatening social, educational, political, or economic cues that are communicated individually, institutionally, or societally to marginalized groups" (p. 25). It plays the same tune as the microaggression of African-American under-representation. A mere 2% of accountants, as measured by the AICPA's 2019 trends report, are Black, effectively telling Black students, "This profession is not for you!"

Professions in the United States have increasingly become infatuated with models of standardized training. These training models are understood to be catalysts of knowledge, and any diversion from these models leaves people in shock, scrambling for answers. Law enforcement is a good example that relies on standardized training. Hours upon hours of training are spent preparing officers for worst case scenarios – where force must be used to subdue a stereotypical "bad guy" – while less time is spent analyzing the most common interaction between officers and the public, everyday traffic violations. While situations using force are tragic and are seen throughout Black communities, training programs do not account for common decency, virtue, or positive behavior.

Society has yet to fully understand what causes deviations from standardized training programs or how to deal with them in real time. How do we prevent bad cops? How do we deal with doctors who do more harm than good but are blanketed in malpractice insurance that enables them to move on to the next patient? How do we deal with an egotistical defense lawyer or prosecutor who is more interested in money or conviction rates than the truth? How do we deal with accountants who memorize definitions for the ethics exam but seize the opportunity to enact racial practice in the workplace where they can? When training programs are relied upon as catalysts for knowledge and standardization, dissatisfactions and inequities are ignored. This leaves us with a question: how can the Racially Conscious Accountant be more?

CPA Licensing and the Racially Conscious Accountant

We propose that CPA licensing has a central role to play in the disenfranchisement of the racial Other similar to old discriminatory Country Clubs of days gone by, those that excluded Blacks, limiting entry only to those ensconced in whiteness. In the past, Black accounting students learned capitalistic methods of evaluating, analyzing, and offering opinions, their acquisition of knowledge used in pursuit of CPA licensure, but was it truly worthwhile? In the Accounting Country Club, Blacks can caddy but never play a round of golf for themselves, let alone win. By no means should they have a white caddy in this space! Education can allow the Racially Conscious Accountant to see how rigged the game is, and in doing so, seek to disrupt the established order, one that sees the best work go to those who are *pale* and *male*.

The Racially Conscious Accountant understands how and why Black colleagues are disqualified from the Accounting Club, excluded from partaking in the weightless knapsack of goodies that is white privilege (McIntosh, 1997). It is the moral responsibility of the Racially Conscious Accountant to open the knapsack, widen the gates of the Club to accounting's Black and Brown Other, simply because it is the right thing to do, the definition of social justice. Certification is advertised as an asset, a passport to market shelter, giving wealth to those who possess it, Black or otherwise – a key to middle-class luxuries. However, it does not provide full access to the Club for Black and Brown CPAs, nor can licensure be traded for something more valuable. One must "use it or lose it" – even though it falls short of the claims on the label for certain CPAs.

Is the act of licensing for the Black and Brown accountant a trap they are encouraged to enter with a promise of wealth – the path of capitalism, facilitating asset transference from generation to generation, the passing of wealth intergenerationally? While the sales pitch holds up for those who can fully join the Club – the pale, male, and middle class – students marked as Black, Brown, or poor (regardless of race) cannot. Those students spend most of their prime years paying down education debt from expensive undergraduate programs – the 150-hour requirement forcing students to borrow money for Master's degrees. Layered on top are licensing fees, fingerprint fees, AICPA and state society dues, the cost of continuing education, exam preparatory courses, and test-taking fees. These certification costs deter Black entry into accounting – professionalism "weeding out" potential Black and Brown CPAs who consequently remain outside the Club.

As a result, Black students who want to enter accounting are forced to put aside their lived-experience gained from their communities in order to acclimate to a curriculum that never accounted for them and an industry that does not truly accept them. When Black students view accounting as an option for a career, they encounter a wall of whiteness on which their Blackness stands out like a credit balance on a cash ledger. Things must change, but how?

What's Next?

For the Racially Conscious Accountant to exist as conceived here, accounting education must change. In many respects, accounting education is designed by, and for those whom the profession values most, the male and pale with sights set on the CPA exam. Championing their cause has led to standardization, creating barriers to licensure for those less valued. Accounting education advocates white-centric knowledge which is often culturally inaccessible for Black and

Brown accountants and others of color. In addition, the expensive 150-hour requirement presents a barricade for those most financially challenged, i.e., minority communities and poor whites. These impediments effectively close accounting's door to many Black and Brown candidates even though the profession cannot afford for this to be the case.

An accounting curriculum that maintains the story of accounting as an unbiased technocracy does so with a resulting message of "for whites only," an environmental microaggression. This type of curriculum has lost the potential to effectively attract Black and Brown students. Put another way, if a Black student decides they want to learn accounting in order to build their community, the study of redlining and its economic effects past and present is of great importance. The CPA-focused accounting curriculum fails to support those ambitions.[3] The Racially Conscious Accountant is one who sees this and works tirelessly against it. Why? Because they have knowledge and awareness of accounting's storied and murky history. They understand that accounting is a racial project, and its purpose is to convince the public that accountants can be trusted because they represent what is most expected, the "neutrality" of whiteness (Lewis, 2015). Since the body of knowledge in accounting is racially ambiguous, no questions are raised. The Racially Conscious Accountant must raise those questions, to make a racial ruckus, paving the way for the beleaguered Other to enter the profession in greater numbers than before and feel welcome doing so.

References

AICPA. (2019). *Trends in the supply of accounting graduates and the demand for public accounting recruits*. https://us.aicpa.org/content/dam/aicpa/interestareas/accountingeducation/newsandpublications/downloadabledocuments/2019-trends-report.pdf

Alston, C., Rukasuwan, L., & Lewis, A. (2023, September/October). What can the profession do? Looking closely at each piece of the puzzle. *The CPA Journal*, *36*. https://www.cpajournal.com/2023/12/04/what-can-the-profession-do/

Chan, R. Y. (2016). Understanding the purpose of higher education: An analysis of the economic and social benefits for completing a college degree. *Journal of Education Policy, Planning and Administration*, *6*(5), 1–40.

Hylton, K. (2009). *'Race' and sport: Critical race theory*. Routledge.

Labaree, D. F. (1997). Public goods, private goods: The American struggle over educational goals. *American Educational Research Journal*, *34*(1), 39–81.

Lewis (2015). Counting black and white beans: Why we need a critical race theory of accounting. *European Journal of Contemporary Economics and Management*, *2*(2), 1–13.

Macdonald, K. M. (1995). *The sociology of the professions*. SAGE Publications Ltd.

[3]Redlining is a prejudiced practice where services such as mortgage lending are blocked to inhabitants of particular places based on race. It was widely practiced in the mid-20th century against African Americans which prevented them from buying homes in predominantly white areas (Rothstein, 2017).

McIntosh, P. (1997). White privilege and male privilege: A personal account of coming to see correspondences through work in women's studies. In R. Delgado & J. Stefancic (Eds.), *Critical white studies: Looking behind the mirror* (pp. 291–299). Temple University Press.

Rothstein, R. (2017). *The color of law*. Liveright Publishing Corporation.

Sue, D. W. (2010). *Microaggressions in everyday life: Race, gender and sexual orientation*. John Wiley & Sons.

Chapter 17

The Cost That Comes With Not Caring: An Autoethnographic Critical Reflection of Race Equity in Education

Iwi Ugiagbe-Green

Manchester Metropolitan University, UK

Unlike the other contributions to this book, this chapter is one that tells a personal journey of an accounting academic working in race equity in academia in England in the United Kingdom. I am a cisgender woman racialised as Black and of African and Caribbean heritage. I was born and educated in England. I am from a low-income family, whose parents relied on the State for housing and financial support, for all my childhood. On leaving University, I trained, qualified and worked as a chartered certified accountant for 10 years, serendipitously starting my academic career 12 years ago. I feel it is important for me to explain some details of my life history, in order that you, the reader, understand my perspectives and insights of my lived experience that I share with you in this chapter.

This chapter will chronicle some of my personal, but as it turns out, not unique experiences of working in race equity in higher education in the United Kingdom, as a mid-career woman academic activist (Zerai, 2002). My lived experience as a Black woman shapes the lens through which I see myself. My 'Blackness' is a proud and indelible part of my identity, of who I am and how I experience the world. It is within this context that this autoethnographic, critical reflection is written. Bhaskar (2020) suggests that we should approach the ontology of persons in terms using the South African philosophy of Ubuntu, which means roughly 'I am because you are'. A foundational principle of Ubuntu is that one's being, their personhood, is relational to that of others.

Autoethnography is an approach to research and writing that seeks to describe and systematically analyse (*graphy*) personal experience (*auto*) to understand cultural experience (*ethno*) (Ellis, 2004). There are some who view this method as self-indulgent, narcissistic, introspective and individualised (Atkinson, 1997; Coffey, 1999). However, it is my view that using this method validates the right to tell my truth as an expert of my own experience. I share Gillborn's (1998) view

Voices of Change, 227–238

doi:10.1108/978-1-83753-030-420251039

that good ethnography is not about revealing an explicit truth but about presenting a convincing case for the argument being made.

The convincing argument to be made in this chapter does not focus on the need for race equity work in accounting education. That is a given. The argument I put forward in this chapter using my critical reflections underpinned by an ontology of persons (Bhaskar, 2020) is to propose the need for an ethics of care (Noddings, 1984) in not only accounting education but everything that we do as educators.

Critical reflection is focused on uncovering hegemonic assumptions, which permeate the context invading and distorting one's life, both in the intimate and social spheres (Mortari, 2015). Critical theorists attribute to critical reflection, the task of unmasking the tacit hegemonic assumptions that infuse our context of life, to interrupt the reproduction of systems of class, race and gender oppression (Giroux & McLaren, 1989; Kanpol, 1999). My critical reflections propose that it is through these hegemonic structures that harm to those who are marginalised and minoritised is inflicted.

I hold a fundamental epistemological belief that underpins my approach to writing this chapter, in which I integrate ontological theory and lived experience. That belief is that knowledge is socially constructed through human definition and interpretation shaped by cultural and historical contexts (Subramaniam, 2010). My understanding of my lived experience is derived by my interpretations and sense making of defining and categorizing groups of people, experience and reality in cultural contexts in my work.

This chapter is written in a conversational style, to reflect that I am speaking to you, the reader, about my experiences through this text. I am making myself vulnerable to you, your thoughts and opinions. You will not agree with everything that I say here, but I am the expert of my own experience. I am not revealing aspects of myself to convince you of explicit truth. I am putting forward an argument for an ethics of care (Noddings, 1984) to be centred in all our work as accounting educators. I am reliving some of the trauma I have endured in working in accounting education because it's important. In our work as educators, the accounting students for whom we advocate are not statistics. They are not data points. They are not a problem to be fixed. They are not an instrument to be used for self-promotion and gratification. These students embody society's future. They are people who should move through the world with joyful curiosity and hope and understanding of how they can use their knowledge, skills and expertise to contribute to a better world.

Everyone, regardless of their history, should experience our higher education system with care and compassion. It should be a place of learning, nurturing, liberation and healing. We should all be working to support our students' development into the best versions of themselves that they choose to be. We should be creating the conditions in which they go on and be global citizens of the world and make it a better place for all. To do this, we need to centre ethics of care (Noddings, 1984). We cannot begin to address the fact that the glass ceiling is impenetrable for many racialised people of a profession where only one in 250 partners of the top eight accountancy firms in the UK is Black (BAME, 2020). A system of care helps organisations view structural and individual level racism through a trauma-informed lens through which to consider interventions and revisions to policies, procedures and practices.

> The ethics of care. . . conceptualizes persons as deeply affected by, and involved in, relations with others; to many care theorists persons are at least partly constituted by their social ties. The ethics of care. . . does not assume that relations relevant for morality have been entered into voluntarily by free and equal individuals as do dominant moral theories. Held (2006, p. 46)

Noddings (1984) explains that care is always relational. It is a basic human need. Virtually, all care theorists make the relation more fundamental than the individual. The need for an ethics of care in race equity work in accounting education is particularly pertinent. Those of us on the margins in the accounting profession know all too well of its need. This is not about morality. It is about our humanity as people. It is about social justice. If our profession really cared about race equity, it would not be afraid to examine its historical ties to colonialism, imperialism and the slave trade. It would have no issue with challenging ideologies, structures and policies that continue to perpetuate white wealth and white norms over and above racially minoritised people. Instead, the profession continues to act as gatekeeper, with racially minoritised people in both education and practice, on the margins, through its lack of care. A profession that really cared about its racial imperviousness would resourcefully, systematically and strategically review its education, policies, structures and identity, to dismantle racial hierarchies in the profession. And yet, Lewis (2020) critiques the profession's professed 'colour-blindness' and reluctance to do so, by stating that 'accounting fails to address the underpinnings of race because it chooses not to see it' (p. 2).

My work, as an academic race equity activist working in accounting education, anchors me. I position myself as an activist because I try to use my different roles to combine scholarly expertise with expressed activist goals and social justice advocacy. It is a force that centres me. My work, though challenging, provides me with purpose and fulfilment. The challenge I face in my work includes the obvious pushback, whataboutisms, denial, apathy and so on from others. However, the biggest challenge has been the toxic, performative, self-interest–driven motivations of some academics working in this space, for whom this work is an opportunity for self-promotion. For whom this work is a chance to climb the greasy pole to senior leadership and for whom to get there, to exploit emotional labour and shamelessly leverage the endless hours of work undertaken outside of the standard workload allocation by others who receive little recognition or reward. These people will dismiss the care and compassion that is essential to our work in pursuit of targets and metrics or awards and accreditations. For many of these people, care does not feature in their work, never mind be centred in what they do or how they do it.

Some of you reading this will have already surmised that in this chapter, I will express anger, frustration, hurt and pain. I do so in solidarity with some many colleagues, working in race equity who are emotionally exhausted by the lack of care in our accounting profession and cost that is borne by all of us, particularly those who are marginalised and minoritised as a result.

My bumpy road into academic activism started five years ago, when one morning, a group of six wonderful Black women accounting and finance undergraduate students turned up unannounced to my shared office, while I was doing some last-minute preparation (those who know me know this is not unusual!) for a meeting I had in the afternoon. They rang the bell and asked my lovely colleague on reception if they could see me. I overheard the request and after a moment's hesitation, driven by the panic realising this meant less time for me to do my 'last-minute' preparation for the meeting in 3 hours' time smiled incongruously at my colleague and said:

> Of course!... Please ask them to take a seat.

As instructed, they all sat down, chatting animatedly while they waited for me to join them in one of our adjoining offices where we would regularly meet students.

Now, I am not going to go through all the dialogue of this exchange, only to say that it is no exaggeration to say that what happened next changed me and the direction of my career forever. One short opening sentence that led to nearly two hours of dialogue and five years since that day, of academic advocacy and activism.

> We are so glad that you are here. You are the only one and you really care.

For context, I had been working at the institution for a matter of months. I was suffering daily from imposter syndrome. I had moved from a less prestigious university to this one and was conscious that I did not share a similar background to that of many of my peers and most of the students I was supporting in my new role.

Our conversation centred on me being the only Black member of Faculty and my authentic student-centred approach to a pedagogy of care and compassion (I didn't even realise then it was a theory, for me, it is just a way of being). The conversation that day spanned all sorts of aspects of their racialised experiences both in and outside of the classroom. They spoke of common microaggressions encountered from some of my colleagues, their mental health and well-being issues and a feeling that there was no provision within the university that really understood the cultural sensitivities and factors influencing how they were feeling. They wilfully explained a longing to integrate with peers outside of their own friendship group but a real fear of rejection existed, based on their experiences of invisibility in the classroom and being ignored at student parties. They spoke of their 'imposter syndrome' and how they felt that they would not achieve their potential and that they would become another statistic of underachievement (my words, not theirs).

In short, on that day, they resurfaced experiences that I had when I was a student 10 years prior and had continued to experience in the workplace but had buried in the pursuit to fit in and get on. As they were talking, I was reflecting.

Our conversation surfaced feelings of shame in me. Yes, I had actively listened when each of them had told me on an individual basis in our one-to-one meetings that they were feeling lonely and displaced, but what had I done to change things? Why should these students have suffered in silence and only feel a sense of hope by my presence as a Black woman academic. It is wrong. It is unfair, and I was not going to move forward in shame and anger. I was going to do something about it. I was going to change things.

Change things, did I? Well, not quite.

I did do something about it. I set up an informal mentoring scheme in partnership with one of the Big Four professional services firms for these women. I checked in with the women regularly, holding them to account for their work and progress. We met for coffee and informal chats, for me to make sure that they were OK. I did not dismiss their experiences or how they were feeling, giving them space to talk about it, while I listened. They were seen and they were heard. This wasn't revolutionary but was noticed by colleagues within my faculty. I was challenged on why I was targeting a specific demographic of students with my mentoring scheme. There was a strong sense that I was not widening our provision but excluding certain groups of students (whom by all accounts were doing well already). I was openly accused of favouritism.

Yes, in the faces of these women, I saw my sisters, my daughter, my nieces, my friends, but my favourite student (I know you're not supposed to have them, but I didn't teach this person, so in my view it was ok) was a white student from a working-class (low economic) background from the Northeast of England. They had a stammer and a very challenging and chaotic life. When I met with this student (a regular occurrence), I would always ensure I had some food to offer, as I knew it was likely they had not eaten. I cared for and about them, as much as I did for these Black women. However, I resolutely make absolutely no apology for 'always going on about race', but to be accused (as I am frequently) of not caring about 'white working-class people' is an insult and assault on me and my character, particularly given that I married one (not that I should need to justify myself with this fact either).

I am forever proud of the fact that these women all left as a happier, more fulfilled and accomplished version of themselves into excellent jobs, armed with the 'good degrees' (2:1 and 1:1 degrees), that they had worked hard to achieve, and I forever take pride in my small role in that.[1]

But my shame and regret in not previously advocating for these students to challenge accepted behaviours, practices and policies paved the way to the bumpy road of academic activism. This formally began with a research fellowship awarded by the Centre of Teaching Excellence at my (then) university to address racialised degree award gaps. These are differential gaps in the awarding of 'good degrees' to different racialised student groups. It should be of no surprise that

---

[1]In Britain, a 2:1 degree, also known as Upper Second-Class Honours in general, parallels a grade point average (GPA) of 3.3–3.7. In the American grading system, a 1:1 degree or First-Class Honours is comparable to a GPA of 3.7–4.0.

during the last two decades, white students year on year have achieved a 'good degree' at much higher rates than any other racialised student group (Ugiagbe-Green & Ernsting, 2022). The current degree award gap between white students and 'Black, Asian and 'minority ethnic' students is 10.7% (Advance, 2023). You are more likely to achieve a good degree if you are a white student who achieved BBC at 'A Level' than a Black student who achieved AAA at 'A Level' (UUK, 2019).[2] Racialised degree award gaps in universities are high on universities' agenda because the regulator has set a sector target reduction of 5.5% by 2025 (which is unlikely to be achieved given the current sector gap of 10.8%). As such, there are a lot of people in UK higher education sector tasked by their universities with working on racialised degree award gaps.

One of the joys of the Fellowship was the honour of sharing space with colleagues in various communities of practice that focused on enhancing and improving students' experience. It is telling that I was often the only person from my department (except for one colleague who was often in education focused spaces) within these communities of practice. These spaces were collegial and joyful. I learned much from colleagues and was able to access kindness and compassion at times when I have really needed it. I was making great strides across the institution with my work on racialised degree award gaps. Many colleagues (outside of Business School) were genuinely interested in what they could do to make a difference and I sensed a shift in culture. Everything was going well. At least, it seemed to everyone within my networks and communities of practice that it was.

What colleagues did not know is that I did not receive the time buyout as agreed by the conditions of my Fellowship that should have provided me with 2 full days a week to do my race equity work. I was essentially working 40% over my standard work allowance (which was already slightly over workload) to work within the Business School. I was overworked and I was suffering. What colleagues did not know is that I carried out postgraduate dissertation meetings with my accounting and finance Master's students, the day after I learned at my 12 weeks scan, I had miscarried the baby that I thought I was still growing. I had booked annual leave for a few days in anticipation of sharing our joyful news with family and friends. Instead, on that fateful day, my out of office sombrely and apologetically explained that due to unforeseen circumstances, I would be uncontactable for the rest of the week. On seeing my out of office, a student with whom I had a dissertation support appointment in a few days' time, then raised a complaint with senior management in my department, copying me in regarding my extended unplanned absence. I was asked to reply and explain my absence to the student (and yes, at this point senior management did know what had happened). What colleagues didn't know was that a few weeks after my return, I was up at 4 a.m.

---

[2]Typically, UK A-Level (advanced level) qualifications determine entry into Universities in the UK University system. Usually, three subjects are taken graded A to E in final exams. A student who receives AAA is an exceptional scholar across their chosen disciplines. The point is that an exceptional Black student beginning their university journey is likely to fare worse than a good to average white student in terms of eventual degree attainment by the completion of their course.

almost every day marking assessments for nearly 400 students on my own because despite having asked for help from my senior leaders in the department on returning after 3 weeks' sick leave (taken a few weeks on returning from my few days of annual leave), following my baby loss, I received none. There was no care. I was enduring all of this while trying to care for my two primary school aged children who I was homeschooling with my partner, due to COVID-19-related national lock downs.

Fast forward a few months, the marks were in (late, having also been chased to work harder to get them in on time), the children were back at school and I was working through the emotional wreckage of what I had endured. I was a bit broken but resolved I would lobby for the two days a week I was entitled to continue the work in the next academic year. I was informed by the Centre for Teaching Excellence that there was no guarantee I would be able to continue with my Fellowship because my department's demands for my time took priority. My department deemed that my role in teaching accounting and supporting students as their personal tutor/Head of Year was more important than my research and work on racialised degree award gaps, which I was informed by a colleague had been expressed as 'a distraction' in a meeting that I was not present in.

On hearing this news, I was bereft, but I chose to prioritise my mental health and left the university. Colleagues were flabbergasted; everything had been going so well? I was effecting some change and making a small difference. Importantly for me, I was honouring the gift of trust from those Black women and was doing the work. But I asked myself, at what cost? I was emotionally and physically burned out. I was broken and so, so sad. On leaving, colleagues assumed I was leaving for a big promotion. During one of my final meetings, one Professor who was a member of the senior management team in my department, so knew about the circumstances of my leaving, told me, 'I can understand why you would want to get us on your CV and return to a post-92. Institution'.[3] It doesn't happen often, but I was speechless. There was no acknowledgement whatsoever of the harm and pain that had been inflicted on me.

A few days after starting my new role in my (wonderful) post-92 institution, I learned that a large research bid to do some scholarly work to support Black and Black heritage people into doctoral study that I had submitted was successful. There is an important context to this that I need to explain, before moving on. The conditions of the national research call were that higher education institutions could only submit three bids and could be the lead institution on only one bid. I had never written a large bid document before and had no support to do so. At the time of submission, I knew I was leaving my former institution (I was on a 6 month notice period) and had

[3]Post-1992 universities in the United Kingdom are institutions granted university status after the Further and Higher Education Act of 1992. They are perceived as less prestigious than pre-1992 contemporaries who focus on research, and traditionally have better funding. This leads to the impression that pre-1992 Universities are of a higher quality educational standard and are more rigorous. The insinuation is that I merely used the better pre-1992 university to enhance my CV but did not want to suffer the rigorous academic standards required to stay.

not yet started at my new institution. I had an idea (a specific targeted support programme, with a range of different work packages relating to a framework I had developed through my race equity research) in response to the research call. The evaluation plan was devised by a lovely collaborator I had worked with at my former institution during my Fellowship. Incidentally, it was she who alerted me to the call and encouraged me (numerous times) that we submit a bid. By the time she convinced me we should put something in, we had three weeks (!) to do it. However, I was in between institutions, and both of whom it turned out were already submitting bids. I approached a different institution that I had also worked with during my Fellowship, to see if they would like to be involved in the project and they said yes. They were submitting two partner bids for the call, so would be the lead institution on the bid I had written with my evaluation collaborator. It was brilliant. They committed significant resources and funding to the proposal. I was asked to add some costings to the bid I had written; I consulted with a few colleagues I had approached to be involved in the programme to sense check the bid and everything was sent to the institution for approval. I subsequently submitted the bid to the funders and crossed all my fingers and toes. Five months later and we were informed that we were successful! Absolute elation following a very difficult year.

It is fair to say that everyone (except our ever-trusting evaluation partner) was surprised it was successful. Now, I can only speculate on why this happened, but once the project started, there was minimal involvement from the institutions involved. As it turned out, initially, this was a positive thing because I had the freedom to develop the programme I had conceived and get it implemented. There had been a delay to announcing the projects that had been successful and a strict embargo that delayed the start of the project by nearly two months. Nevertheless, I worked all hours, returning to my 4 a.m. starts to get the programme content written, all the associated workshops in place and almost everything programme related in place within two months. We managed to recruit people onto the programme as hoped, and although there were several issues, the first year of the project was seemingly a success. We achieved some brilliant outcomes; two people on the programme had gone on to access (fully funded) PhD opportunities, several students had been awarded prizes on their degrees, all (Black and Black heritage) undergraduates on the programme had achieved 'good degrees', people had been promoted at work, some students had accessed graduate job roles or postgraduate taught degrees. The programme had been impactful and had made a real difference, right?

Yes, well. . .

What some of my colleagues did not know was that behind the scenes, I had been fighting to be formally recognised as the principal investigator (PI) of the project. I had written the bid (with the evaluation plan being written by my collaborator). I was the only Black woman leading the project team, and it had been acknowledged I had written the bid, that I had designed and written the content of the programme, that I had co-ordinated all workshops and learning activities on the programme, I had implemented the programme on a learning platform that was completely new to me. And I alone had worked with our evaluation partner to design our theory of change for the evaluation (despite repeated invitations from myself and the evaluation partner to join us on the evaluation). A member of the project team who had embraced being spotlighted by their institution for their contribution to the project, had diminished the transformative knowledge production of the project telling me it 'was not a real research project'. My labour was acknowledged. I had received the funding letter from the funding council as the submitter of the bid. However, because I did not work at the lead institution, I could not possibly be the PI. I sought independent advice on this, and it turns out, no, you do not need to work at the lead institution to be the PI on a research project.

I consider myself an afro-feminist, but in my career, it is certainly true that I have allowed people, particularly men, to tell me what I can and cannot do. However, this project was too important to me to allow that to happen this time. I had invested too much of myself to allow myself to be a victim of misogynoir (Bailey, 2021) this time. So, I challenged the instruction that I was not the PI and could not refer to myself as the PI on this project, and that this would be afforded to a colleague at the lead institution. My response and approach to challenging this position was deemed unprofessional. Not because I was rude or I was personally attacking anyone but because for once, I was disruptive. I was not silent. I made people feel uncomfortable. I let everyone know what was happening and that I was not happy about it. I was not going to be in a position this time where I had to say to myself, 'well colleagues did not know'. Everyone knew what was going on. I was not going to be complicit in my pain this time, by neglecting myself and negating what I knew to be right, in the interests of not causing a fuss, even when it was put to me by a colleague at the lead institution on the project that I was enacting the 'angry Black woman trope'. I was angry and I am Black – so what? I am not allowed to be angry because I am Black. Please.

There was one regret in all of this. On reflection, by being so open with our evaluators (with whom I had a great relationship but who have an important presence in the sector) about the issue, I had compromised the position of some colleagues who other than being invaluable administrative support to the programme were not involved in what was happening. I did care about that, so I personally apologised to them. What I was not remorseful for was that I made those who were responsible for my pain once again feel uncomfortable. I am also not sorry that people who did not know from the lead institution perceived me to be arrogant by expressing my frustration, explicitly outlining my labour and not accepting what I had been told and being quiet about it. Recognition as PI on this project meant so much more to me than anyone could ever acknowledge or know. It was validation of the pain I had endured doing the Fellowship. It was validation that my work was not 'a distraction'. It was validation that I could do research and do it well. I had been told by my supervisors during my PhD that I would never get my doctorate. My research was not valued by my previous department; it was 'a distraction'. Being PI on this project was not only career defining, but it was validation for those Black women students. Their gift of trust meant something for me and for others like them. That I could use their pain in the most beautiful way and create opportunities for others like them. It was validation that I was good at what I do and was being given the opportunity to do more. It mattered more than anyone would know.

I continued working on the project, but it set the tone for what was another emotionally turbulent and bumpy experience working on race equity issues. As the project progressed, the institutions became more involved and more people (quite rightly) joined the project. Oversight, accountability and governance structures and processes took shape and were put in place. I must stress (as an accountant, if nothing else) that this activity was ultimately a good thing for the project. However, decisions started being made that I did not agree with. My voice was being ignored; I was excluded from channels of communication and began to feel a loss of control. I started to navigate project meetings in an exhausting state of internal flux, wanting to speak up but feeling disempowered to do so. The adjustment in working with different people and no longer being able to lead on decisions was difficult, but I resolved it was collaboration and I needed to commit to making it work, for the students, if nothing else.

However, it became increasingly obvious that the direction of travel was not going to change and my commitment to the programme took a very different shape from my collaborators. I felt the values of the programme were being compromised and eroded and was having a really difficult time dealing with it, as it was clear that nobody else perceived the issues in the same way. I internalised these feelings but started to feel anxious and stressed. My mental health declined once more. Everything I had hoped to achieve in terms of outcomes was being achieved but again at what cost? Everything felt like a monumental battle. I felt it was me and everyone else on the project (except for our evaluation partner), pulling in different directions. However, this time, I did not make the same mistake as I had done a year before. This time round, I had communicated my difficulties as they happened, with trusted colleagues outside of the project. I felt vindicated when upon sharing with those colleagues that I was leaving the project, they retorted, 'I am surprised you did not go sooner'. It was a painful decision to leave. I did not leave unscathed. I lost valued associates and damaged my relationship with the project team irrevocably, but I have absolutely no regrets.

When news started to break that I had left the project, several other Black women contacted me. It was heartbreaking to hear Black women on other race equity projects express that they have left or are thinking about leaving their projects too, sometimes under similar circumstances. They shared all sorts of stories that mirrored elements of my own story. I was told of cases of once confirmation that the project was successful, of PIs abandoning the project and leaving more junior racially minoritised staff with little expertise and experience of project management to run the projects. Black women have shared how they have been challenged for their (perceived to be) radical, liberatory approach to some work packages; for example, choosing to work with community activists and that some white colleagues on the project had deemed this approach unprofessional and unnecessary. Black women have shared common stories of the heavy emotional burden that they have carried on projects, of the constant need to justify their approach and decision making and of how they care in a way that no others on the project care. It would seem in this work, there is a framing of what is deemed acceptable practice, of hierarchical power relations and performativity, that is often at odds with the heart that we as Black women bring to our work. Many of these women often undertake unremunerated work which is integral to help mobilise projects, work that would otherwise be at standstill. Many of us continue because the work is just too important. I did not, and despite no regrets, leaving the project is a pain I will carry with me forever.

I take no joy in reflecting on these experiences. It pains me greatly that these are the experiences of Black women in this work, who are without question always working to make things better. The personal sacrifice we endure is too great to be motivated by anything else. So why stay? There is immense joy and satisfaction to be experienced in this work. It is not virtuous to strive for better experiences, better outcomes for our racially minoritised students and colleagues. It is a matter of survival that we survive this system. For us, and those who come after us.

The impact of my race equity work has certainly brought me some individual recognition and rewards. It has undoubtedly been a source of pride and joy to work for an institution, where my work is seemingly no longer perceived as a 'distraction' but as work of some value. However, I am under no illusions. I do not present myself as 'the angry Black woman', though expressed anger is completely legitimate. We have race equity issues in my institution, like every other institution in our higher education sector. There is a lot to be angry about. However, I present myself in a way that I am deemed to be an acceptable voice of challenge. After five years of working in this space, I am somewhat skilled at navigating the political conditions and whataboutisms, in which much of my race equity work is situated. I am purposeful in my intent not to incite feelings of fragility, as a tactic to progress. I wrestle with the feelings that suppressing my anger and frustration brings, but it in pursuit of things that are bigger than me or how I feel.

We are all guided by individualism and our personal framing of ethics. We are all biased and flawed, but our work as accounting educators is always interpersonal (even in the advent of Artificial Intelligence). Our accounting profession needs to acknowledge the plurality of our values and constantly evaluate the effect of this in all aspects of the profession, what is taught, by whom and for whom. As accounting educators, we need to model care in our behaviour. It is important that the profession openly manifests care, through transparent critique and better understanding of their relations and practice with marginalised and minoritised members.

We need open and honest conversations about the performativity of some of the 'Equality, diversity and inclusion' work in the profession and to get real about lived experience of those of us (often marginalised and minoritised and often women) working authentically in race equity. We need an ethics of care (Noddings, 1984), that is centred as importantly as our professional competency frameworks. Because as the experiences that I have shared in this chapter, those of my accounting students and also those of my fellow Black women academics show us, the absence of an ethics of care in accounting education comes at great cost.

References

Advance HE. (2023). *Equality in higher education: Statistical reports 2023*. Advance HE. (advance-he.ac.uk). https://www.advance-he.ac.uk/news-and-views/equality-higher-education-statistical-reports-2023?_cldee=QPRHUjUc8RUSA09ih70r6CXkJv50YxCVmcr_Zbeb2w98-TT0PjQBcZ-McFmzKPbD&recipientid=contact-19e02e7087beed1183fe002248c6c021-2e4622341afe4f17bd316012be2ff987&utm_source=ClickDimensions&utm_medium=email&utm_campaign=news-nov23&esid=6021bd6e-ea8a-ee11-be36-002248c6f978. Accessed 12 03, 2023.

Atkinson, P. (1997). Narrative turn or blind alley? *Qualitative Health Research*, *7*, 325–344.

Bailey, M. (2021). *Misogynoir transformed Black women's digital resistance*. New York University Press.

BAME. (2020). Accountancy daily. https://www.accountancydaily.co/bame-2020-one-250-partners-black-top-eight-accountancy-firms. Accessed 12 03, 2023.

Bhaskar, R. (2020). Critical realism and the ontology of persons. *Journal of Critical Realism*, *19*(2), 113–120. https://doi.org/10.1080/14767430.2020.1734736

Coffey, A. (1999). *The ethnographic self*. Sage.

Ellis, C. (2004). *The ethnographic I: A methodological novel about autoethnography*. AltaMira Press.

Gillborn, D. (1998). Racism, selection, poverty and parents: New Labour, old problems? *Journal of Education Policy*, *13*(6), 717–735. https://doi.org/10.1080/0268093980130604

Giroux, H., & McLaren, P. (Eds.) (1989), *Critical pedagogy, the state, and cultural struggle*. State University of New York Press.

Held, V. (2006). *The ethics of care: Personal, political, global*. Oxford University Press.

Kanpol, B. (1999). *Critical pedagogy. An introduction*. Bergin & Garvey.

Lewis, A. (2020). *Counting black and white beans: Critical race theory in accounting*. Emerald Publishing Limited.

Mortari, L. (2015). Reflectivity in research practice: An overview of different perspectives. *International Journal of Qualitative Methods*, *14*(5). https://doi.org/10.1177/1609406915618045

Noddings, N. (1984). *Caring: A feminine approach to ethics and moral education*. University of California Press.

Subramaniam, B. (2010). Imperfect oracle: The epistemic and moral authority of science. *Contemporary Sociology*, *39*(6), 687–688. https://doi.org/10.1177/0094306110386886f

Ugiagbe-Green, I., & Ernsting, F. (2022). The Wicked problem of B(A)ME degree award gaps and systemic racism in our universities. 04 October 2022. Sec. Race and Ethnicity. *Frontiers in Sociology*.

Universities UK (UUK). (2019). *Closing the gap report: Black, asian and minority ethnic student attainment at UK universities*.

Zerai, A. (2002). Models for unity between scholarship and grassroots activism. *Critical Sociology*, *28*, 201–216.

Conclusion

Joanne Sopt

San Francisco State University, USA

In the wake of the murder of George Floyd, a forum on accounting and race emerged. It has been a space for both academics and practitioners to share experiences, resources, and ultimately create a bond with each other. This book is a direct output of individuals within the forum expressing a desire to have their voices in print. This book had at its core the goal for authors to say what they wanted to say. Some of the topics discussed were decolonization, caste, racism, white supremacy, violence, and exploitation. These all represent words that are difficult to justify to reviewers and editors when trying to publish under the constraints of major academic journals.

What emerged is a richness of perspectives, writing styles, data sources, and choice in how to conduct research and teaching. Many shared details from their own personal experiences within the field of accounting such as working as a Black accounting professional and academic (Davis, 2024; Ugiagbe-Green, 2024) and as a DEI professional (Etienne, 2024). Streeter and Hammond (2024) provided an update on the work that has been done to improve the numbers of Black CPAs in the United States based on their personal work. Gittens (2024) connected the accounting literature on small developing countries to her experiences working in government accounting in Antigua and Barbuda and living the frustrations of interacting with multilateral organizations. Ufodike (2024) was able to weave his personal narrative as a Nigerian into the debates around diversity, equity, inclusion, and belonging (DEIB) efforts. Other contributors shared their own personal intellectual journeys around race such as Saatkamp (2024) and Rukasuwan (2024) which contain valuable resources for others who aim to have a more historical and critical understanding of accounting. All of these experiences shared the common goal of exposing how important the centrality of race is to the contributors' personal understandings of the world around them. It also allowed for the chapters to be interconnected and read in a powerful way. Unpacking racism in particular can lead to further unpacking of other repressive forces such as capitalism and accounting's role within it. What we can observe is how linked these systems of domination are to each other.

Voices of Change, 239–245

Published under exclusive licence by Emerald Publishing Limited
doi:10.1108/978-1-83753-030-420251042

The use of emotion and personal narratives was a refreshing change from reading work that is meant to mask the human from the article as much as possible. Mixing different data sources such as government statistics and newspaper articles in the chapter from Alston (2024) created an overall picture of the notoriously slippery concept of fraud. It provided a way to connect the dots among fraud risk, charter schools and under-represented minorities. Lewis and Hurt (2024), in an act of resistance, propose steps to encourage active anti-racism in the field of accounting.

Methodology and theoretical choices in research can provide space for marginalized perspectives to be shared. Musundwa and Hammond (2024) shared the power and sensitivity of oral history to uncover deeper understandings of individuals that belong to communities that are usually ignored. Twyford et al. (2024) promoted the potential of Critical Race Theory, counter accounts, and critical dialogic accounting and accountability to capture these perspectives within a framework so that they can be heard. Finally, Kyriacou (2024) highlighted the creativity that can emerge when using a transdisciplinary approach which is sorely needed in accounting to break free from the system of classification that it is built on.

Several chapters also discussed the choice around pedagogical approaches in opening up understandings in the classroom by incorporating race-focused content in accounting coursework particularly around the historical origins of accounting and current-day barriers (Lewis & Hurt, 2024; Rukasuwan, 2024; Saatkamp, 2024). Musundwa et al. (2024) provided background information on what decolonization means from the perspective of the accounting curriculum along with some concrete suggestions.

This book is also a continuation of previous studies and recent special issues in accounting journals which all have a motivation to diversify voices in accounting away from the white heteronormative perspective. The *Accounting, Auditing & Accountability Journal (AAAJ)* special issue focused squarely on race and published research articles that articulated the connections among accounting, accountability, race, racism, capitalism, and neoliberalism (Agyemang et al., 2024). Common themes between the *AAAJ* and this book are the importance of history (Walker, 2023), lived experiences in the accounting profession and academia (Gago-Rodriguez et al., 2024; Musundwa & Moses, 2024), counter accounts, and Critical Race Theory. They also focused on environmental issues and its intersection with race by highlighting the disturbing trends of environmental racism and climate apartheid (Perkiss, 2024). Accountability in workplace practices was another important theme (Dhanani et al., 2024).

The *Social and Environmental Accountability Journal* highlighted articles that focused on the intersectionality of race with other diversity attributes such as gender, ethnicity, and sexual identity (Lima et al., 2024; Tanima & George, 2024) similar to Ashong-Lamptey (2024) on his chapter on race, ethnicity, and class. The editorial of Egan et al. (2024, p. 91) provided areas for future research and a call to:

> to actively find our diverse voices, both through our personal experiences and through empirical insights of personal importance to us, to collectively collaborate at dismantling the

> social constructions of the glass and lavender ceilings, actively removing barriers for all minority, 'marginalised and managed' groups (Ghio, McGuigan, & Powell, 2023)!

The *Issues in Accounting Education* special issue centered on DEIB initiatives in accounting education. It highlighted additional voices and narratives such as the working conditions and institutional pressures of Black faculty both from personal experiences at predominately white institutions (Dawkins, 2023) and those working at Historically Black Colleges and Universities (HBCUs) (Smith et al., 2023). The editors concluded that if the profession wants more diversity among its membership, "the education of its members must reflect, embrace, and promote diversity, equity, and social justice" (Ghio, McGuigan, et al., 2023, p. 4).

Finally, the *Accounting Horizons* special issue made an important point about translating buzzwords into action (Brown-Liburd et al., 2024). The articles shed light on the experiences of Black professionals. Raddatz et al. (2024) captured the experiences of Black, Indigenous, and people of color (BIPOC) auditors having to anticipate discrimination in the workplace and the adverse effect it has on them. Dey et al. (2024) highlighted the extra work of Black accountants around practice development and social interaction skills compared to white accountants. Musundwa and Hammond (2024) revealed the barriers in becoming and thriving as a Black accountant in South Africa. Other articles focused on accounting academia such as the online economic and accounting forums that harbor toxic racist communication (Alberti & Morris, 2024) and the lack of charitable giving to HBCUs compared to predominately white institutions (Cowle et al., 2024). These articles revealed the problems in the field of accounting, and Brown-Liburd et al. (2024) rightly called for action to address them.

As noted, this book and other special issues have responded to the lacuna of race-related articles in accounting as highlighted by Annisette and Prasad (2017). This book in particular reveals just how far we still need to go to have race equity in the field of accounting by providing recent lived experiences from the authors. Ghio et al. (2024) also provided figures on the lack of importance placed on race within diversity research in accounting. Out of the 428 articles selected from 1979 to 2021, only 3.7% focused solely on race with an additional 6.3% that included race as an element of investigation in addition to other diversity attributes. From that metric alone, we see how much more research is needed for this work to gain additional traction and impact in academia. In contrast, the majority of diversity studies were on gender with 62.4% of those articles only focusing on gender and an additional 12.2% of intersectional studies including gender. Ufodike (2024) highlighted the positive impact that gender initiatives have had on corporate behavior but also mentioned that it has been felt predominately by white women. However, the author expressed hope that all of these equity initiatives on race will matter and that we should not be too focused on getting it exactly right for "seeking perfection is a pursuit for divinity" (Ufodike, 2024).

In reality, there is no known obvious solution on how to move forward. We know many of the problems as revealed in this book and previous research. Streeter and Hammond (2024) highlighted that a current issue is why firms are not hiring Black accounting students even though the students know they can do the work. Ufodike (2024) mentioned the tensions that exist in the DEIB space and how different diversity initiatives can be seen to be in competition with each other. On an individual level, Etienne (2024) stated that emotional intelligence and resilience is needed to confront one's bias which is difficult work. The chapters in this book have shed light on the challenges working in this space along with the real threats of job security in our hyper-racial times (Annisette & Prasad, 2017). The fear of having one's career destroyed for voicing a position that contradicts the white perspective is real. Knowing this, we thank the authors for sharing their voice. We should use their shared knowledge to reflect on what can be done now and, in the future, to address the root of the problems.

However, in this book, we have chapters such as Ugiagbe-Green (2024) that provide a path on how we should conduct this work going forward. An ethics of care (Noddings, 1984) is crucially needed for an impact to be felt beyond what can be quantified. For example:

> in our work as educators, the accounting students for whom we advocate are not statistics. They are not data points. They are not a problem to be fixed. They are not an instrument to be used for self-promotion and gratification. These students embody society's future. (Ugiagbe-Green, 2024, p. 228)

But yet again, we are faced with additional struggles of being tasked to do the work with colleagues who do not exhibit care toward marginalized students and those carrying the burden of such programs such as Black women. This all can result in being physically burned out and feelings of being "so, so sad" (Ugiagbe-Green, 2024).

We encourage you, the readers, to make your voice heard. Take the time to read and re-read the chapters, have conversations about them, reflect on paths forward, and act on them. Share them with the authors and editors. This takes collective work. Neoliberalism and capitalism thrive on individualism which oftentimes is the result of despair. This book started with good intentions, and the same spirit of connectedness and community is needed to continue with this work. As noted by Agyemang et al. (2024, Resistance and Emancipation section), "at the heart of resistance movements is the demand to be recognised as equal, as human." Scobie and Laird (2024) in the *AAAJ* special issue found evidence of "accounting's role in…individual and collective practices including walking, thinking, writing, drawing and dancing" to contribute toward resisting racial capitalism (Agyemang et al., 2024, Resistance and Emancipation section). How can accounting incorporate the positive elements of our humanity that is needed to carry on this work?

Many point to intersectionality as a next step. However, it should not be viewed as the newest buzzword but as a point of action. In addition to intersecting different identities in the diversity space, how can we see and act on race intersecting with environmental degradation as noted by Perkiss (2024)? How can we see and act on race intersecting with current day tragedies and systems of oppression in Gaza in addition to Congo as mentioned by Agyemang et al. (2024)? What social justice issues do you see around you that also intersect with race? We encourage you to analyze the situations around you through the lens of race to see what new questions you can personally be asking. We also encourage you to email us, the editors, to join the Accounting and Race Forum.

The book concludes where the Accounting Manifesto (Alawattage et al., 2021) began:

> If you have come here to help me, you are wasting your time. But if you have come because your liberation is bound up with mine, then let us work together. – An Aboriginal activist's phrase from the 1970s[1]

These are impactful words that help fuel and re-center the work when needed. And for those who perceive themselves to be liberated, we implore you not to forget those systems of oppression that continue to wreak havoc in the world and more specifically for this book regarding race in the field of accounting.

References

Agyemang, G., Dhanani, A., Ejiogu, A. R., & Perkiss, S. (2024). Researching race, accounting and accountability: Past, present and future. *Accounting, Auditing & Accountability Journal*, *37*(7/8), 1637–1664.

Alawattage, C., Arjaliès, D. L., Barrett, M., Bernard, J., de Castro Casa Nova, S. P., Cho, C. H., Cooper, C., Denedo, M., Drujon D'Astros, C., Evans, R., Ejiogu, A., Frieden, L., Ghio, A., McGuigan, N., Luo, Y., Pimentel, E., Powell, L., Pérez, P. A. N., Quattrone, P., ... Sorola, M. (2021). Opening accounting: A manifesto. *Accounting Forum*, *45*(3), 227–246.

Alberti, C. T., & Morris, L. (2024). Online toxic communication about the accounting academic job market. *Accounting Horizons*, *38*(1), 7–26.

Annisette, M., & Prasad, A. (2017). Critical accounting research in hyper-racial times. *Critical Perspectives on Accounting*, *43*, 5–19.

Brown-Liburd, H. L., Ghio, A., & Roberts, A. A. (2024). Diversity, equity, inclusion and belonging: Practice problems of real consequence. *Accounting Horizons*, *38*(1), 1–5.

Cowle, E. N., Draeger, M. A., & Smith, K. W. (2024). Accounting firm investment in diverse talent: Evidence from charitable giving to historically Black colleges and universities (HBCUs). *Accounting Horizons*, *38*(1), 49–67.

Dawkins, M. C. (2023). Life experiences of a Black accounting student and faculty member. *Issues in Accounting Education*, *38*(1), 19–33.

[1]As noted in the Accounting Manifesto, "This phrase is often attributed to Murri activist and educator, Lilla Watson. However, she maintains the phrase emerged as a collective expression from an Aboriginal Rights group in Queensland (see: http://unnecessaryevils.blogspot.com/2008/11/attributing-words.html)."

Dey, R. M., Lim, L., Dickins, D., & Quamina, L. (2024). Skills required to succeed in public accounting: Perceptions of Black and white accountants. *Accounting Horizons*, *38*(1), 69–78.

Dhanani, A., Chaidali, P., Sharma, N., & Varoutsa, E. (2024). Responding to race inequalities in the national health service (England) accountability and the workforce equality standard. *Accounting, Auditing & Accountability Journal*, *37*(7/8), 1665–1694.

Egan, M., Voss, B. D. L., Mcguigan, N., & Powell, L. (2024). Finding our voices–exploring diversity, inclusion and accounting by the marginalised and managed diverse. *Social and Environmental Accountability Journal*, *44*(2), 87–92.

Gago-Rodriguez, S., Lazcano, L., & Bada, C. (2024). A fairy tale with an unhappy ending: The organizational regulation of 'Latina accountant identity' in Spain. *Accounting, Auditing & Accountability Journal*. https://doi.org/10.1108/aaaj-03-2023-6318

Ghio, A., McGuigan, N., & Powell, L. (2023). The queering accounting manifesto. *Critical Perspectives on Accounting*, *90*, 102395.

Ghio, A., McGuigan, N., Stewart, O. J., Tharapos, M., & Wood, L. I. (2023). Diversity, equity, and social justice in accounting education. *Issues in Accounting Education*, *38*(1), 1–5.

Ghio, A., Occhipinti, Z., & Verona, R. (2024). The consideration of diversity in the accounting literature: A systematic literature review. *European Accounting Review*, *33*(5), 1667–1691. https://doi.org/10.1080/09638180.2024.2330089

Lima, J. P., Miranda, C., & Casa Nova, S. (2024). Is there no sin down south of the equator? Brazilian auditors' perception of the gendered and racialized dynamics in audit firms. *Social Environmental and Accountability Journal*, *44*(2).

Musundwa, S., & Hammond, T. A. (2024). Black chartered accountants in post-Apartheid South Africa: Global implications for the profession. *Accounting Horizons*, *38*(1), 111–122.

Musundwa, S., & Moses, O. (2024). The lived experiences of South African Black accountants within the framework of the chartered accountancy profession sector code. *Accounting, Auditing & Accountability Journal*, *37*(7/8), 1726–1760.

Noddings, N. (1984). *Caring: A feminine approach to ethics and moral education*. University of California Press.

Perkiss, S. (2024). Climate apartheid: The failures of accountability and climate justice. *Accounting, Auditing & Accountability Journal*, *37*(7/8), 1761–1794.

Raddatz, N. I., Raddatz, P. A., Sorensen, K., & Ogunade, K. (2024). The adverse effects of the "anticipation of racial discrimination" on auditors who are Black, Indigenous, or people of color (BIPOC): An exploratory study with research propositions. *Accounting Horizons*, *38*(1).

Scobie, M., & Laird, L. (2024). 'A war waged with numbers'. Accounting and accumulation by alienation in Australia's border industrial complex. *Accounting, Auditing & Accountability Journal*, *37*(7/8), 1795–1819.

Smith, K. W., Davis, M., Malone, C., & Owens-Jackson, L. (2023). Faculty that look like me: An examination of historically Black colleges and universities accounting faculty motivation and job satisfaction. *Issues in Accounting Education*, *38*(1), 35–58.

Tanima, F., & George, S. (2024). When the personal is political: Sharing our lived experiences as women of colour in academia. *Social Environmental and Accountability Journal*, *44*(2).

Walker, S. (2023). Accounting and racial violence in the postbellum American South. *Accounting, Auditing & Accountability Journal.* (online first). https://doi.org/10.1108/AAAJ-01-2023-6245

Index

Printed and bound by CPI Group (UK) Ltd, Croydon, CR0 4YY

02/06/2026

14891180-0001